Working with Texts, Second Edition

Reviews of the first edition

'Extremely wide-ranging in its texts, its topics, and its treatment of both. The overwhelming feeling I had every time I opened it was a sense of the joy and fun of engaging with such a lively variety of texts and interesting commentaries.'

Amos Paran, *ELT Journal*

'A most flexible book ... an invaluable resource both for the quality and presentation of its source material and for the clarity and economy of its writing.'

Renee Stanton, *English & Media Magazine*

'[This] book, through which a wide range of insights are made eminently accessible, without condescension ... give[s] the serious student not only a wide range of knowledge, but also a high degree of communicative competence.'

Jean-Pierre van Noppen, *Language and Literature*

'An ideal choice for foundation courses in language studies ... it is informative, challenging, engaging and entertaining. ... Major topics are explored via a wonderful range of texts and snippets, taken from truly contemporary English and popular culture in all its energetic and competitive diversity.'

Michael Toolan, *University of Birmingham*

'New directions for understanding language are opened up here, for exactly those readers who have been denied access for so many years to a well-thought-out, well-designed and accessible introduction to the way in which language works.'

David Birch, *Central Queensland University, Australia*

Feedback from users of the first edition

'The selection of texts is varied and imaginative, and commentaries are detailed.'

John Keen, *University of Manchester and Chief Examiner,*
A-level English Language

'Very good introductory course in English grammar and structure from a textual point of view. Excellent materials. Wonderful activities.'

Hortensia Curell, *Autonoma University, Barcelona, Spain*

'Very interesting. Good opening text for tutorial work in language-based humanities courses.'

Jacqui Miller, *Liverpool Hope University College*

'Excellent for insights into texts ... a fresh, interesting approach and authentic, varied texts. Enjoyable to use.'

Maggie Ward Goodbody, *Bath University*

'Apart from historical linguistics, this book has *everything* I teach in the Intro class. On top of its comprehensiveness it looks *very* teachable.'

Ingrid Piller, *Hamburg University, Germany*

Working with Texts

The second edition of *Working with Texts: a core introduction to language analysis* is a fully revised and updated version of a well-established introductory language textbook. Covering a wide range of language areas, the book uses an interactive, activity-based approach to support students' understanding of language structure and variety. The second edition includes:

◎ new material on differences between spoken and written language; children's language; new technologies and language change;
◎ an updated range of texts, including literary extracts, advertisements, horoscopes, junk mail, comedy sketches, political speeches, telephone discourse and Internet chat;
◎ more extension work to support student-directed study;
◎ a new concluding section, which offers further analyses to help students draw together the different aspects of the book;
◎ updated Further reading and a list of URLs for students to visit.

Ronald Carter is Professor of Modern English Language in the School of English Studies, University of Nottingham, the editor of the Routledge INTERFACE series and co-editor of the Routledge *Applied Linguistics* series. **Angela Goddard** is Senior Lecturer in Language at the Centre for Human Communication, Manchester Metropolitan University. **Danuta Reah** is principal moderator, **Keith Sanger** a team leader, and **Maggie Bowring** a moderator for English Language A-Level Investigation.

The Intertext series

◎   Why does the phrase 'spinning a yarn' refer both to using language and making cloth?

◎   What might a piece of literary writing have in common with an advert or a note from the milkman?

◎   What aspects of language are important to understand when analysing texts?

The Routledge INTERTEXT series will develop readers' understanding of how texts work. It does this by showing some of the designs and patterns in the language from which they are made, by placing texts within the contexts in which they occur, and by exploring relationships between them.

The series consists of a foundation text, *Working with Texts: A core introduction to language analysis*, which looks at language aspects essential for the analysis of texts, and a range of satellite texts. These apply aspects of language to a particular topic area in more detail. They complement the core text and can also be used alone, providing the user has the foundation skills furnished by the core text.

Benefits of using this series:

◎   **Unique** – written by a team of respected teachers and practitioners whose ideas and activities have also been trialled independently.

◎   **Multi-disciplinary** – provides a foundation for the analysis of texts, supporting students who want to achieve a detailed focus on language.

◎   **Accessible** – no previous knowledge of language analysis is assumed, just an interest in language use.

◎   **Comprehensive** – wide coverage of different genres: literary texts, notes, memos, signs, advertisements, leaflets, speeches, conversation.

◎   **Student-friendly** – contains suggestions for further reading; activities relating to texts studied; commentaries after activities; key terms highlighted and an index of terms.

The series editors:

Adrian Beard is Head of English at Gosforth High School, Newcastle upon Tyne, and a chief examiner for A-Level English Literature. He has written and lectured extensively on the subjects of literature and language. His publications include *Texts and Contexts* (Routledge).

Ronald Carter is Professor of Modern English Language in the School of English Studies at the University of Nottingham, is the editor of the Routledge INTERFACE series and co-editor of the Routledge *Applied Linguistics* series. He is author of *Vocabulary* (2nd edn; Routledge, 1998) and co-author of *The Routledge History of Literature in English* (2nd edn; Routledge, 2001). From 1989 to 1992 he was seconded as National Director for the Language in the National Curriculum (LINC) project, directing a £21.4 million in-service teacher education programme.

Angela Goddard is Senior Lecturer in Language at the Centre for Human Communication, Manchester Metropolitan University, and was Chief Moderator for English Language A-Level Project Research at the Northern Examination and Assessment Board (NEAB), 1983–1995. She is now chair of examiners of A-Level English Language. Her publications include *Researching Language* (2nd edn; Heinemann, 2000).

Core textbook:

Working with Texts: A core introduction to language analysis (2nd edn; 2001)
Ronald Carter, Angela Goddard, Danuta Reah, Keith Sanger, Maggie Bowring

Satellite titles:

The Language of Sport
Adrian Beard

The Language of Politics
Adrian Beard

The Language of Speech and Writing
Sandra Cornbleet and Ronald Carter

The Language of Advertising: Written texts
Angela Goddard

Language and Gender
Angela Goddard and Lindsey Meân Patterson

The Language of Magazines
Linda McLoughlin

The Language of Poetry
John McRae

The Language of Conversation
Francesca Pridham

The Language of Newspapers
Danuta Reah

The Language of Humour
Alison Ross

The Language of Drama
Keith Sanger

The Language of Fiction
Keith Sanger

The Language of ICT: Information and Communication Technology
Tim Shortis

Working with Texts

A core introduction to language analysis

Second Edition

- ◎ Ronald Carter
- ◎ Angela Goddard
- ◎ Danuta Reah
- ◎ Keith Sanger
- ◎ Maggie Bowring

Routledge
Taylor & Francis Group

LONDON AND NEW YORK

First published 1997
Reprinted 1998, 1999, 2000 (twice), 2001
This second edition published 2001
by Routledge
11 New Fetter Lane, London EC4P 4EE

Simultaneously published in the USA and Canada
by Routledge
29 West 35th Street, New York, NY 10001

Reprinted 2002, 2003

Routledge is an imprint of the Taylor & Francis Group

Typeset in Stone Sans/Stone Serif
by Florence Production Ltd, Stoodleigh, Devon
Printed and bound in Great Britain
by TJ International, Padstow, Cornwall

British Library Cataloguing in Publication Data
A catalogue record for this book is available from the British Library

Library of Congress Cataloguing in Publication Data
Working with texts : a core introduction to language analysis / Ronald Carter . . .
[et al.].—2nd ed.
    p. cm. — (Intertext)
Includes bibliographical references and index.
ISBN 0–415–23464–6 (alk. paper) — ISBN 0–415–23465–4 (pbk: alk. paper)
1. Language and languages—Problems, exercises, etc.   2. Written
communication—Problems, exercises, etc.   3. English Language—
Written English—Problems, exercises, etc.   I. Carter, Ronald.
II. Intertext (London, England)
P107.W67 2001
420.1′41—dc21   00–065292

ISBN 0–415–23464–6 (hbk)
ISBN 0–415–23465–4 (pbk)

contents

notes on authors

Maggie Bowring is an English Language A-level moderator and has taught English Language in further education colleges for more than ten years. She currently teaches on A-level and degree courses at Barnsley College in South Yorkshire. She is co-author of *Something(s) to do with English Language* (1990) and *Somemorething(s) to do with English Language* (Pavic Publications, Sheffield Hallam University, 1994).

Ronald Carter has taught English in secondary schools and in further and higher education. From 1989 to 1992 he was National Director of the Language in the National Curriculum (LINC) project. He is currently Professor of Modern English Language in the School of English Studies at the University of Nottingham. He is editor of the Routledge INTERFACE series and co-editor of the *Routledge Applied Linguistics* series. He is author of *Vocabulary* (2nd edn; Routledge, 1998) and co-author of The Routledge History of literature in English (2nd edn; Routledge, 2001).

Angela Goddard has taught English in all phases of education, and currently works in the Centre for Human Communication at Manchester Metropolitan University. She co-ordinated the LINC Project for the Manchester area 1990–2, and was NEAB's Chief Moderator for A-Level English Language Project Research, 1983–95. She is now a chair for examiners of A-Level English Language. Her publications include *Researching Language* (2nd edn; Heinemann, 2000), *The Language of Advertising* (Routledge, 1998) and (with L. Mean-Patterson) *Language and Gender* (Routledge, 2000).

Danuta Reah has taught English in further and higher education. She is a principal moderator for English Language investigation and runs INSET courses in English Language. Her publications include *Something(s) to do with English Language*, 1990, and *Somemorething(s) to do with English Language* (Pavic, Sheffield Hallam University, 1994) and *The Language of Newspapers* (Routledge, 1998). Her fiction, which is published internationally, includes *Silent Playgrounds* (HarperCollins, 2000).

Keith Sanger has taught English at secondary school and sixth-form college level. He currently teaches English Language and Drama at NEW College, Pontefract. He has an MA in Modern English Language from Leeds University, and is a team leader for A-level English Language examiners. His publications include *The Language of Fiction* (Routledge, 1998) and *The Language of Drama* (Routledge, 2000).

acknowledgements

We are grateful to the copyright holders below for use of copyright material in this book.

Boddington's beer mat: Boddington's; Cover of *City Life*: Luke Bainbridge, Editor in Chief, *City Life*; 'Why we read' and 'Why do we/adults write?': Angela Richardson and Veronica Kaiserman, LINC Primary Advisor Teachers, Tameside, Stockport and Manchester Consortium; *Ladder of Years* by Anne Tyler: Copyright © 1995 by ATM Inc. Reprinted by permission of Alfred Knopf Inc.; NSPCC advert: NSPCC, London; Demon advert: Demon Internet Ltd; Boots advert: Boots the Chemist Ltd; Steve Bell cartoons: Steve Bell; Graphic novel *The Doll's House* by Neil Gaiman: Copyright © 1990 D.C. Comics. All rights reserved. Used with permission; 'England v. Spain': 'Keegan must throw the art of passing' by Martin Thorpe. Copyright © Guardian Newspapers Ltd; Amnesty International advert: Amnesty International; 'Coco Chanel first introduced . . .' by Karl Plewka: *Observer*; 'Off Course' by Edwin Morgan: Carcanet Press; Severn Trent Water advert: Severn Trent Water; 'This is a Photograph of Me' by Margaret Atwood. Reproduced with permission of Curtis Brown Ltd, London, on behalf of Margaret Atwood. Copyright © Margaret Atwood 1966. In North America, from *The Circle Game* by Margaret Atwood. Copyright © 1998 by Margaret Atwood. Reprinted by permission of Stoddart Publishing Co. Ltd; Friends of the Earth Leaflet, 'It's time you joined us': Friends of the Earth, London; Extract from *Boys and Girls*: Ladybird Books, 1964; Yakult advert: Yakult UK; Sting CT advert: Monsanto PLC; Manchester City Planning material: David Kaiserman, Head of Planning and Environmental Health, Manchester City Council; 'Not Waving But Drowning' by Stevie Smith: Virago Press; Little, Brown & Co., London; Kellogg's advert: Kellogg Company of Great Britain Ltd; Quaker advert: Quaker Trading Ltd; Ovaltine advert: Sandoz Nutrition Ltd; Macallan advert: The Macallan Distillers Ltd; Subaru advert: Subaru UK; Conservation areas advert: High Peak Borough Council; Extract from *K is for Killer* by Sue Grafton: Molly Friedrich for Sue Grafton; Macmillan Publishers; BT advert 'Why can't men be more like women?' and 'Boldly Go/Super Boldly Go': British Telecommunications PLC; Iberia advert: Iberia Airlines; InterCity advert: Saatchi & Saatchi;

Conversations with Kirstie, Callum and Edward: Julia Gillen; Pub sign of 'The Quiet Woman': the proprietor; Patwa and Standard English material: Judy Craven and Frances Jackson, *Versions: Writing in Creole and Standard English*, Manchester Education Committee, 1985; 'The Fat Black Woman Goes Shopping' by Grace Nicols: Virago Press; Little, Brown & Co., London; Planet Talk advert: Planet Talk; Extract from *Chunky* by Victoria Wood: Methuen.

Some illustrations have been redrawn. The publishers have made every effort to contact copyright holders although this has not been possible in some cases. Outstanding permissions will be remedied in future editions.

introduction

The contributors

The authors of this book are practitioners, with much experience of language teaching, curriculum development work, in-service training, examining and writing. The ideas and activities here have arisen from their own practice; they have also been trialled independently.

Aim of this book

The aim of this book is to provide a foundation for the analysis of texts, in order to support students in any discipline who want to achieve a detailed focus on language. No previous knowledge of language analysis is assumed; what *is* assumed is an interest in language use and a desire to account for the choices made by language users.

How this book is structured

The book is divided into six units which, taken together, cover the main aspects of language that it will be important to consider in any rigorous textual description:

> *Unit one: Signs and sounds* explores some aspects of meaning in written sign systems and in the sounds that constitute the basic ingredients of spoken language;
> *Unit two: Words and things* examines the nature of the lexical system;
> *Unit three: Sentences and structures* considers the effects of various types of grammatical patterning;
> *Unit four: Text and context: written discourse* focuses on the cohesive devices that tie texts together across sentence boundaries;

Unit five: Text and context: spoken discourse looks at some important aspects of spoken varieties, both in naturally occurring and in mediated texts.

Unit six: Applications points forward to the ways in which language and analysis can be taken further into investigative research.

Although the units represent distinct areas of language, these areas are not independent of each other in practice, when language is actually being used: for example, written symbols are combined to form words, and lexical patterning is an important aspect of written discourse. But in order to study language rather than simply use it, some systematic ways of paying attention to its various components are necessary. When working through this book, it is obviously important to understand each of the language areas being considered in the units; but it is equally important not to lose sight of language as a whole system while thinking about its parts. Practical reminders about the holistic nature of language occur in this book in a number of ways: in cross-references between the units, where some features of language are considered more than once, but from different perspectives; in analytical activities, where questions and commentaries on texts will focus on certain salient features, but will also suggest the larger picture to which these features contribute; in the developmental structure of the book, where later units will enable earlier skills to be re-applied and further enhanced; and in the final unit, where students are pointed towards the planning of their own research projects.

The intention, then, is that the book should build a composite picture which enables students to appreciate the nature of texts as a whole while being able to discuss meaningfully the contributions made by different aspects of language.

Ways of working

Wherever possible, the features of language referred to are shown in operation, within texts. This means the book is not intended to be a passive reading exercise but, rather, a set of active learning materials: instead of simply being told about features, readers are asked to consider how they work within texts and in particular contexts. The wide range of different genres covered is intentional, to show that skills in analysing language can be successfully applied whatever the text, and to break down the idea that only high-status texts such as literary forms are worthy of scrutiny: literary texts are considered here, but there is equivalent, if not more, discussion of such texts as notes, memos, signs, advertisements, informative leaflets, speeches and spontaneous conversation. For students of literature, comparative studies across a range of textual types can enable interesting questions to be asked about the nature of literary language.

Commentaries are provided after many of the activities. These commentaries, which highlight and discuss some of the main points of language use, are not intended to be model answers or definitive accounts: rather, they are a way to compare readers' perceptions with those of the authors. It is hoped that readers will use these commentaries in the way that best supports their own learning. Links to the relevant satellite titles are made throughout the core text, and the final unit provides both guidance on the initial stages of research planning and a selection of texts and commentaries that act as a sampler for the INTERTEXT titles.

While this book may form the basis for work in groups, it can also be used by individuals working alone. When readers work alone, the feedback that can often come via other group members is not available; the commentaries can, at least in part, make up for that.

At the end of some activities, suggestions are given for extension work. It is a common feature of many A-Level and undergraduate courses that students undertake their own language investigations. The ideas within the 'Extension' sections have this type of work in mind. As a core text, this book can only offer brief suggestions and pointers; the satellite titles that form part of the INTERTEXT series as a whole are designed to pursue many of these topics in considerably more detail.

Terminology and further reading

Because no previous knowledge of language analysis is assumed, the first usage of what is considered to be a technical term is emboldened in the text. Some of these terms are explained in context, but a brief explanation of most of these terms can be found in the 'Index of terms' at the back of this book. Suggestions for further reading are also provided.

Notes on the Second Edition

This new edition reflects some of the interesting changes that have taken place over the last few years in linguistic study:

- ◎ Computer-based communication tools such as Internet chatrooms have generated new types of text for study. We include some material from such sites, and ask to what extent electronic discourse disrupts our conventional notions of speech and writing.
- ◎ As well as providing new sites for communication, the Internet is also proving invaluable as a resource, giving us access to archives of language and to many different aspects of theoretical knowledge. A list of useful URLs is included at the back of the book.
- ◎ New approaches to research have sometimes overturned previous assumptions about language, or have provided fresh insights into the way language is used. Several examples of data searches from language corpora are included in order to show that corpus linguistics has much to offer, even at quite a simple level.
- ◎ Work on corpora has been particularly revealing of the features and strategies of speech. Spoken language is dealt with in closer detail in this new edition, which includes a greater variety of speech genres.
- ◎ New collaborations across subject disciplines have opened up fresh opportunities for applied language study. As the INTERTEXT series develops, we continue to support applied language work in a range of different areas via our satellite titles. This new edition offers greater transparency to students by explicitly demonstrating the connections between aspects of the core book and their applications in the satellite titles of the series.

one

Signs and sounds

1

From speech to writing

In this section you explore the different functions of speech and writing and the signs and symbols used to represent speech and writing.

Space-shifting

Here you consider the use made of spaces and textual layout in a wide range of different texts.

Who's in the picture?

This brief section looks at signs and symbols involving human subjects.

SOUNDS

In this more extensive section you begin to analyse the sounds of English and how they are produced. You cover consonants, vowels, sound symbolism and are introduced to phonetic alphabets.

Texts used include

◎ Signs and logos
◎ The use of birds to connote particular services or companies
◎ Computer-mediated communication (**CMC**)
◎ Alphabets
◎ Early writing by young children
◎ Jokes, riddles and written symbols
◎ Extracts from novels
◎ Poetry and poems
◎ Cartoons which use signs and symbols
◎ Advertisements
◎ Visual shapes and sound patterns in texts
◎ Word repetitions and contrasts

Signs

WHAT IS A SIGN?

Language is sometimes referred to as a **semiotic** system.

This means that it is thought to be a system where the individual elements – 'signs' – take their overall meaning from how they are combined with other elements. The analogy that is often used to illustrate this principle is the system of road traffic lights: the red, amber and green lights work as a system, and the whole system has meaning which is not carried by any one of the lights alone, but by the lights in a certain combination and sequence. In the same way, written letters of a language are signs that have to be in a certain order to make sense to the reader, and the sounds of a language are signs that only have meaning to a hearer when they occur in predictable groups. To take this idea to its logical conclusion, it is clearly possible for the elements mentioned to occur in unpredictable ways – such as for a red and green light to occur simultaneously in a set of traffic lights, or for an invented word to have an odd spelling, such as 'mldh'; but, in these cases, we still make sense of what is happening – by explaining away these occurrences as 'breakdowns' or 'mistakes'. We are still therefore referring back to a system of rules, in defining such phenomena as deviating from what we expect.

Cultural analysts would go beyond language to look at all aspects of society as systems of signs: for example, films are a system where different signs are combined in patterned ways; dress codes embody rules where different elements can occur in many varied combinations; the area of food contains many rules about what can be combined with what, and when different foods can be eaten. In all such aspects of culture, conventions are highly culture-bound – in other words, different cultures have different semiotic systems.

Activity

This activity will focus on signs in the most traditional sense – road signs – and will explore the idea of how we read them. Look at the signs in Text: Road signs. These are all from an edition of the Highway Code published in the 1930s.

The originator of the idea of semiotics – the Swiss linguist Ferdinand de Saussure – suggested that there were at least two types of sign in cases such as these: **iconic** and **symbolic**. An iconic sign tries to be a direct picture

3

of what it refers to (although this may consist of a generalised line drawing rather than a picture in the photographic, literal sense). A symbolic sign is not a picture of what is being referred to (**referent**), but a picture of something that we associate with the referent.

◎ Which of these signs are iconic, and which symbolic?

◎ Where a sign is symbolic, how does it work – what are the associations (**connotations**) that are called up in the reader's mind?

Text: Road signs

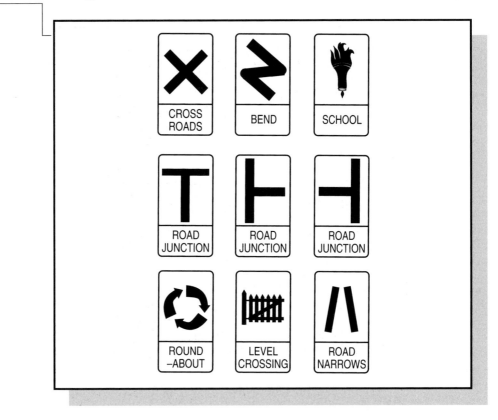

Commentary

All the signs are iconic apart from the sign for 'school'.

The 'school' sign, rather than picturing a school, symbolises a school by using a torch. This type of torch is often used on public statues, and carries classical references to such ideas as 'shedding the light of knowledge on dark areas', 'lighting up a path towards progress and civilisation' – ideas which are represented by the torch still used to mark the Olympic games. This same idea is in the word 'enlightenment', which is often used to describe a particular period in history when people looked towards classical civilisation (Ancient Greece and Rome) as ideal states.

Such associations are being played with in the Boddington's beer mat below, where the symbol (a cut-out shape) resembles both a torch and an ice-cream cone, and where the phrase 'the cream of' synthesises ideas of cream-as-luxury-foodstuff with that of high quality in general (as in 'la crème de la crème') and, ultimately, with the 'creamy' pint of Manchester-based beer.

THE CREAM OF MANCHESTER
WWW.BODDINGTONS.COM

Although all the other signs are iconic, the sign for 'crossroads' is slightly different from the rest in that it doesn't necessarily suggest the actual shape of roads coming up: instead, it takes the idea of the cross as a written symbol, and bases itself on that shape. Note that, outside the context of road signs, this shape can have other, highly symbolic, meanings – such as a 'kiss' on a personal letter, 'wrong' when written on an answer, or 'multiply' in mathematics.

Extension

Collect some examples of symbolic signs.

You might start by looking for more examples of the torch: for example, the contemporary Prudential Insurance logo; the Statue of Liberty; the logo of the Conservative Party.

Also look at a modern version of the Highway Code: how have the roads signs above changed? Do modern road signs work mainly in an iconic or symbolic way?

Activity

The fact that certain symbols call up powerful associations in the minds of readers is not lost on advertisers. The old adage 'a picture paints a thousand words' is demonstrated daily in the texts that advertising agencies produce.

In Text: Bird images are seven logos taken from texts advertising goods and services. Although each one is a picture of a bird, in each case the advertiser was using the bird image for its associations or connotations.

For each logo, write down the connotations that come to mind when you see it. Don't try to guess which product or service was being advertised, but rather concentrate on the image itself.

Text: Bird images

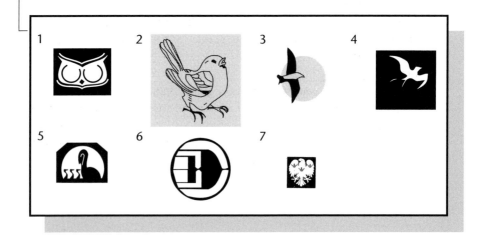

Commentary

The products/services and possible connotations are as follows:

1   Owl: from a small ads/services page in a local paper. The column headed by the owl logo was advertising children's reading clubs. We have connotations of the 'wise kindly old owl'; perhaps the fact that the owl has large, forward-facing eyes makes us associate the bird with reading and therefore acquiring knowledge. Or it could be that we associate reading with night-time activity, a time when the nocturnal bird is alert.

2   Sparrow: the logo of a local paper, placed in the top right-hand corner of the front page, just below the title of the paper, which was the *Enquirer*. Sparrows are thought to be bold, inquisitive birds – qualities which the newspaper would presumably like to be associated with.

3   Seagull: from a holiday company. We associate seagulls with the seaside, and therefore leisure-time activities. The picture shows the seagull flying across the sun: to see the bird at this angle, we would have to be lying on our backs – presumably basking in the warmth and sunshine of a summer's day.

4   Swallow: from a futon company. Associations we have for this type of bird are likely to include grace, elegance, freedom – soaring high in the air, swooping and diving. These birds also often feature in oriental art, and the futon itself is Japanese.

5   Pelican and chicks: from an insurance company. The adult pelican is known to peck out its own feathers in order to line the nest for its chicks. Whether all readers would bring this idea to the image is doubtful, but even so the image of an adult bird with its chicks calls up associations for us of protection and security.

6   Swallow: from an airline company. The idea of 'flying high' would be something any airline would like to suggest. The design of the picture is very stylised and mechanistic, so in contrast to the futon company's 'natural' image, this picture suggests power and man-made speed, calling up the shape of an aircraft with its engines creating a slipstream of air.

7   Eagle: a bank. The eagle suggests power and strength. It has been used to symbolise the power of nation-states, as in the famous American bald eagle. It therefore calls up ideas of large, powerful institutions with extensive resources at their disposal.

There is nothing natural about the associations we have for these images: for example, the owl is, in fact, blind at night; and it would be absurd to suggest that a swallow felt 'freer' than a sparrow, that a sparrow thought of itself as cheeky, or that a seagull knew what a seaside resort was. These ideas are imposed on members of the animal kingdom by humans – a process so well recognised that we have a name for it – **anthropomorphism** (from Greek 'anthropos', human, and 'morph', shape). Further examples of this would be the 'cuddly' bear, the 'cunning' fox, the 'evil' snake. They are not universal ideas, but are culture-specific, and different cultures may well have very different connotations for the same animal.

As well as cultural associations, individuals of course bring their own experiences and feelings to images: a cuddly bear may not seem so cuddly if you've been attacked by one.

Signs such as the ones you have just been studying are powerful rhetorical devices, for a number of reasons: they call up strong associations in the mind of the reader; they are economic, using no verbal language at all, and taking up minimal space; meanings can be fluid, so there is space to manipulate, adapt and change; signs can suggest several ideas at once, so they can be multi-purpose.

The ideas behind such signs – here, animals having certain characteristics – are used frequently in literary texts as forms of symbolism: for example, a poem could use a verbal description of a bird to suggest ideas about personal freedom. Such a poem could go further, by also setting out its lines in the shape of a bird's wings. The use of verbal text as a visual art form in poetry is often referred to as 'concrete poetry', and you can probably remember occasions in school when you were asked to create a text of that kind. (For an example, see p. 128.)

AS SIMPLE AS ABC

In looking at logos, it's clear that, even if readers are not consciously analysing and interpreting them, logos bring to mind a range of associations.

Just as logos are signs, so too are our common alphabetic letters and punctuation marks. But we don't go through the same process with them – or do we?

Look at the signs in Text: Signs and logos, which are all based on the English alphabet and punctuation system. Apart from the triangular road sign, these are all company logos.

Which alphabetic letters are being featured, and what do you think each of the signs is trying to suggest?

Text: Signs and logos

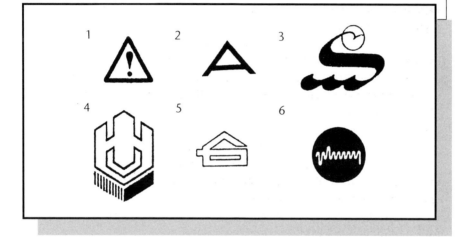

1   The exclamation mark suggests emotive expression – presumably as a result of the shock or surprise that the driver may experience if s/he encounters the impending road feature unprepared. Notice how quickly we process the meaning of this sign, and how complex the meaning actually is. We know not to take this sign iconically – we do not expect to be showered by exclamation marks! This sign is therefore doubly symbolic – as a road sign, and as a punctuation mark.

2   This is a roofing company, using the letter 'A' to represent a traditional roof shape.

3   This is a South African cruise-line company. The letter 'S' is deployed very cleverly: to represent a ship and the sea in its shape, and to suggest **sound symbolism** (linking sounds with certain ideas) by calling up the 's' sound as well, to remind us of the sea. (See later in this unit for

9

more exploration of sound symbolism.) In addition, the top of the 'S' becomes a seagull flying across the sun. Perhaps this company is capitalising on the fact that this has become a well-known symbol as a result of the success of another company – Thomson's – but hopes that we will associate the symbol with holidays in general rather than just the Thomson name.

4   and 5. These are both building-society logos, using an H and a G respectively. The associations we have may be for different types of building, the three-dimensional 'H' resembling a castle structure (an 'Englishman's home') while the 'G' appears as a more modest residence, such as a bungalow.

6   This is Plessey Radar. The writing looks like the company name, with the added suggestion of the kind of electrical impulse produced by a sophisticated piece of equipment – a radar screen, perhaps in a military installation. On the other hand, the machine could be registering a human pulse in a hospital context: a company with a scientific profile would benefit from being seen as humane and concerned with saving life.

English alphabetic letters are not symbols in the way the earliest forms of our writing were, where written symbols pictured what they represented: such symbols, called 'pictograms' or 'pictographs', have been discovered in many parts of the world – for example, Egypt (dated around 3000 BC) and China (1500 BC). The pictogram would be similar to one of the letters A, G or H in the previous activity standing for the whole concept of 'house' in all contexts and occurrences.

WHERE IT'S @

New communication technologies, such as computer-based communication, have given us new forms of written language and images, and new sites for their exploration. For example:

◎   As readers of paper-based texts, we have become accustomed to the static nature of icons, symbols and logos, but many websites now use animations that require a different sort of reading from that of a 'still' text;

◎   Some of our traditional punctuation marks have undergone something of a status shift. For example, the mark above – @ – only ever used to be used in business invoices, and the full stop – the bane of the schoolteacher's life – is now the essential ingredient in all website addresses. And . . .

◎ Whoever would have thought that punctuation could become a form of artwork? In the form of emoticons (written symbols put together to form a picture), punctuation appears to have a new, expressive function. Here are two examples. You need to incline your head to the left to understand them:

;-) (winking face)   :-p (sticking your tongue out)

◎ We have become so familiar with the kinds of texts that appear on the computer screen that they have begun to influence our paper-based texts, thus establishing a kind of reflexivity. The way in which one text can refer to or imitate another is sometimes called **inter-textuality**.

Activity

Look at Text: *City Life*, which is the front cover from a traditional paper text – a Manchester-based listings magazine. How is this front cover imitating the types of text you find on computer screens? Try to explore this in as much detail as you can. For example:

◎ Which different computer-based texts (and types of software) is this cover drawing on?
◎ How does the paper text imitate the types of interactive process that computer screen-readers regularly go through?
◎ Are there aspects of this cover that are more typical of traditional, paper-based magazines than of computer texts?

(Note: there is no commentary on this activity.)

Note: see satellite texts: *The Language of Magazines, The Language of ICT*

Text: *City Life*

In organising this unit, it was tempting to delay reference to computer texts until after the next section, which is about what we can learn from looking at children's writing, and at their views on literacy. But computer literacy is no longer the domain of a few adult specialists: even very young children know about computer texts, just as they know other forms of technology such as the telephone. However, the teacher who collected the material for the next section on children's views of reading and writing did not place a strong focus on computer texts when she did the activity. For this reason, you might think about how different the children's responses might have been if computers had been emphasised as sites for literacy. If you are interested in this area, you could do some research of your own along these lines.

FROM SPEECH TO WRITING

By the time we have reached adulthood, most of us have forgotten what it felt like to move from spoken to written language, and to encounter, not just a whole new set of conventions in terms of the features of writing, but a new set of rules about functions as well: just what are the purposes of written language? Why bother to have it at all? Why pay so much attention to it?

Activity

Read through the comments in Text: Why we read, and Text: Why do we/adults write? They are from classes of 7–8 year olds, asked about the purposes of writing and reading. What ideas come through here, and how do their ideas compare with your own – what do *you* see as the functions of written language?

Why We Read

Why do
We
Pri
because
We would
Our
going fo.
Coun[...]

We Read for a lot of things for one thing We need to Read because... if there is a sign that said "DANGER" and you cant Read it than something bad will happen.

1. We read because if we had to sing We would not be able to read the music.

2. To learn how to spell things.

3. To read nice books that you enjoy.

4. To spell properly.

5. To teach other people.

6. To read prices when you go in a shop.

7. When you go into a book shop you would now what book to get.

We read to our children to Educat them

frogs
fet

e read?

ed

on tins
we didnt
be wasting

time
to the
to ask.

to find out what has
happened in the past

We need to read so we can tell
what temperature an apple crumble
goes in.

Spelling	Prices
What.	£500,
Why.	11p.
We.	£299.
read.	£400.
dog.	44p.
cat.	62p.
bowl.	£4.62.
Light.	

to find out
whats on on tv

Spelling.

1) To teach other people to Spell
proptley with out getting it wrong

2) Prices.

To read the prices when you go
Into a Shop So you dont give
them the wrong price.

Why do we read

1) To find what happened's in the past.

2) if mum gives us a shopping list and we cant
read it you might get the wrong thing.

3) it makes you use a dictionary.

4) it helps you to spell things.

5) Because reading is good for us

tchis need
read
spells to
read
spell book

J.J.

...cause of checks and writing letters cards and to tell things to People they dant see.

They write to get atention and to cheques and lots of other things like that. Oh and Bills.

My mum writes Crosswords.
my Dad writes cheques.
my Grandma writes bets for the horses.
So does my Grandad

My mother writes letters to her friends

Grown ups write crosswords and shopping lists.

They write cheques Letters Bank and holliday Letters.

They write to relitaves to tell them what happend.

Grown-ups write to the milk man

because they need to.

I dont no

My mum and dad use a computer to write essays and important things for work.

Why do grown-ups write ?

Why do we write?

We write because in the future we will be awful to spell. To become clever and work.

You write to become clever and get a job

I write mostly for pleasure and because I want to. I write for school and to keep up ideas for my best stories.

Sometimes you write to ~~commu~~ communicate with people or to remember something.

For fun. and edjercashon. and writeeng bookes.

So people can read it instead of hearing it

Because it gives my hand excercise

I write to communicate

Sometimes I have to.

I write because it is relaxing and you sometimes learn from it

I write because its nice to know that you can and it gives my mind a rest.

because it is a way to explan.

Because I am told

We write so we can learn and if you cant write you cant read and then you can't learn.

I write because I enjoy writing sometimes.

I write because the teacher makes us.

17

Commentary

Some of the ideas that are expressed by the children could be grouped as follows:

1   The importance of literacy in terms of day-to-day functioning: reading recipes, seeing signs for danger, not being cheated in shops, finding out what's on TV, leaving notes for the milkman, writing shopping lists and cheques, and putting bets on. These are all ways of controlling and negotiating our world, and illustrate the importance of reading and writing as forms of instrumental, everyday communication.

2   Written language is seen as the repository of knowledge and therefore a means of educating ourselves. Writing produces tangible permanent artifacts – books – and as such is the archive of a culture's ideas and attitudes. To gain access to this store, we need to be able to read.

3   Written language is associated with being 'clever' and getting a job. In contemporary society, we take for granted the idea that literacy should be a universal entitlement. But compulsory schooling only started in 1870; traditionally, while spoken language was universal, writing was a very particular skill, learned only by those who were formally educated. In medieval times, writing was a professional skill – 'scribing' – for which money would be charged.

Even though we now view literacy as a basic skill for everyone, we still have a legacy which connects literacy with power in all sorts of ways, from the most obvious – the importance we give to written exams and application forms, the way we pay large sums of money to lawyers to write our legal documents and 'translate' them for us – to the slightly more subtle – the importance of signing your name (as opposed to giving a verbal agreement), the way libel is seen as a valid legal concept, while slander is not taken as seriously.

4   Both the pleasure and the labour of using literacy skills come across here. Unlike speech, which is spontaneous and feels relatively effortless, both writing and reading are skills which require concentration and subtle co-ordination of hand and eye movements, aside from all the different types of linguistic processing that they entail.

Observing children's transition from spoken to written language can give us many insights into how written texts work for us as adults.

Text: Jonathon is a piece of writing by Jonathon, age 4, reporting on his day out to Blackpool. In it, the writer uses initial letters to stand for whole words; the child's teacher wrote the full lines of text, after Jonathon read his writing back to her.

Using initial letters to stand for whole words is a common stage for early writers: it signals that a crucial connection has been made between speech and writing, but that not enough of each whole word can be mapped out in order to represent it graphically. Initial letters can be a useful aide-mémoire, to recall the whole word if necessary at some later stage (as here – it was two days later that Jonathon read his text back to the teacher); in learning the manual skill of writing, the hand quickly tires. This method is therefore a good way of writing a long text – something any teacher in the vicinity would be encouraging. Note also the importance of drawing in early texts such as these, where pictures are often an integral part of the writing. It is only the adult world that puts strong boundaries around these two types of activity, putting them into the separate categories of 'art' and 'writing'; for children who have yet to learn about the way adults divide up the world of representation, one type of symbolic mark must be much like another. It is well known that early drawing (what adults sometimes disparagingly call 'scribbling') is good preparation for the very fine movements needed to produce alphabetic letters.

Text: Jonathon

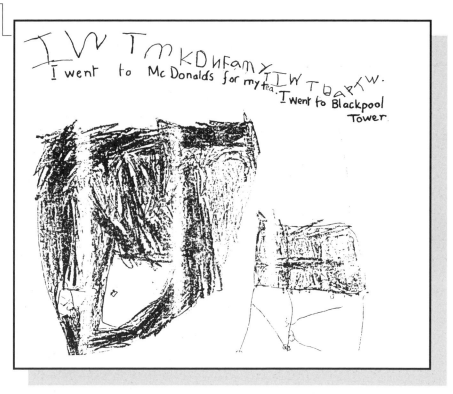

Where, in adult texts, do we use single letters or abbreviated forms of words on a regular basis? How do such alterations work? Are our reasons for doing this the same as Jonathon's? To get you started, read through Text: Estate agent's advert, then abbreviate the words as far as you can without removing the ability of the reader to reconstitute them:

Text: Estate agent's advert

Beautifully restored nineteenth-century farmhouse with two reception rooms, a large kitchen, three bedrooms, a bathroom and separate toilet. There is gas central heating throughout the house. Outside the property, there is a substantial double garage, and extensive gardens and outhouses. All the carpets and curtains are included in the selling price, which is £85,000 or nearest offer.

Commentary

In abbreviating the description of the house, you will have omitted many of the vowels (except where a vowel starts a word) but retained many of the consonants. This approach is at the basis of other examples of abbreviation, such as in 'T-line' shorthand. However, some words have such a distinctive profile, or are used so often in abbreviated form, that we come to understand them even when given only the first part of the word, especially when we see them used in a particular context – for example, the estate agent's material could have had 'beaut', '19thC', 'rec', 'sep', 'ext' and 'incl'. Some phrases are often abbreviated to initial letters (called **initialisms**) where this occurs on a regular basis: for example, GCH regularly means 'gas central heating', and ONO 'or nearest offer'. The latter examples are not very different from the child's strategy of initial-letter use; this same technique is also used regularly in personal ads (where GSOH in lonely hearts' columns means 'good sense of humour' and WLTM means 'would like to meet'), and in road signs – such as P for 'Parking' and H for 'hospital'. **Acronyms** also feature single letters, but they are then pronounced as whole words, whether recognised as a collection of letters (as in NATO) or not (as in laser – 'light amplification by the stimulated emission of radiation').

The reasons for our uses of initialisms and acronyms in adult texts could be determined by any one or several of the following factors: financial cost of advertising space (e.g. estate agents, personal ads); demands on the memory made by having to remember the whole word or series of words (e.g. acronyms); the need for speed in writing (e.g. shorthand), reading (e.g. roadsigns) or speaking (e.g. initialisms which enable us to refer quickly to institutions or artifacts – BBC, TV, CD-ROM, PC).

Extension

Collect as many examples as you can find of texts that use abbreviations, initialisms and acronyms. When you have collected your material, sort your examples into groups according to the techniques they use. Try to draw some conclusions about the reasons for the usages you have collected. If you are unsure about the comprehensibility of some of your examples, test them out on some informants of your own.

One area that hasn't been covered, but which you could explore in your data collection, is that of jokes, puzzles and riddles which involve playing around with written symbols. For example, some use single letters (but not necessarily initial letters) to stand for whole words, as in the following hoarding outside a church:

WHAT'S MISSING FROM THIS CH—CH?

You might find some more examples like this in children's comics and magazines, or in some types of English school textbook.

Another area to consider is abbreviated language use in computer chat-rooms, or in e-mails. For example, the following are quite common:

btw = by the way
pls = please
f2f = face to face
IRL = in real life
asl = age, sex, location (asked of participants in chatrooms)
ru = are you
2 = to, too
y = why
afk = away from the keyboard
bak = back at the keyboard
cya = see you

Activity

Another area where children can teach us a lot about the resources of written texts is that of sound effects. The writing system has a range of ways to call up some of the aspects of sound that we learn to pay attention to as part of the meaning of spoken language.

Read through the two children's stories in Text: Omar, and Text: Lauren.

How are these children using aspects of written language to try to suggest sound?

Text: Omar

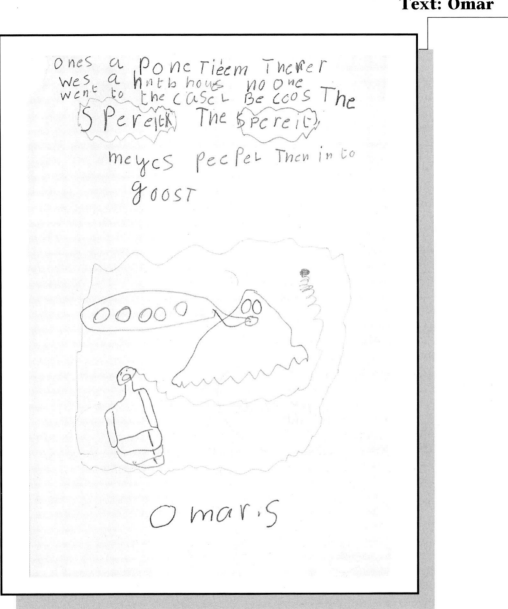

Ones a Pone Tieem Therer
wes a hntb houe no One
went to the cascl Be ccos The
S Pere(t) The S Pcre(t)

meycs pecPeL Then into

goost

Omar.S

~~The~~ my brithday

When it was my brithday I went to
a island for a picnic.. I take
Simone and megan. We went in a boat
Waen we got there we played for
a pitr then we had . The picnic
~~then~~ we came to going home the
boat had gone I Started to
cry. I whant to go home
Simone had a ~~idey~~ I deau We can
make a ward out of pebbles.
What is the ward going to
Say ~~holpt~~ help??? yes Side
megan. Losts get going I ho
I ho its of to work We
go There ~~we have~~ ~~work~~
Wave finish At home mum
and dad had Send a
Sertch party. At the island
the were sitting woting.
A l helicopter they Saw the
Words h.e.l.p then we all
Side hepp. the helicopter
came with laders we ~~clamnd~~
Clamnd up.

Omar (age 5) enhances his story with a picture where a ghostly figure makes 'ooooo' sounds, in an attempt to provide something of an atmospheric soundtrack. This also occurs within the text itself: the reader knows that the words 'The Spirit, The Spirit' need to be pronounced in a 'spooky' way, as a result of their having wobbly lines round them. It's difficult to say exactly where this convention is from, but likely contenders could be comics and those science-fiction films where the screen 'dissolves' as the narrator goes back in time to remember 'when it all began'. (Note the very logical sound-based spelling, 'ones a pone tieem' for 'once upon a time'.)

Lauren (age 7) uses a range of devices to suggest features of spoken language: the enlargement of letters and the darker print in the words 'gone' and 'help?' suggest increased volume – in the first word, as a result of shock, and in the second, to signal a voice calling out. The question mark on 'help' indicates a speaker's raised voice when asking another character whether that is the right word to use. While the characters work to build their word out of pebbles, there is a soundtrack: 'Hi ho, hi ho, it's off to work we go'. This is particularly appropriate, as in *Snow White and the Seven Dwarfs*, from which the soundtrack comes, the dwarfs sing this as they go off stone-breaking in the mines. The sense of time passing, as the characters go through a laborious routine of repetitive work, is therefore achieved.

Towards the end, there is a clever use of full-stops to indicate that the letters in the word 'h.e.l.p.' are written (in pebbles, of course) rather than spoken.

If writers can use aspects of writing to suggest sound, this is unlikely to remain unnoticed by the advertisers of hi-fi equipment.

Text: Metz & Rahmen is an advert for personal stereos.

Identify the written language devices being used by the advertisers to refer to or represent aspects of sound. (Note: there is no commentary on this activity.)

Text: Metz & Rahmen

Lots of people settle for any old personal stereo —they jusst put up with the hissSing and accept that sometimes only one earpiece works at a time. They TURN UP THE VOLUME until the sound is so distorted that its just a NIGHTMARE Then, just when they're listening to their favourite music, their batteries *conk out on them.....* or their headphones *drop to bits* in their lap. Not with Metz & Rahmen.

EEZZZy listening that's a dream .

(((M&R)))

Note: see satellite text: *The Language of Advertising*

Activity

Writers of fiction often try to give the reader a sense of spoken language, in a variety of ways: they may want to construct a 'voice' for the narrator, so that the reader can distinguish this address from the language used by the characters; there are the various voices of the characters themselves when they are talking to each other; and there are 'inner voices' in the form of the thoughts of the characters, relayed to readers by the narrator.

Below is an extract from *Ladder of Years*, by Anne Tyler, published in 1995. It is the opening of the novel.

◎ How does the writer use graphological features – in particular, punctuation and variations in typeface – to suggest aspects of spoken discourse?

◎ How much cannot be conveyed by such features, but has to be explained by the narrator directly, in the form of description?

Text: *Ladder of Years*

This all started on a Saturday morning in May, one of those warm spring days that smell like clean linen. Delia had gone to the supermarket to shop for the week's meals. She was standing in the produce section, languidly choosing a bunch of celery. Grocery
5 stores always made her reflective. Why was it, she was wondering, that celery was not called 'corduroy plant'? That would be much more colorful. And garlic bulbs should be 'moneybags,' because their shape reminded her of the sacks of gold coins in folktales.

A customer on her right was sorting through the green onions.
10 It was early enough so the store was nearly empty, and yet this person seemed to be edging in on her a bit. Once or twice the fabric of his shirt sleeve brushed her dress sleeve. Also, he was really no more than stirring those onions around. He would lift one rubber-banded clump and then drop it and alight on another. His fingers
15 were very long and agile, almost spidery. His cuffs were yellow oxford cloth.

He said, 'Would you know if these are called scallions?'

'Well, sometimes,' Delia said. She seized the nearest bunch of celery and stepped toward the plastic bags.
20 'Or would they be shallots?'

'No, they're scallions,' she told him.

Needlessly, he steadied the roll of bags overhead while she peeled one off. (He towered a good foot above her.) She dropped the celery into the bag and reached toward the cup of twist ties,
25 but he had already plucked one out for her. 'What are shallots, anyway?' he asked.

She would have feared that he was trying to pick her up, except that when she turned she saw he was surely ten years her junior, and very good-looking besides. He had straight, dark-yellow hair
30 and milky blue eyes that made him seem dreamy and peaceful. He was smiling down at her, standing a little closer than strangers ordinarily stand.

'Um . . .,' she said, flustered.

'Shallots,' he reminded her.
35 'Shallots are fatter,' she said. She set the celery in her grocery cart. 'I believe they're above the parsley,' she called over her shoulder, but she found him next to her, keeping step with her as she wheeled her cart toward the citrus fruits. He wore blue jeans, very faded, and soft moccasins that couldn't be heard above 'King

40 of the Road' on the public sound system.

'I also need lemons,' he told her.

She slid another glance at him.

'Look,' he said suddenly. He lowered his voice. 'Could I ask you a big favor?'

45 'Um . . .'

'My ex-wife is up ahead in potatoes. Or not ex I guess but . . . estranged, let's say, and she's got her boyfriend with her. Could you just pretend we're together? Just till I can duck out of here?'

'Well, of course,' Delia said.

50 And without even taking a deep breath first, she plunged happily back into the old high-school atmosphere of romantic intrigue and deception. She narrowed her eyes and lifted her chin and said, 'We'll *show* her!' and sailed past the fruits and made a U-turn into root vegetables. 'Which one is she?' she murmured

55 through ventriloquist lips.

'Tan shirt,' he whispered. Then he startled her with a sudden burst of laughter. 'Ha, ha!' he told her too loudly. 'Aren't you clever to say so!'

But 'tan shirt' was nowhere near an adequate description. The

60 woman who turned at the sound of his voice wore an ecru raw-silk tunic over black silk trousers as slim as two pencils. Her hair was absolutely black, cut shorter on one side, and her face was a perfect oval. 'Why, Adrian,' she said. Whoever was with her – some man or other – turned too, still gripping a potato. A dark, thick

65 man with rough skin like stucco and eyebrows that met in the middle. Not up to the woman's standard at all; but how many people were?

Delia's companion said, 'Rosemary. I didn't see you. So don't forget,' he told Delia, not breaking his stride. He set a hand on her cart to steer it into aisle 3. 'You promised me you'd make your

70 marvelous blancmange tonight.'

'Oh, yes, my . . . blancmange,' Delia echoed faintly. Whatever blancmange might be, it sounded the way she felt just then: pale and plain-faced and skinny, with her freckles and her frizzy brown curls and her ruffled pink round-collared dress.

75 They had bypassed the dairy case and the juice aisle, where Delia had planned to pick up several items, but she didn't point that out because this Adrian person was still talking. 'Your blancmange and then your, uh, what, your meat and vegetables and da-da-da . . .'

> 80 The way he let his voice die reminded her of those popular songs that end with the singers just absentmindedly drifting away from the microphone. 'Is she looking at us?' he whispered. 'Check it out. Don't make it obvious.'
>
> Delia glanced over, pretending to be struck by a display of converted rice. Both the wife and the boyfriend had their backs to her, but there was something artificial in their posture. No one 85 could find russet potatoes so mesmerizing. 'Well, she's mentally looking,' Delia murmured. She turned to see her grocery cart rapidly filling with pasta. Egg noodles, rotini, linguine – Adrian flung in boxes at random. 'Excuse me . . .,' she said.

Commentary

David Crystal's *The Cambridge Encyclopedia of the English Language* (1995) lists four main functions for punctuation: grammar, where features such as full stops and commas mark out grammatical units; prosody, where such symbols as speech marks, question marks and exclamation marks indicate that someone is speaking, and that their voice is behaving in certain ways; rhetoric, where some forms of punctuation – most notably, colons and semi-colons – map out aspects of argument or explanation (as in this paragraph); and semantic nuance, where features of emphasis such as quotation marks suggest a particular attitude to a word or phrase being 'marked out'.

Anne Tyler uses punctuation to mark out grammatical units in the same way as writers of many other types of text. There are two examples of the rhetorical function listed above: these are a colon in line 72, which points forward to the explanation that follows it, and the semi-colon in line 66 which balances the sentences either side of the punctuation mark, bringing them into more dramatic parallel than a comma would do, and leading up to a rhetorical question (a question posed for effect, rather than one requiring a real answer).

What is noticeable, however, is Tyler's extensive use of the prosodic and the semantic nuance functions. This is hardly suprising, given that these are concerned with constructing a sense of voice, and with establishing attitudes.

Examples of the prosodic function: within the language of the characters themselves – speech marks, lines of dots suggesting a voice trailing off, question marks, exclamation marks, italics to suggest emphasis; within the language used by the narrator – brackets and dashes in lines 23, 63 and 64, 87 and 88 to suggest a change in pace as a result of adding extra information.

Examples of the semantic nuance function: quotation marks in the narrator's report of Delia's thoughts in lines 6 and 7; the same in the narrator's commentary in lines 39 and 59.

Despite these extensive markers, there is still much about the way the characters speak that has to be described by the narrator. Here are some examples: 'she called over her shoulder'; 'he lowered his voice'; 'she murmured through ventriloquist lips'; 'he whispered'; 'he startled her with a sudden burst of laughter'; 'he told her too loudly'; 'Delia echoed faintly'; 'the way he let his voice die reminded her . . .'.

These examples illustrate that, in the end, written language cannot do justice to the subtleties of speech. All it can do is to give us some signposts as readers, via devices such as punctuation marks, to help us create the idea of speech in our heads.

Note: see satellite text: *The Language of Fiction, The Language of Drama*

Extension

Collect some texts that are using features of written language in order to suggest aspects of speech. You could focus on a particular area: for example, children's early writing; advertising; literature.

SPACE-SHIFTING

In computer language, space is treated as if it were a mark on the page; it therefore has the same status as a punctuation mark or a letter. The fact that this seems like an odd notion is evidence of how much we take space in written texts for granted, both in its existence and where it should occur: in English, words have gaps between them, lines of writing are separated by space, pages have no-go areas called 'margins', application forms announce sternly 'do not write below this line'. Rules about space are part of the way we formulate rules about textual shape.

Space is actually meaningful in a variety of ways. To begin with, different languages have very different rules about orientation – Arabic reads from right to left, Chinese from top to bottom – therefore ideas about where spaces should occur will be different, leading to different written patterns.

It's also clear that we have notions, as readers, of an appropriate amount of space in and around texts: for example, we talk about some forms of writing being off-putting because they look too densely packed, or some texts looking rather hectic and 'busy', perhaps because the writing in them is set at odd angles on the page or contains overlaps; we might also say that writing looks rather 'lost' on a page because it doesn't fill the space adequately. Such ideas about crowds and loneliness appear to vary according to a number of factors associated with the reader – age being one significant dimension: the size of print, the amount of space left on the page, and the ratio of verbal language to pictures will be very different in a children's reader compared with a book such as this one.

Activity

As well as the space around texts, the space inside texts is meaningful. For example, if we expect a text to occur, then its absence, or partial absence, can be startling. This is illustrated by Text: NSPCC, which uses the strategy of absence to make the powerful statement that the true text is too upsetting to print. Think about the following:

◎   Why has the advertiser decided to leave the lines and full stops in this text, rather than just offering a blank space?

(Note: there is no commentary on this activity.)

Text: NSPCC

This is a 12-year-old's account of the abuse she suffered from her father.
The more shocking details of her story have been removed.

Tomorrow is FULL STOP day. Wear the badge. Phone 09069 123 888 for yours. **Cruelty to children must stop. FULL STOP ● NSPCC™**

Calls cost £1 per minute at all times. Calls will not exceed 3 minutes. All profits from the phone line will go direct to the NSPCC. Registered charity 216401

Space, defining the shape of a text, is also one powerful way of recognising different types of writing (also called **genres**). This activity will test out how far it is possible to identify different written genres without being able to read any of the actual words the texts contain. First, brainstorm as many distinctively different types of writing as you can think of. Here are some examples, to start you off:

- shopping list
- menu
- recipe
- letter
- poem
- newspaper article.

When you have exhausted your list, without writing any words, draw the shape of each of your texts by using lines to represent the shape of the writing, and boxes to show artwork such as photographs. You can use any number of different lines, plus asterisks, bullet points, arrows, or any ornamental features you want to include. Here is an example of a shopping list:

When you have finished drawing your texts, swop them with those from other students in your group, without saying what the texts are: see how many can be guessed accurately. There may well be more than one possible outcome for a particular shape: where this happens, try to see what the various 'guesses' have in common in terms of their nature and purpose. (Note: there is no commentary on this activity.)

Activity

Because particular written genres are associated with certain textual designs, the idea of textual design can be used by one text to suggest another. This was discussed with reference to the *City Life* magazine cover (p. 12), where the concept of intertextuality was introduced.

Look at Text: Demon Internet, which consists of an envelope, plus contents in the form of a card plus 'Post-it' note. The context for these texts were that the recipient cancelled their subscription to the Demon Internet service. How does this mailing use our knowledge of a range of other texts to construct its message?

Text: Demon Internet

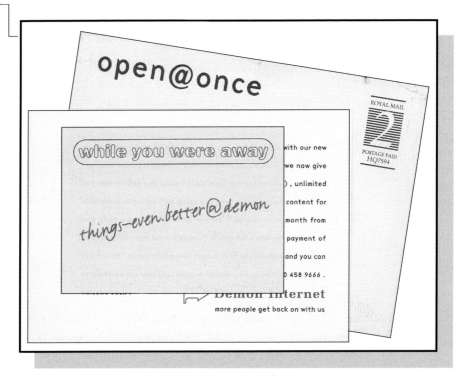

we were sorry when you left us . so let us tempt you back with our new

upgraded standard service , still only £10+vat a month . we now give

you 15mb of free web space (triple what you had before) , unlimited

email addresses and a free games web site . plus LineOne™ content for

only £3.20 a month after three months' free trial (one month from

september 25) and our fax to email service for a one-off payment of

£19.99+vat . re-registering your account is absolutely free and you can

keep exactly the same host name as before . call us on 0800 458 9666 .

welcome back .

Demon Internet
more people get back on with us

Commentary

The envelope uses the @ symbol to indicate that this is a communication about new technology, with the @ substituting for the word 'at' in the phrase 'open at once'. This phrase commands the imaginary recipient – the **narratee** – to take urgent action. Inside, the 'Post-it' note imitates the kind of message written by the receivers of phone calls: evidence for this is the phrase 'while you were away' at the top, which also refers to the fact that the recipient of the mail was 'away' from the Demon service. Interestingly, the pseudo-**URL** (Internet address) 'things-even.better@demon' is handwritten, suggesting that the 'phone call' convinced someone other than the recipient – another narratee – that good deals were to be had. When the 'Post-it' note is peeled off, the card sets out some of the suggested improvements to the service. The text on the card endorses the fact that Demon are old hands at Internet communication by using unconventional capitalisation: lower case letters have become a **signifier** of computer-based texts. It also personalises the communication by using direct address – 'you' – to the recipient. By the end of the text, it is assumed that the recipient has signed up again: it says 'welcome back'. The slogan at the end is another piece of intertextuality in being a version of the regular Demon slogan, which is 'more people get on with us'. Both slogans demonstrate a double meaning in the phrase

3 5

'get on', referring both to getting on the Internet and having good relationships with people.

This communication represents a growing number of texts that are interactive – that is, they are constructed to be handled and manipulated by the recipient. Such texts feature commonly in 'junk' mailings.

Activity

Text: Boots No. 7 is another piece of 'junk' mail that was addressed personally to the recipient. This text also uses strongly intertextual strategies. Read it through carefully and answer the following:

◎ Which other texts are being referred to throughout the mailing?
◎ Why are the intertextual references you have identified above being used?
◎ How do the verbal texts relate to the images and other graphological features being used? Pay particular attention to the typeface and layout (it may be useful for you to know that the original envelope was black with emerald green lettering).

(Note: there is no commentary on this activity.)

Note: see satellite texts: *The Language of Advertising, The Language of ICT*

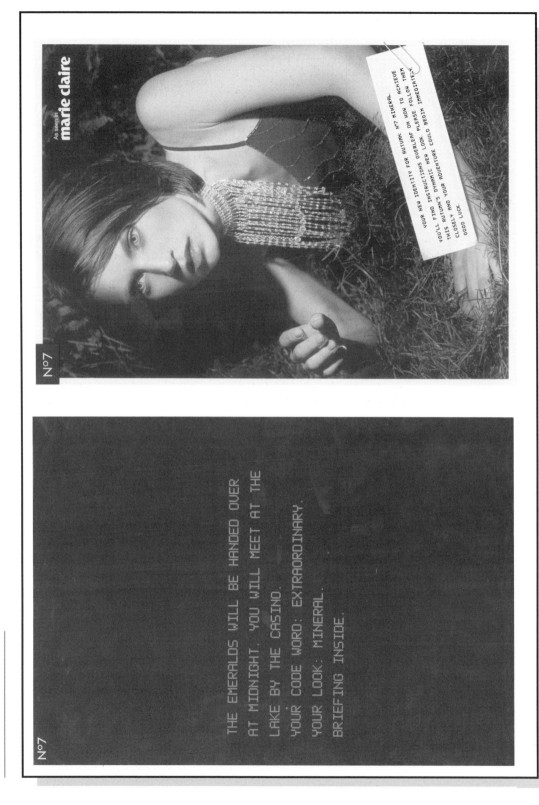

N°7

ONLY FOR EYES OF ADDRESSEE:

03446004 8   DM97000210 3

MS A GODDARD
2 PIKES LANE
GLOSSOP
DERBYSHIRE
SK13 8EA

20361

TO: MS A GODDARD
FROM: S.LAYTON, N°7

MESSAGE READS:

HERE IS YOUR NEW IDENTITY FOR AUTUMN – N°7 MINERAL. AN EXPLORATION OF
METALLIC GREENS AND GREYS, BURNISHED COPPER AND A GLINT OF GOLD – INSPIRED
BY THE COOL, OXIDISED HUES OF NEWLY MINED PRECIOUS METALS. DIG DEEP INTO
YOUR OWN SENSE OF ADVENTURE. THIS IS A GO-ANYWHERE, DO-ANYTHING LOOK.

THESE ARE THE PRODUCTS YOU SHOULD MAKE YOUR TOP PRIORITY.

NEW MINERALS COLOUR PERFECT TRIO...OLIVE SUPERLASH MASCARA...OLIVE PRECISION
EYE PENCIL...METALLIC TRUFFLE COLOUR LOCK™ LIPCOLOUR...NEW MALTESE COLOUR
LOCK ULTRA™ LIPCOLOUR...COPPER COLOUR LOCK ULTRA™ LIPCOLOUR...MERLIN COLOUR
LOCK™ NAIL ENAMEL...GREENGAGE COLOUR LOCK™ NAIL ENAMEL...LIMITED EDITION
GOLDEN SHINE STICK.

YOUR REWARD:

CHOOSE ANY TWO OF THE PRODUCTS LISTED ABOVE OR ANY OTHER TWO FROM THE N°7
RANGE* AND YOU WILL RECEIVE A FREE DAILY SKINCARE PRODUCT.

RENDEZVOUS: NEAREST N°7 COUNTER
CRITICAL DATES: 30/9/98 – 20/10/98

TO CREATE YOUR NEW IDENTITY, YOUR INSTRUCTIONS ARE ENCLOSED.
READ AND PROCEED INTO ACTION.

MESSAGE ENDS.

*QUALIFYING PURCHASES EXCLUDE DAILY SKINCARE, OFFER SUBJECT TO AVAILABILITY.

010807

FOR YOUR EYES:

USE NEW N°7 MINERALS COLOUR PERFECT TRIO. APPLY THE
AMAZON-INSPIRED BLUES AND GREENS IN COLOUR BLOCKS ON THE
UPPER LID OR AROUND THE EYE. TURN UP THE INTENSITY BY
APPLYING OLIVE PRECISION EYE PENCIL TO UPPER AND LOWER
LASH LINES. AND FOR MAXIMUM IMPACT, COAT LASHES WITH
OLIVE SUPERLASH MASCARA.

FOR YOUR FACE:

FOR A POWERFUL RADIANCE, APPLY N°7'S LIMITED EDITION
GOLDEN SHINE STICK HIGH ON CHEEKBONES. TO BE MORE STRIKING
YET, ADD TOUCHES DOWN CENTRE OF NOSE AND EYEBROW ARCH.

FOR YOUR LIPS:

LUSCIOUS AND MYSTERIOUS, N°7 COLOUR LOCK™ LIPCOLOUR IN
METALLIC TRUFFLE OR COLOUR LOCK ULTRA™ LIPCOLOUR IN NEW
MALTESE IS EASY TO APPLY: LONG LASTING COLOUR IN ONE
SWEEP. NOTE: COLOUR LOCK ULTRA™ LIPCOLOUR WITH ITS UNIQUE
MOISTURE SEAL™ LASTS UP TO 12 HOURS.

FOR YOUR NAILS:

APPLY TWO LAYERS OF COLOUR LOCK™ NAIL ENAMEL IN MERLIN
OR GREENGAGE FOR A LIGHT BUT METALLIC EFFECT.

WHO'S IN THE PICTURE?

At the beginning of this unit, the focus was on signs and symbols involving non-human images. But as you saw more recently in this unit, images can also feature people and, as with all the signs that have been studied so far, there is no such thing as simple neutrality: the way people are represented can call up powerful connotations that work alongside the verbal language in a text. Analysing images in the form of photographs, paintings and drawings is clearly a large area in its own right. To do justice to this, a range of academic areas would need to be addressed – including art, media studies, cultural studies and anthropology. But the fact that analysing images may open up several more academic areas doesn't mean that language analysts can simply ignore visual aspects, since images form an important part of the way we 'read' the world. What is offered here, then, is a set of headings and questions as a starting point: if you want to explore this area further now, look through this book, fix on some of the texts that use images as part of their message, and apply the ideas below to them. On the other hand, you may decide to come back to these questions later, as you deal with the texts that form part of each unit.

Content: what is the content of the picture?

◎ What artifacts are in the picture?
◎ Are there any non-human beings in the picture?
◎ What people are included?: consider gender, age, ethnicity, occupation, social class, region, sexuality.
◎ What is the setting?

Genre: how is the content being presented?

◎ What is being suggested by the content and how it is set up? For example, does it involve a story of some kind, where certain types of people might own the artifacts in the picture, or where some action has occurred before the image was 'captured'?
◎ How does the reader use his/her cultural knowledge to make sense of the picture and the way the items relate to each other within it?

Techniques: what are some of the mechanisms and effects?

◎ What method of representation has been chosen, and why (for example, photograph, line drawing, painting, computer-generated image)?

◎ How is the viewer's position established by the techniques used (for example, camera angle, perspective, body language and eye contact of the 'actors')? Is the viewer in a more or less powerful position than the people or things in the picture?

◎ Does the picture presume that the viewer is interacting with it in some way?

◎ What colours and dress codes are present? What technical treatments have been used (for example, glossy surfaces, sepia tints, soft-focus photography)?

Inter-relationships

◎ How do features of the image relate to the verbal aspects of the text?

◎ Does the whole text refer to or base itself on another text and if so, why?

◎ If so, what part does the picture play in this?

Agencies and audiences

◎ On the evidence of the answers to the previous questions, what cultural attitudes and values are being presented by the producers?

◎ What assumptions are made about the audience's views, interests and composition?

Sounds

Just as signs connote ideas for language users, so do sounds.

Sound as a system is primary: it is the first code learnt by individuals in their lives; it also came before writing historically as a system of communication for humans in general. However, the fact that speech is primary does not mean that our responses to sound are simple and straightforward. The way we talk about sound, for example, is often metaphorical, where we describe sounds not in terms of our hearing, but in terms of our other senses: we say some sounds are 'big', 'small' or 'rounded' (sight); some are 'piercing', 'hard', 'soft' or 'abrasive' (touch); others are 'sweet' (taste). We have developed systems for the interpretation of sounds that may or may not have a base in physical reality; in the end, whether our attitudes to sound are physically based or culturally constructed, the result is the same – sounds still have an *effect* on us. The aim of this unit is to familiarise you with the physical nature of sounds, so that you are more accurately able to assess the way we interpret them, both in speech and in written texts.

A SOUND ALPHABET

The Roman alphabet, which is what you are reading now, cannot represent the sounds of spoken English with total accuracy and uniformity. It has been estimated that there is only about a 40 per cent correspondence between the sounds and written symbols of English. For example, one spelling can have many different pronunciations (consider how 'ough' is pronounced in 'through', 'cough', 'dough', 'thorough' and 'ought'); one sound can be represented by different written symbols ('meat', 'meet' and 'metre' all contain the same vowel sound, but this sound is spelt in different ways).

Because of the problems outlined above, linguists use a set of symbols called the International Phonetic Alphabet, or IPA, to represent sounds. Even if you have never heard its official name, you will have come across the IPA in dictionaries, where the pronunciation of a word is often given in brackets, before the definition. The IPA covers the sounds of all the world's known languages. This book will only be using that part of it that describes the sounds of the English language. Some of the symbols will already be familiar to you because they exist in the Roman alphabet; others won't be, but they will be explained later. When you work with the symbols that follow, remember that the underlined part of the word given as an example of each sound refers to how that sound would be produced by someone with a **Received Pronunciation** (RP) accent. This is the accent you would be likely to hear when listening to a British national TV news broadcaster. It is an accent which does not mark the speaker as coming from a particular region (but does give messages about the user's social-class membership). If you speak with a regional accent, you may find some differences between the chart and the sounds you would make in pronouncing certain words.

Text: IPA symbols

IPA symbols for English sounds

Consonants

p - pip
b - bib
t - ten
d - den
k - cat
g - get
f - fish
v - van
θ - thigh
ð - thy
s - set
z - zen
ʃ - ship
ʒ - leisure
h - hen
tʃ - church
dʒ - judge
m - man
n - man
ŋ - sing
l - let
r - ride
w - wet
j - yet

Short vowels

ɪ pit
ɛ pet
æ pat
ɒ pot
ʌ putt
ʊ put
ə patter

Long vowels

i: bean
ɜ: burn
ɑ: barn
ɔ: born
u: boon

Diphthongs

aɪ bite
ɛɪ bait
ɔɪ boy
əʊ roe
aʊ house
ʊə poor
ɪə ear
ɛə air

(Note: the headings under which vowels are grouped will be explained later.)

Activity

In order to become familiar with the alphabet, write your name using the appropriate symbols. Forget the spelling of your name, and concentrate on the sounds that are produced when you say it aloud. Exchange your writing with someone else, and get them to read back what you have written.

Then have a go at transcribing the sentence below, assuming that the speaker had an RP accent. In some cases, the sounds in a word will be influenced by the words either side of it, so take notice of how the sounds blend together as the sentence as a whole is said, rather than taking each word strictly in isolation. This instruction itself says a lot about the difference between speech and writing: we don't necessarily speak in 'words' with pauses around them – the very concept of a word is an idea derived from writing.

> Would you please queue at the end of the corridor?
>
> (Answer and commentary on p. 69)

SPEECH PRODUCTION AND DESCRIPTION: CONSONANTS

Sounds in English are produced as a result of air from the lungs coming up through the vocal cords and being manipulated in various ways. We describe consonants by answering three questions about how they are produced physically:

1 How is the airstream manipulated? *Manner of articulation*
2 Where does this happen? *Place of articulation*
3 Are the vocal cords vibrating or not? *Voiced or voiceless sound*

Plosives: p b t d k g

These sounds (or '**phonemes**') are all explosions: they are created by obstructing the flow of air by bringing parts of the mouth together, then letting go suddenly. To explore this, place the palm of your hand in front

44

of your mouth and, one by one, make each of these sounds in an exaggerated way. You should be able to feel the air from your mouth hitting your palm. English plosives (also called 'stops') are differentiated from each other in two ways: they are made in different places in the mouth (place of articulation, above), and they use different amounts of voice (as 3, above). While /p/ and /b/ are produced using the two lips (bilabial), /t/ and /d/ involve contact between the tongue and the teeth ridge (alveolar); /k/ and /g/ are made by closing off air at the back of the mouth (velar). See the diagram below.

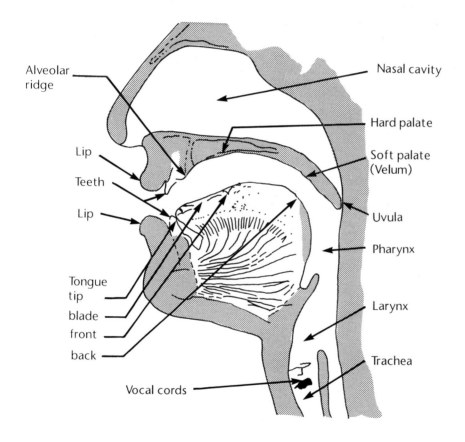

Each of these pairs of sounds has one voiced and one voiceless phoneme, as follows:

Voiceless	Voiced
p	b
t	d
k	g

To understand the idea of voice, put your fingers on your 'Adam's Apple' and alternate between the voiceless and voiced phonemes several times: you should be aware that your vocal cords are vibrating when you say the voiced sounds. If all the plosives sound voiced to you, this will be because you are adding a vowel (which are all voiced) and your voiceless plosives are picking up some of the vowel's voiced quality. For example, you might be adding the vowel /ə/. If you are doing this, make the voiceless sounds as if you were whispering them.

Fricatives: f v θ ð s z ʃ ʒ h

While plosives are produced by completely obstructing the airflow, fricatives involve a lesser obstruction where air is forced through in a steady stream, resulting in friction rather than explosion. Plosives cannot be kept going in the way fricatives can: to illustrate this idea, say an /s/ until you run out of breath; now try to keep a /p/ sound going. You will find that all you can do for the latter is to produce a number of separate /p/ sounds, one after the other.

Fricatives, like plosives, are distinguished from each other by their place of articulation, and by voice, each pair below being made up of a voiceless and voiced phoneme – apart from 'h', which is voiceless but has no voiced partner:

Voiceless	Voiced
f	v
θ (as in 'thigh')	ð (as in 'thy')
s	z
ʃ (as in 'ship')	ʒ (as in 'leisure')
h	

As with plosives, go through these phonemes, exploring where they are made in the mouth and sounding out their differences in terms of voice. (If your version of 'h' sounds voiced, this is because you are adding a vowel again, and saying something like 'huh'. The 'h' sound above is the sound that you would make if you were whispering.)

Some linguists regard /h/ as a weak and vulnerable fricative because of its isolation, and point to its absence from many regional accents to support the view that it may eventually drop out of the English language altogether.

Affricates: tʃ **(as in 'church')** dʒ **(as in 'judge')**

There are only two of these consonant sounds in English. They have double symbols to represent the fact that each one is a plosive followed by a fricative. If you make these sounds in very slow motion you may be able to hear this sequence. /tʃ/ is voiceless and /dʒ/ is its voiced partner.

Nasals: m n ŋ **(as in 'singing')**

The distinctive feature of these sounds is that they are produced in a particular manner: the airstream comes out through the nose rather than the mouth. They differ from each other in being made in different places: /m/ is bilabial, /n/ is alveolar, and /ŋ/ is velar. When you have a cold and air cannot escape from the nose, nasals become plosives, as in the second version of 'good morning' below:

gʊd mɔːnɪŋ
gʊd bɔːdɪŋg

Laterals: l

This sound is sometimes referred to as a 'liquid' sound, and is made by placing the tip of the tongue on the teeth ridge and sending air down the sides of the mouth. The easiest way to experience this airflow is to put the tongue in the right position to say an /l/, then breathe in instead of out: you should be able to feel the air flowing along the sides of your tongue. This is the reverse of what happens when you say an /l/ normally.

Approximants: r w j

The final three consonants are usually grouped together because they share the property of being midway between consonants and vowels; in some linguistic descriptions you will see them called 'semi-vowels'. They all involve less contact between the organs of speech than many of the other consonants: compare /r/ with /p/, for example. While /r/ and /j/ are produced in the palatal area (roof of the mouth), /w/ is a bilabial.

Glottal: ?

This does not appear on the list of symbols because it doesn't represent a sound as such. It is a closure of the vocal cords, resulting in shutting off the airstream, and it is sometimes produced as an alternative to certain plosive sounds. To explore this, say the words 'butter' and 'water', but 'swallow' the /t/ in the middle of each word. The glottal stop is a strong feature of some regional accents, and written texts often represent it by an apostrophe: for example, 'I've go' a lo' of li'le bo'les'.

Below is a summary of the consonant system in English. The chart shows place and manner of articulation; a colon marks voice, where there is a pair of sounds contrasted by this feature, voiceless sounds being to the left and voiced to the right. /r/ and /j/ are together because they are both palatal sounds, but they are not separated by a colon because they are not a voiceless/voiced pair.

Manner of articulation	Bilabial	Labio-dental	Dental	Alveolar	Palatal	Velar	Glottal
Plosive	p : b			t : d		k : g	ʔ
Affricate					tʃ : dʒ		
Fricative		f : v	θ : ð	s : z	ʃ : ʒ		h
Nasal	m			n		ŋ	
Lateral				l			
Approximant	w				r j		

Place of articulation

48

IT'S NOT WHAT YOU SAY,
IT'S THE WAY THAT YOU SAY IT

Some of the sounds you have been studying vary considerably on a regional and ethnic basis: for example, Cockney and Afro-Caribbean Patwa speakers have no /h/ phoneme; /ŋ/ is regularly replaced by /n/ in the West Country, and by /ŋg/ in some Northern accents; glottal stops are a common feature in many regional accents. Such regional variations are often stigmatised, being regarded as 'bad', 'sloppy' or 'lazy' speech in some quarters. It's important to realise that these judgements are social, rather than linguistic: they are examples of how language can be used as a shibboleth – a way of more powerful groups marking out their own forms of language as prestigious and 'correct' and that of others as inadequate in order to forestall social movement and prevent others' access to power.

Being able to describe these aspects of language phonetically can help you to understand and explain the differences between linguistic facts and social attitudes. One aspect that should be apparent, if you work further on accent variation using the IPA, is that quite extensive and complex sets of attitudes are based on rather small features of language: for example, that a speaker has specific character traits, a certain degree of social status, or a particular level of intelligence as a result of whether s/he uses one phoneme or another.

Activity

In Text: Mother of the Nation, and Text: Leader's speech, both cartoons by Steve Bell, a certain type of accent is suggested by altering the spelling of words (known as 'eye-dialect'); this accent is then linked with particular attitudes and values as expressed by the speakers.

Discuss the stereotypes that are often associated with this type of accent. Compare the stereotypes you have identified with those often associated with regionally accented speakers. (Note: there is no commentary on this activity.)

Text: Mother of the Nation

Text: Leader's speech

Extension

1   Collect some written material where the writers have tried to represent accent on the page, and analyse their approaches: for example, have they altered the spellings of words, or used apostrophes to show glottal stops? How do their strategies compare with the real phonetic features of that accent? (If you can't spend time doing some phonetic analysis yourself, you can find information on accent variations in linguistic text-books.) You will find further work on the representation of speech in Unit 5.

2   Record some TV adverts, and analyse how differently accented speakers are used. For example, which products are sold by the use of regionally accented voiceovers or actors, and which by RP-accented voices? What qualities are associated with particular accents? Are male and female regional and RP speakers used in the same ways? What accents are given to non-white speakers of English in adverts? How are foreign-accented speakers used?

SOUND SYMBOLISM

Another important use of the IPA is to help us understand any possible basis for sound symbolism. This is the process by which we use the different sounds produced by our speech organs to stand for some of the sounds around us in our environment. When we form these sounds into whole words that themselves stand for noises, like 'bang', 'crash', and 'thud', this is called **onomatopoeia**. This area is by no means clear cut, however. Take, for example, the sound effects often seen in comics, as in Text: Comic 'noises'. Are these really an accurate description of noises, or do we just interpret them as such because we are used to the convention of the words meaning specific things? Are they understandable outside the context of the page where they occurred, without all the picture and story cues to support comprehension? Would someone who had never read a comic understand them? And are they language-specific: would someone who isn't an English speaker interpret them the same way, even though that person's organs of speech produce all the same sounds as ours? (You might be interested to know that German cockerels go 'kikeriki', while the French for a dog's 'woof-woof' is 'oua-oua'; and that the Spanish for 'bang' or 'crack' is 'pum' or 'paf'.)

51

Text: Comic 'noises'

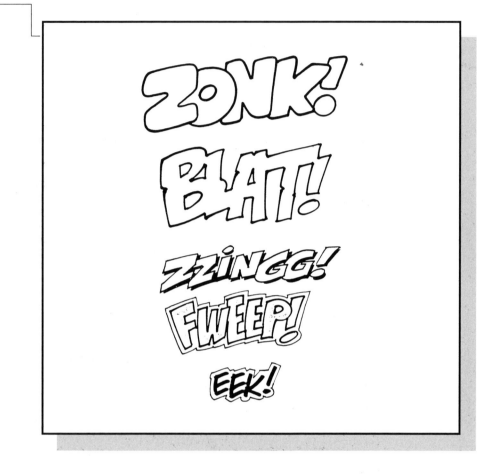

Activity

The aim of this activity is to look carefully at the relationship between the sounds we produce and the sound effects we try to achieve in texts.

Read the poetry extracts in Text: Sound effects.

In each case, the language is highlighting certain types of sound, which have been underlined. Look back at the phonetic information given earlier, think about the way the sounds are produced physically and decide why the writers might have used them:

Text: Sound effects

1   From a poem by Wilfred Owen describing a battle in progress:

Only the stuttering rifles rapid rattle

2   From a poem by Geoffrey Hill about the Crucifixion:

While the dulled wood
Spat on the stones each drop
Of deliberate blood

3   From a poem by Peter Redgrove describing wind around a house:

Limped up the stairs and puffed on the landings
Snuffled through floorboards from the foundations

4   From a poem by Sylvia Plath addressing a sleeping baby:

All night your moth breath
Flickers among the flat pink roses

5   From a poem by Tennyson describing the sounds of doves and bees:

The moan of doves in immemorial elms
And murmuring of innumerable bees

6   From another poem by Wilfred Owen describing the sounds of a summer's day:

By the May breeze murmurous with wasp and midge

Commentary

Examples 1 and 2 are plosives, 2 using more voiced sounds. Example 1 suggests the explosive force of bullets (compare this with the sounds in 'rat-a-tat'); 2 tries to evoke the duller thud of drops on a hard surface.

Examples 3 and 4 use voiceless fricatives, suggesting the light friction of wind and breath.

Examples 5 and 6 use nasals, 5 suggesting the repeated and overlapping calls of doves and continuous hum of bees; 6 uses nasals in combination with fricatives and an affricate. The humming of wasps is combined with the lighter hissing noises of smaller insects.

Summary of broad categorisations

- Voiced/voiceless: louder, heavier, a fuller sound/softer, lighter, a thinner sound
- Plosives: percussive sounds – banging, striking, tapping
- Fricatives and affricates: friction – hissing, scratching
- Nasals and approximants: continuous sound or motion – flowing, rippling, humming

Activity

Some of the effects in Text: Sound effects are cumulative: particular sounds are repeated within a short space (termed 'alliteration' when the sounds are at the beginning of words). Individual words occurring on their own may or may not have in-built sound effects: for example, while 'murmur' may suggest the hum of mumbled talk – as 'mumble' itself may – the word 'immemorial' has no particular sound profile.

But it appears that some groups of words have acquired an 'aura' of meaning, as a result of an accumulation of another kind: that of simple force of numbers in the lexicon. These are much harder to explain. To explore this, brainstorm as many words as you can that belong to the following sets, then try to draw some conclusions about the operation of certain sounds.

slip, slide . . .	bump, lump . . .
glitter, glow . . .	smash, crash . . .
flip, flutter . . .	puff, bluff . . .
twist, twiddle . . .	

(Note: there is no commentary on this activity.)

'Meeting at Night' (1845) is a poem by Robert Browning.

How does Browning use sound – particularly consonants – to reinforce the action that takes place in the poem and the emotions that are involved?

Text: 'Meeting at Night'

The grey sea and long black land;
And the yellow half-moon large and low;
And the startled little waves that leap
In fiery ringlets from their sleep,
As I gain the cove with pushing prow,
And quench its speed i' the slushy sand.

Then a mile of warm sea-scented beach;
Three fields to cross till a farm appears;
A tap at the pane, the quick sharp scratch
And blue spurt of a lighted match,
And a voice less loud, through its joys and fears,
Than the two hearts beating each to each!

Commentary

The poem is organised into two 6-line rhyming stanzas. In stanza 1 the narrator is rowing his boat at night across the sea towards land. Stanza 2 describes his journey across land and culminates in the lovers' meeting of the title.

The dominant consonant sounds in the first stanza are:

◎ the voiced lateral /l/, sometimes referred to as a 'liquid' and associated with the flowing, rippling qualities of water
◎ the voiceless plosives /k/ and /p/ – soft percussive sounds
◎ the voiceless fricatives /ʃ/ and /s/ – soft hissing sounds
◎ the voiceless affricate /tʃ/ – soft percussive, immediately followed by soft hissing.

55

The way that these sounds are distributed across the lines of the stanza helps to suggest the action and sound of the oars. The plosives enact the vigorous movement of the oars entering and pulling through the water and the fricatives are suggestive of the sound made by the disturbed water after the oars are taken up ready for the next stroke. The 'soft' voiceless quality of most of the sounds contributes to the emotional atmosphere of the poem – the action takes place at night, imparting an air of secrecy to the proceedings and the oarsman is perhaps driven by a sense of quiet determination. In line 5 the poet describes the boat coming to a halt as it drives into the sand of the beach. Here he introduces the voiced plosive /g/ in the word 'gain' – a loud percussive sound – and follows this with a concentration of voiceless plosives (/p/), fricatives (/ʃ/ and /s/) and the affricate (/tʃ/) – sounds that suggest the sudden stopping of the boat, the disturbance this creates in the water (the affricate /tʃ/ which involves both a plosive and fricative sound) and the gradual restoration of the sound and motion of waves lapping gently onto the beach and around the finally stilled boat.

In the second stanza the narrator crosses the beach and fields to arrive at the farm. 'A tap at the pane' echoes the rhythm of his action and the voiceless plosives /t/ and /p/ suggest that his tapping is cautious and muted. He doesn't want to alarm the occupant. The following line and a half use another series of voiceless sounds to describe a match being struck inside the house in response to his tapping. Think about striking a match. It involves friction (scratching sounds) and combustion (percussive sounds). The fricatives and affricates reinforce the sound of a match being rubbed against sandpaper and the plosives contribute to the image of the match bursting into flame. All these sounds are voiceless until the point where the match takes light. We could perhaps interpret this as the moment when the lovers recognise each other, the tension that has built up in the poem is released, the door is opened and the 'two hearts' are united in the final two lines.

Extension

Explore the use of sound symbolism based on consonants by collecting a range of data. Here are some areas to consider:

1   Plosives are often used in newspaper headlines to give a sense of energy and drama: for example, in words like 'probe', 'cut', 'hit', 'snap', 'quit', 'scoop' and 'block'. (These words are also monosyllabic, giving them extra force.) Collect some headlines and investigate the types of words used in them.

2   Product brand names are carefully chosen by manufacturers to have a certain 'ring'. Choose some different products and list their brand names and slogans. Do certain sounds recur, or are certain sounds associated with particular types of product? For example, the names 'Twix', 'Crunchie', 'Snickers', 'Kit Kat' and 'Picnic' all contain plosives, perhaps because the manufacturers want to suggest a crisp, cracking noise. Are fricatives used for scouring creams and liquids, or air fresheners?

Slogans can often use alliteration, for example:

Best Buy Bold (washing powder)

P-P-Pick up a Penguin (chocolate bar)

The Power to Hit Pain Precisely (analgesic)

3   Some newspapers also use phoneme substitution as a regular technique in their headlines. Rather than exploiting sound symbolism, this process is one of rule-breaking: the reader expects one sound and gets another which creates a new and relevant word or phrase – sometimes with deliberately comic effect. You can see this process in certain kinds of 'corny' joke:

Q: What did the duck say as it flew upside down?
A: I'm quacking up.
Q: What do sea monsters live on?
A: Fish and ships.
Q: What do cats read?
A: The Mews of the World.

But the same technique can be used for serious purposes too. Adverts can exploit the way phoneme substitution can call up two phrases at once, as in using 'Limited Emission' to describe a car with a catalytic converter (and calling up the sophistication and exclusiveness of 'Limited Edition' at the same time).

See if you can find some examples of sound substitution from newspaper headlines, advertising copy and jokes.

4   The jokes above are one example of how much we like to play with sound. Collect some further examples of sound play, in the form of tongue twisters and popular sayings.

Note: see satellite texts: *The Language of Advertising, The Language of Poetry*

SPEECH PRODUCTION AND DESCRIPTION: VOWELS

Vowels also play their part in our interpretation of language.

Vowels are always voiced. Unlike consonants, they do not involve any obstruction of the airway; vowel sounds are more to do with the shape and position of the tongue, and whether the lips are spread or rounded.

English vowel sounds are grouped into two categories: 'pure' vowels and 'diphthongs'. While the former are single sounds, diphthongs are a combination of two sounds where the speaker starts with one sound and glides towards the other. Here are the relevant symbols:

Short vowels		Long vowels		Diphthongs	
ɪ	pit	iː	bean	aɪ	bite
ɛ	pet	ɜː	burn	ɛɪ	bait
æ	pat	ɑː	barn	ɔɪ	boy
ɒ	pot	ɔː	born	əʊ	roe
ʌ	putt	uː	boon	aʊ	house
ʊ	put			ʊə	cruel
ə	patter			ɪə	ear
				ɛə	air

(Note: the phonetic system in this book marks long vowels with a colon (:). You may encounter descriptions in other textbooks where this mark is not used, but you will still be able to understand the sounds because the symbols themselves do not differ.)

In order to get a sense of these sounds, go through them, first alternating between short and long vowels and trying to feel the difference between them – for example, contrasting the vowel sound in 'pit' with that in 'bean'; then sound out some diphthongs, trying to feel the way these sounds are sequences of vowels.

The diagrams below show where English vowel sounds are made in the mouth. The shape of the diagram (called a 'vowel trapezium') is an abstract version of the space inside the mouth: 'high', 'mid' and 'low' refer to how near the tongue is to the roof of the mouth or bottom of the jaw; 'front', 'central' and 'back' refer to how far forward or retracted the body of the tongue is; the shapes drawn around the sounds themselves are explained below.

○ = made with rounded lips

□ = made with spread lips

◖ = starting with rounded lips and ending with spread lips

◗ = starting with spread lips and ending with rounded lips

'Pure' vowels

Diphthongs

(Note: the arrows show the direction of movement for these sounds.)

How now brown cow

As with consonants, vowels can mark out the region of origin, ethnicity or social class of a speaker: for example, Northern speakers have no /ʌ/, so will pronounce 'put' and 'putt' in the same way; speakers of Afro-Caribbean Patwa will use /a:/ instead of /ɒ/ in 'pot'; an older form of RP, characteristic of the language of the royal family and upper-class speakers from years ago, is sometimes called 'marked RP'. In this accent, speakers would use /ɔ/ instead of /ɒ/.

Activity

Now that you have looked at vowels, read through the Steve Bell cartoons again (on p. 50). Previously, you discussed the stereotypes that are associated with this 'marked RP' accent (there is a reference to this accent as an older form, often heard on early radio and TV broadcasts, in the first cartoon strip).

Now map out the way Steve Bell has altered the vowel sounds in order to construct the idea of this accent for the reader. List the words whose spelling has been altered, then compare this pronunciation with the regular RP version. An example has been done below, to start you off:

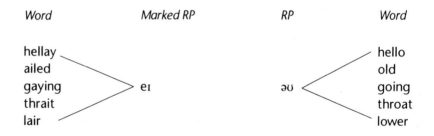

Word	*Marked RP*	*RP*	*Word*
hellay			hello
ailed			old
gaying	eɪ	əʊ	going
thrait			throat
lair			lower

(Answers on p. 69 ff)

Extension

Choose an accent that you know well, and write some 'eye dialect' yourself, where you try to simulate the accent by altering the spelling. Think about vowel sounds as well as consonants.

In a previous activity, you collected some texts in order to examine how accent is represented on the page. How far did you find alterations in spelling to suggest vowel sounds? Are vowel alterations in 'eye dialect' more likely to be done in humorous texts than in those for serious purposes? What strategies are used in dialect poetry?

A bit of a teeny weeny ding-dong

As with consonants, vowels are used to suggest certain ideas: for example, /i:/ is often associated with diminutive size, as in the words 'teeny', 'weeny', 'wee'. We often put /i:/ on the ends of words in 'baby talk', using 'cardies' for 'cardigan', 'jarmies' for 'pyjamas', 'drinky' for 'drink', 'walkies' for 'walk', and so on.

As well as individual sounds appearing to have symbolic value, vowels also have cumulative force, either in repetition or in contrast: for example, 'teeny weeny' as a phrase is more effective for the repetitions in it; 'ding dong' draws attention to itself partly through the contrast of the high front /i:/ with the low back /ɒ/. (Note the effect of the consonants here, too: the striking note of the voiced plosive, followed by the drawn out resonance of the nasal.)

Activity

We have many expressions that exploit vowel sounds by using either repetition or contrast. Below is a list of some of them. Sort them out by referring back to the vowel trapezium and symbols you studied earlier: which of these use repetition, and which use contrast? Group them into categories, identifying which vowels are being used. When you have finished, think about the nature of these terms: what type of language do they represent? Where would they be used – by whom, and in which contexts?:

helter skelter   flip flop   topsy turvey   wishy washy   fat cat
hoity toity   lovey dovey   hip hop   see saw   mishmash
spick and span   big wig   knick knack   harum scarum   tick tock
tit for tat   jet set   eebie jeebies   hanky panky   sing song
willy nilly   shilly shally   nitty gritty   ping pong   hotch potch
pitter patter   namby pamby   hugger mugger   collywobbles
hoi polloi   jim jams (for pyjamas)   airy fairy   arty farty
roly poly

(Answers on p. 70)

Rhyme, pararhyme, assonance and reverse rhyme

Some of the expressions above use rhyme as part of their effect: for example, willy nilly, nitty gritty. This aspect of patterning is learnt early as part of our childhood experience of language, via songs, nursery rhymes and the chants that accompany play. As well as full rhyme, though, there are other types of near-rhyme that set up relationships between sounds, and these can be used where full rhyme may seem too neat and tidy or childlike (although sometimes full rhyme can be very effective in serious texts, as a deliberate device).

First, it's important to realise that rhyme of all kinds is based on the sounds of words rather than the spelling. Here, the operation of **homophones** (words that are spelt differently but have the same sound) can have an important role.

Activity

The following are homophones in RP. How many different words can be represented by these sounds?

1	ni: dz
2	a: mz
3	bru: z
4	kɔ: s
5	səʊl
6	kɔ: t
7	lɛsən
8	kwɔ: ts
9	kɔ: z
10	rəʊz
11	sɛnt

(Answers on p. 71)

The following words are homophones for some regional speakers, who would pronounce both words in each case as the first example. Can you identify where the speakers would be from? A random list of possibilities is given after the wordlist:

---

1   ant   aunt
2   stir   stair
3   moo   mew
4   caught   cot
5   tree   three

Liverpool; Afro-Caribbean Patwa; Northern England; Norfolk; Scotland.

(Answers on p. 71)

The homophonic principle can work across word boundaries as well as within them. For example:

Q: Where did Humpty Dumpty leave his hat?
A: Humpty dumped 'is 'at on the wall.

Q: Where do all policemen live?
A: Lettsby Avenue.

Q: What did Neptune say when the sea dried up?
A: I haven't a notion.

and the book title *Dangerous Cliffs*, by Eileen Dover.

Supply your own answer to this question:

Q: If frozen water is iced water, what's frozen ink?

(Answer on p. 72)

63

Supply the answers to the following jokes, and identify the homophones involved:

> Q: What trees come in twos?
>
> Q: What fly has laryngitis?
>
> (Answers on p. 72)

Activity

Some of the expressions you sorted earlier use contrasting vowels within the framework of the same consonants: for example, 'sing song', 'shilly shally'.

This is known as **pararhyme**, and can be found in many different types of text as a shaping strategy. For example, it is used in the poem 'Strange Meeting' (1918) by Wilfred Owen in order to set up echoes between words, without providing the sense of completeness that would come with full rhyme. The narrator describes an imaginary journey down into hollow spaces in the earth where he encounters a dead enemy soldier who was one of his victims during the battle.

Identify some examples of pararhyme in these initial lines of the poem, and try to describe the effects produced. (Note: there is no commentary on this activity.)

Text: 'Strange Meeting'

> It seemed that out of battle I escaped
> Down some profound dull tunnel, long since scooped
> Through granites which titanic wars had groined.
> Yet also there encumbered sleepers groaned,
> Too fast in thought or death to be bestirred.
> Then, as I probed them, one sprang up, and stared
> With piteous recognition in fixed eyes,
> Lifting distressful hands as if to bless.

These lines also use a form of sound patterning called **assonance** – the repetition of vowels, without the other components that entail full rhyme: for example, the vowel sounds in 'down' and 'profound'; or in 'dull tunnel'. This pattern is seen in the expression 'collywobbles', from the earlier list.

A final aspect of patterning that can be useful to focus on when explaining sound effects in language is **reverse rhyme**. This is the repetition of an initial syllable rather than the final one which is necessary to full rhyme: for example, <u>star</u> and <u>star</u>ling, or <u>grey</u> and <u>gra</u>iny.

Activity

The two texts for this activity – the poems 'Kubla Khan' (1816), by Samuel Taylor Coleridge (the first thirty lines have been printed here), and 'Ballade Made in the Hot Weather', by the late nineteenth-century poet W.E. Henley – both use sound as a strong element in their construction of sensation.

Explore how sound contributes to the overall meaning of the poem in each case. (Note: there is no commentary on this activity.)

65

Text: 'Kubla Khan'

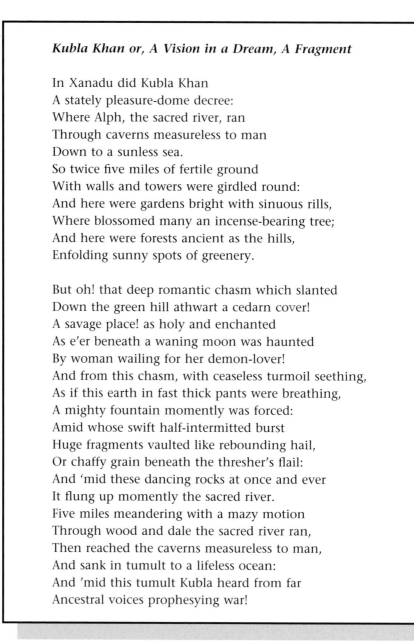

Kubla Khan or, A Vision in a Dream, A Fragment

In Xanadu did Kubla Khan
A stately pleasure-dome decree:
Where Alph, the sacred river, ran
Through caverns measureless to man
Down to a sunless sea.
So twice five miles of fertile ground
With walls and towers were girdled round:
And here were gardens bright with sinuous rills,
Where blossomed many an incense-bearing tree;
And here were forests ancient as the hills,
Enfolding sunny spots of greenery.

But oh! that deep romantic chasm which slanted
Down the green hill athwart a cedarn cover!
A savage place! as holy and enchanted
As e'er beneath a waning moon was haunted
By woman wailing for her demon-lover!
And from this chasm, with ceaseless turmoil seething,
As if this earth in fast thick pants were breathing,
A mighty fountain momently was forced:
Amid whose swift half-intermitted burst
Huge fragments vaulted like rebounding hail,
Or chaffy grain beneath the thresher's flail:
And 'mid these dancing rocks at once and ever
It flung up momently the sacred river.
Five miles meandering with a mazy motion
Through wood and dale the sacred river ran,
Then reached the caverns measureless to man,
And sank in tumult to a lifeless ocean:
And 'mid this tumult Kubla heard from far
Ancestral voices prophesying war!

Text: 'Ballade Made in the Hot Weather'

Ballade Made in the Hot Weather

To C.M.

Fountains that frisk and sprinkle
The moss they overspill;
Pools that the breezes crinkle;
The wheel beside the mill,
With its wet, weedy frill;
Wind-shadows in the wheat;
A water-cart in the street;
The fringe of foam that girds
An islet's ferneries;
A green sky's minor thirds –
To live, I think of these!

Of ice and glass the tinkle,
Pellucid, silver-shrill;
Peaches without a wrinkle;
Cherries and snow at will,
For china bowls that fill
The senses with a sweet
Incuriousness of heat;
A melon's dripping sherds;
Cream-clotted strawberries;
Dusk dairies set with curds –
To live, I think of these!

Vale-lily and periwinkle;
Wet stone-crop on the sill;
The look of leaves a-twinkle
With windlets clear and still;
The feel of a forest rill
That wimples fresh and fleet
About one's naked feet;
The muzzles of drinking herds;
Lush flags and bulrushes;
The chirp of rain-bound birds –
To live, I think of these!

*Envoy**

Dark aisles, new packs of cards,
Mermaidens' tails, cool swards,
Dawn dews and starlit seas,
White marbles, whiter words –
To live, I think of these!

*An envoy is the summarising final stanza of a poem.

Glossary

mill	a water mill (a construction involving water falling onto a large wheel causing it to revolve. The wheel itself was attached to machinery which was set in motion as it turned.)
water-cart	at the time the poem was written, the village pump would have been the main source of water. In a hot summer the pump might run dry and water would have to be brought in by cart from elsewhere.
girds	surrounds or 'girdles'
ferneries	damp places containing ferns
minor thirds	a combination of musical notes producing a melancholic sound
pellucid	transparent or translucent
incuriousness	a word of the poet's own making suggesting a lack of curiosity or active interest
sherds	same as 'shard', a broken piece or fragment
vale-lily, periwinkle, stone-crop	native English plants
rill	a brook or stream
wimples	ripples
fleet	fast
flags	traditional name for native English iris, a plant that grows in shallow water
swards	areas of mown grass

Extension

Collect some non-literary texts that use sound patterning involving vowels: for example, advertising slogans that use rhyme or pararhyme. You may also find that you see new aspects of sound patterning in the texts that you collected earlier in order to explore consonants.

This unit has not had the space to explore the effects of stress and rhythm in language, but these are often important ingredients in how sound patterns work. When you are collecting and analysing material, give some thought to the way these larger patterns contribute to the overall effects.

Answers to activities

Sentence for transcription (p. 44)

wʊdʒu: pli:z kju: (w) ət ði: (j) ɛnd əv ðə kɒrɪdɔ:

According to how exactly this utterance was said (particularly, how strongly some of the vowel sounds were stressed), there could be some alternatives: for example, the vowel in the word 'you' could be /ə/; the vowels in 'at' and 'of' could be /æ/ and /ɒ/ respectively.

The symbols in brackets are linking sounds, enabling smooth transitions between words.

Steve Bell cartoons (p. 60)

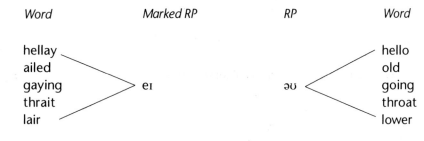

Word	Marked RP	RP	Word
hellay			hello
ailed			old
gaying	eɪ	əʊ	going
thrait			throat
lair			lower

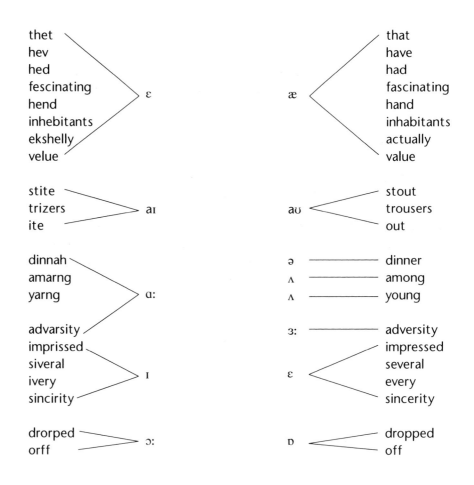

thet	that
hev	have
hed	had
fescinating	fascinating
hend ɛ æ	hand
inhebitants	inhabitants
ekshelly	actually
velue	value
stite	stout
trizers aɪ aʊ	trousers
ite	out
dinnah	ə —— dinner
amarng	ʌ —— among
yarng ɑː	ʌ —— young
advarsity	ɜː —— adversity
imprissed	impressed
siveral	several
ivery ɪ ɛ	every
sincirity	sincerity
drorped ɔː ɒ	dropped
orff	off

Sorting vowel sounds (p. 61)

Repetitions

/ɛ/	helter skelter jet set harum scarum airy fairy
/ɪ/	willy nilly big wig nitty gritty
/æ/	hanky panky fat cat namby pamby
/ɑː/	arty farty
/ɒ/	hotch potch collywobbles
/ʌ/	lovey dovey hugger mugger
/iː/	eebie jeebies
/ɔɪ/	hoity toity hoi polloi
/əʊ/	roly poly

Contrasts

/ɪ/ → /ɒ/	flip flop hip hop sing song ping pong tick tock
	wishy washy
/ɪ/ → /æ/	shilly shally pitter patter mishmash spick and span
	knick knack jim jams tit for tat
/i/ → /ɔ:/	see saw
/ɒ/ → /ɜ:/	topsy turvey

These terms belong to the informal, spoken area of language. Some are so unfamiliar on the page that their spelling is uncertain: for example, is it 'colliewobbles' or 'collywobbles'? 'hoy polloy' or 'hoi polloi'? This is the language of personal anecdote rather than public lecture, although many a public lecture would benefit from the liveliness and energy contributed by these vigorous little items. Many express motion, emotion, muddle and incoherence – 'helter skelter', 'eebie jeebies', 'mishmash', 'hotch potch'; others strike arch attitudes about certain types of people – 'fat cat', 'hoi polloi'; some are straightforwardly onomatopoeic – 'tick tock'. They are all cheeky.

Homophones

(pp. 62–3)

1 kneads, needs
2 arms, alms
3 bruise, brews
4 course, coarse
5 sole, soul
6 caught, court
7 lesson, lessen
8 quarts, quartz
9 cause, cores, caws
10 rose, rows, roes
11 sent, scent, sent

1 Northern England /ænt/
2 Liverpool /stɜ:/
3 Norfolk /mu:/
4 Scotland /kɔ:t/
5 Afro-Caribbean Patwa /tri:/

(pp. 63–4)

Iced ink / I stink
Pear / pair
Horse / hoarse

U n i t two

Words and things

Contents

73

Lexical ambiguity: say what you mean, or mean what you say?
This looks at the way users of text can exploit the capacity of words to carry more than one meaning.

Metaphor: life's a beach and then you fry
This explores the way metaphor operates within text, and looks at some of the effects of metaphoric language.

Idiomatic language: flogging dead crocodiles and keeping your feet under water
Here you will look at some set structures of language having specific meanings that don't necessarily relate to the individual words within the structure.

Computer analysis of words
This looks at differences between the most frequent words we use for speaking and the most frequent words we use for writing. You will also explore how idioms are used in texts.

Denotation and connotation: what are words worth?
This looks at the emotional loading that many words carry, and the way producers of text can exploit this capacity of language to make texts effective.

WORDS AND HISTORIES
This section looks at the origins of the English word stock.

Got any spare words?
This explores the way English has borrowed words from other languages, and looks at these words in a range of texts.

Words mean what I want them to mean
Here the way that words change their meaning over time is explored.

Get your new words here! Creating new words
This explores the different ways in which new words can be created.

Texts used include

◎ Shop and business names
◎ Articles and headlines
◎ Extracts from novels including graphic novels
◎ Students' writing
◎ Advertisements
◎ Notices, letters, menus, etc.
◎ Old English text
◎ Extracts from speeches
◎ Horoscopes
◎ Computer-generated word lists
◎ Newspaper sports reports

What are words made of?

Some questions about words, like 'What is a word?' might be answered by looking at ways in which words in the English language are structured. The study of the structure of words is called **morphology**.

Most users of English would assume that words are the smallest units of language to carry meaning. This, however, is not necessarily the case, which makes questions such as 'What is a word?' even more difficult to answer.

Activity

Look at the following sentence:

> The plogs glorped bliply.

What do the words in this sentence mean?

75

Commentary

Apart from the first word, apparently nothing. They are units of text that currently have no meaning attached to them, unlike units such as 'dog' , 'deckchair' or 'grip'.

Now look at the text again, and answer the following questions:

1   How many plogs were there? One or more than one?
2   What were they doing?
3   Were they doing it now or in the past?
4   How, or in what way, were they doing it?

Most speakers of English will have very little trouble answering these questions. There was more than one plog, because this word carries the plural marker 's'. 'Glorped' is marked as a verb by the use of the past tense marker 'ed', so the reader knows what the plogs were doing, and the fact that they were doing it in the past. Finally, the reader can tell how or in what manner the plogs were glorping – bliply – because the word carries the adverb marker 'ly'.

Just a brief look at text can establish that units smaller than words are carrying meaning. These units are **morphemes**.

Words may be made up of one or more morphemes:

One morpheme   dog, elephant, establish, child

Two morphemes   dog s, elephant ine, establish ment, child ish

Three morphemes   dis establish ment, child ish ness.

In theory, there is no limit to the number of morphemes a word can have, but logic and comprehensibility mean that there tends to be an upper limit, and six morphemes is about it for English:

anti dis establish ment arian ism

There are exceptions found in highly specialised areas of language, for example, terms used in organic chemistry.

Activity

Identify the individual morphemes in the following word list.

> pigs, barked, unlikely, motherhood, salty, cherry, taller, hammer, displease, hardship, superheroes, player
>
> (Answers on p. 121)

Extension

Now classify the morphemes into the following groups:

1   Independent or free. These morphemes can stand on their own.
2   Dependent or bound. These morphemes must be attached to another morpheme.
3   Grammatical. These give grammatical information and mark the role of the word in the sentence.
4   Creative or derivational. These form new words.

Commentary

Many morphemes can constitute words by themselves: pig, bark, like, mother, salt, cherry, tall, please, hard, super, hero, play. These are usually referred to as **free morphemes**.

Others are only ever used as parts of words: s, ed, un, ly, hood, y, er, dis, ship, es, er. These are usually referred to as **bound morphemes**.

It is easy to confuse some bound morphemes with free morphemes that have an identical sound and structure. For example, English has free morphemes 'hood' (a head covering) and 'ship' (a seagoing vessel). It also has the bound morphemes '-ship' and '-hood', that are both used to form nouns. 'Hardship' means a state of deprivation or difficulty, 'hard ship' means something different, a vessel that is difficult to sail, perhaps. 'Motherhood' means the state of being a mother, not the head covering that a mother might wear.

77

It is also easy to confuse part of a word that is a single morpheme, like 'hammer', with a bound morpheme, in this case '-er', that is used to create nouns of agency (as in 'play', 'player') or adjectives of comparison or degree ('tall', 'taller').

Bound morphemes have two functions. One is to act as a grammatical marker, giving information about number, verb tense, aspect and other grammatical functions. These are **inflectional morphemes**. Examples in the data are -s, -ed, -er (comparative), -es. The second is to form new words. These are called **derivational morphemes**. Examples in the data are un-, -ly, -hood, -y, dis-, -ship, -er (to create a noun of agency).

Summary

Meaning therefore exists in units of language smaller than the word, in morphemes. Users of English frequently use the term 'word' when, strictly speaking, they are referring to morphemes. If someone looks a word up in the dictionary, for example 'dogs', they don't look up the plural form, they look up the base morpheme 'dog'. For this reason, and for reasons looked at later in this unit, many linguists prefer the term 'lexeme' to the term 'word'. **Lexeme** refers to a unit of meaning that may be smaller or larger than the traditional term 'word' implies. This unit (i.e. Unit 2) could, therefore, be more accurately called 'Lexemes', but 'Word' is used as being more familiar.

Words and meanings

The previous section looked at meaning in units smaller than the word. This section looks at the relationship between words and meanings, and the way meaning operates in units that are larger than the traditional definition of 'word' allows.

LEXICAL AMBIGUITY: SAY WHAT YOU MEAN, OR MEAN WHAT YOU SAY?

In *Alice through the Looking Glass*, Humpty Dumpty says:

> 'When I use a word, it means just what I choose it to mean – neither more nor less.'

At first, Humpty Dumpty's point seems ridiculous. Common sense tells that each word in the English language has a meaning, and that meaning is well established. Look in any dictionary. Why is it, then, that even the most skilled and experienced users of language can get into trouble, by meaning one thing and saying another. What did Margaret Thatcher really mean when she said that every Prime Minister needed a Willie? (William Whitelaw, usually known as Willie Whitelaw, was a trusted senior member of Thatcher's government at this time.)

Activity

The examples of text below all apparently intend one meaning, but give another. Try to identify the word(s) that have caused the difficulty, and say why this has happened.

These examples are all from letters sent to housing departments.

> I request permission to remove my drawers in the kitchen.
>
> Will you please send a man to look at my water. It is a very funny colour and not fit to drink.
>
> The person next door has a large erection in his back garden which is unsightly and dangerous.

Commentary

If two words in English have the same meaning, this is known as **synonymy**, and the words are called **synonyms**. Examples of synonyms are skin/hide, purchase/buy, obstinate/stubborn. A problem can arise when a word has more than one synonym. 'Hide' means the same as (i.e. is synonymous with)

(1) conceal, (2) skin, (3) place for watching wildlife. If these synonyms aren't closely related in meaning, then the result can be **ambiguity**.

Synonyms

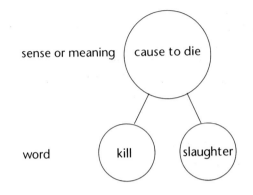

If a word has more than one meaning, this is known as **polysemy**, and the word is called a **polyseme**. An example of a polyseme is pupil (part of the eye, school child).

Polysemy

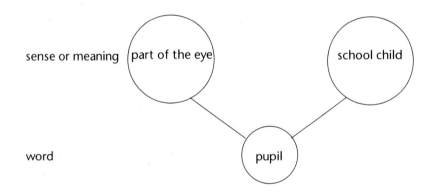

If the synonyms aren't closely related in meaning, or if the intended meaning of the polyseme isn't clear, then the reader or listener may not be able to identify which meaning is intended. There are many kinds of ambiguity, but this section is concerned with **lexical ambiguity**, which occurs when it is not possible to decide on the intended meaning of a word.

In the activity above, some of the words used in these letters have synonyms, or are polysemes. 'Drawers' is synonymous with 'part of an item of furniture' but is also synonymous with 'item of women's underwear'. 'Water' can mean any amount of water from the flow from a tap to the ocean; but also by association 'urine'. 'Erection' can mean 'building' or 'sexual arousal'. If the producer of a text intends one meaning, but the context in which a word is used implies another, the result is confusion, because the text becomes ambiguous.

The examples above are presumably unintentional, but what about examples produced by people whose profession is language? Anyone can make a mistake if they are talking spontaneously, as the following examples show:

GLR reporter	What should you do if your children want to talk about solvent abuse?
Brian Mawhinney	Take a deep breath . . .
George Bush	I'm for a stronger death penalty
Jason Donovan	The lights went up and there I was standing flat on my face.
Brian Gould	We're not the sort of party that does deals behind smoke-filled doors.

But written text is more considered, usually proof read, and it is unlikely that double meanings pass unnoticed. Were the following headlines intentional or not?

Activity

Look at the following newspaper headlines. They are all ambiguous in that there are at least two potential meanings for each one. Try to identify the

> **THREE BATTERED IN FISH SHOP**
>
> **EIGHTH ARMY PUSH BOTTLES UP GERMANS**
>
> **MOUNTING PROBLEMS FOR YOUNG COUPLES**
>
> **FIELD MARSHALL FLIES BACK TO FRONT**

word(s) that have caused the problem, and say why the problem has arisen.The English language, then, has a broader capacity for meaning than a simple one-to-one word and meaning relationship. Producers of text are aware of this capacity and make use of it.

Activity

Text: Shop names is a list of names of various shops, businesses and services. Discuss the ways in which words and meanings are used here. Are all these examples synonyms or polysemes, or can you find other ways of using the relationship between words and meanings? What effects are created by using language in this way?

(For commentary on this activity, see p. 121.)

Text: Shop names

Hairdressers
Curl Up and Dye, Fresh Hair, Look Ahead, Kuttin' Kru, Headlines, Making Waves, Highlights

Bed salesrooms
Bedside Manor, Bedlam

Heating
Gas Flair, Power Dressing

Fur shop
Hide and Sheep

Health food shops
Open Sesame, Just Natural, In a Nutshell, Grain of Truth

Services
Nappy cleaning service: Wee Care
Chimney sweep: Clean Sweep
Drain clearing: Watershed, Blockbusters
HGV driving instructors: Road Train
Dry cleaners: Suits Me
Plumbers: Plumbing Your Way

Collect examples of names of shops and services that exploit the capacity of words to create ambiguous meanings.

Invent names for the following:

> an undertaker, a baker, a fruit shop, a pest controller, a fish-and-chip shop, a solicitor

Check in a local *Yellow Pages* directory. What names do these shops and services use? Which ones do, and which ones don't, play meaning games with language?

These are some examples of names that students invented in response to this activity:

Solicitors	Doowie, Cheetham and Howe; Silk 'n' Briefs
Undertakers	U. Killham and I. Berryem; Croakers; The Body Shop; Graves 'R' Us; Coffin Up
Fruit shop	Going Bananas
Pest controller	Make Mice Day
Florist	Fleurtations; Daisy Chain

The use of this kind of word play is often humorous and almost always light-hearted. Certain trades and professions must give the clearest indications that they take their work seriously. It is, therefore, extremely unlikely that firms such as undertakers or solicitors would play games with language. However, shops and professions that involve only one main service or range of goods are more likely to want to personalize and lighten their trade.

Humpty Dumpty may not be right, but the study of words in use demonstrates quickly that the relationship between words and meanings is more complex than it seems at first. This section looked at the ambiguity that can be created (accidentally or deliberately) by the existence of synonyms and homophones. The situation is even more complex than this, as the next section will discuss.

Note: see satellite text: *The Language of Humour*

METAPHOR: LIFE'S A BEACH, AND THEN YOU FRY

This section looks at the way words can be used to create connections between areas of meaning that may have no direct link, but offer a useful comparison or connection that helps to enhance, clarify, make more vivid or even reinforce existing ideas and concepts.

The existence of metaphor allows for a further expansion of meaning. By linking words or concepts that don't generally have a semantic link, a new meaning can be expressed. **Metaphor** allows producers of text to make connections in a few words that would take lines of writing, or long stretches of speech, to make in a more literal way. The literal translation of a metaphor rarely produces the same effect as the metaphor. Metaphor can be used to make comments on aspects of human behaviour or society without the writer having to spell out literally the point s/he is trying to make.

Metaphor is often seen as something that is more likely to exist in the domain of literature, and not as something that has a lot to do with everyday life. It isn't unusual for people to associate metaphor with written language, and particularly with written language that is literary or has literary associations. Advertising, for example, is often very creative; tabloid newspapers are known for their inventive ways of using the phonological and lexical levels of language. However, metaphor is much more a part of day-to-day uses of language than you might think.

Activity

Look at the example of dialogue in Text: Graphic novel (from *The Sandman – The Doll's House* by Neil Gaiman, Mike Dringenberg and Malcolm Jones III). A group of violent criminals are meeting for a convention. They are casually chatting to each other before proceedings begin.

Identify any popular phrases or well-known sayings that you recognise. (The first two have been underlined.) What is the literal meaning of these?

Why has the writer used these particular phrases in this context?

Commentary

A lot of language that is used regularly involves metaphor. It isn't unusual for somebody describing a situation that has embarrassed them to say, 'I could have died,' or to hear someone say, 'It nearly killed me,' when talking about some major effort. This is not meant literally, but gives a clear expression to the strong feelings aroused by, for example, social embarrassment.

This writer has chosen everyday uses of metaphor that relate to death and violence. The examples used are deliberately commonplace – as readers we probably wouldn't notice them except that so many are used. The effect is interesting. It enhances the role of the participants in the narrative. These are people for whom violence is a way of life, but by drawing attention to the sheer 'everydayness' of such language, the writer is enforcing a point he makes further on in the narrative: violence is so much a part of our lives that we almost fail to notice it.

Activity

The examples of language in Text: Metaphors are all ready-made phrases that are a familiar part of the day-to-day experience of language. They have been classified according to topic. What metaphors are used here? What connections are made to enhance meaning? How does the metaphoric use of language here reflect our cultural attitudes?

Text: Metaphors

Women
Mutton dressed as lamb
She's a bitch.
She's a cow.
She's a slag.

Countries and places
America is our ally.
The rape of Sarajevo
Cuba is the victim of the American blockade.
The evil empire

War
Surgical strike (attack)
Ethnic cleansing
Friendly fire (killed by your own side)

Government and politics
The economy is ailing.
The trade figures are healthy this month.
The Government does not realise how much is at stake.

Commentary

There is clear metaphoric use of language in these examples. Countries and places are treated as people (ally), they suffer as people (rape, victim).

What is more revealing, though, is the connections that are made through these metaphoric uses. Women are associated with animals (cow, bitch), meat (mutton, lamb), or with rubbish discarded after the valuable content has been extracted (slag).

War becomes a medical or beneficial act (surgical, cleansing). Something that kills you becomes benign (friendly). Countries and places become friends or enemies (ally, evil).

Government and politics is described in terms of gambling (at stake), or in terms of health and disease (healthy, ailing).

Cultural attitudes to particular areas of human activity can often be seen in the choices of metaphor used when that activity is discussed. A useful linguistic concept to be aware of here is that of **semantic field**, sometimes called just field, or field of meaning. Particular topics, trades, concepts are associated in the mind of the user of language with particular groups of words. Texts that belong to a particular area of meaning draw from a range of words that relate specifically to that area of meaning. For example, a text that used the words chop, fry, stir, simmer, season, taste, would almost certainly belong to the semantic field of cooking. However, writers can also draw on semantic fields to create metaphorical effects and associations that can enhance the meaning of the text.

Metaphor, then, is very much a part of the day-to-day language, so much so that its presence is often not even noticed by users of language.

It serves to encode and possibly reinforce our attitudes to many aspects of life. Given this, metaphor has the capacity to be a very powerful tool of language.

Activity

Look at the following word list. All these words were taken from the same text. What topic does this text address?

> attrition, sudden death, barbed-wire entanglements, defence, threat

Commentary

Most people assume that these words are from a text about war, possibly the 1914–18 war.

The complete text is given in Text: Newspaper report.

Text: Newspaper report

ENGLAND v SPAIN

An early goal will open up any game but the longer this Wembley quarter-final today remains scoreless, the more it will become a contest of attrition, with the winners likely to be decided by sudden-death overtime or a penalty shoot-out. England are better equipped for an exchange of goals, with Shearer at last producing his prolific league form at international level. Spain have yet to find a consistent striker but the depth of their strength is formidable. They will hope to draw England on to the barbed-wire entanglements of their defence and then use Sergi to catch the opposition on the break. Hierro, Amor and Caminero will pose a threat to Adams coming from the deep. Terry Venables could have done with Ince against Nadal.

Forecast: England 2, Spain 0.

Activity

Comment on the use of metaphor in Text: Newspaper report, and the way in which the writer has drawn upon the semantic field of war to create these metaphors. (Note: there is no commentary on this activity.)

Note: see satellite texts: *The Language of Sport*

IDIOMATIC LANGUAGE: FLOGGING DEAD CROCODILES AND KEEPING YOUR FEET UNDER WATER

The section on metaphor above looked briefly at the daily use of metaphor that is so commonplace that it goes almost unnoticed. A lot of these structures have a fixed and expected form. Some are so fixed that it is not possible to change a word or the structure without losing, or irretrievably changing, the meaning. Such structures are called **idioms**.

Idioms are units of language with a fixed grammatical and lexical content. Their meaning cannot be worked out from a study of the individual words contained in the idiom, and they frequently operate on a metaphorical level.

Idioms therefore function more like individual words than like phrases or sentences, and can be considered as lexemes according to the discussion at the beginning of this unit.

Activity

Complete the idioms in the list below by providing the missing words. Translate the idioms into clear, non-idiomatic English. Is a dictionary helpful here?

1   It's raining _____ *and* _____.

2   Don't feel sorry for him. Those are only _____ tears.

3   You should always *call a* _____ *a* _____.

4   Do it now before you get *cold* _____.

5   Since I gave up smoking, I feel *as fit as a* _____.

Commentary

Idioms present problems of direct translation. It is unusual to be able to substitute one word for another and provide a translation into non-idiomatic English. Frequently, a whole phrase has to be rewritten. Possible translations for the above examples are:

91

1   very heavily
2   insincere, hypocritical
3   speak plainly
4   frightened
5   really well

What problems do idioms present to learners of a language?

Very real ones! First, it is not always possible for listeners or readers to recognise that an idiom exists, and they may assume the literal meaning. Second, without access to a good dictionary that gives examples of idiomatic uses, an idiom is often untranslatable.

Activity

The examples in Text: Translations are all from translations into English by people for whom English is not a first language.

Text: Translations

1   On the menu of a Swiss restaurant: Our wines leave you nothing to hope for.

2   On the menu of a Polish hotel: Roasted duck let loose; beef rashers beaten up in the country people's fashion.

3   On the door of a Moscow hotel room: If this is your first visit to the USSR, you are welcome to it.

4   In an Acapulco hotel: The manager has personally passed all the water served here.

In some cases, these texts have gone wrong because the translator was unaware that s/he was dealing with idiom. In other cases, the translator has unwittingly produced an idiom that has a different meaning from the one that the combination of words would logically suggest.

Try to rewrite these texts into clear English. Identify the idiom that has caused the translation to go wrong.

Commentary

1   'Hope' is synonymous with 'desire'. Unfortunately, 'leaves nothing to be desired' means the opposite of 'nothing to hope for'. A translator who was not fluent in English, and who was working with a thesaurus, could easily fall into this trap.

2   'Free-range' is an expression of very fixed meaning. It may appear to mean the same as 'let loose', but it doesn't. The second mistranslation in this example is not a matter of idiom, but is a problem of lexical ambiguity (see p. 78). 'Battered' is synonymous with 'covered in batter' and with 'beaten up'.

3   'You are welcome' and 'you are welcome to it' have more or less opposite meanings. An inexperienced user of the language would have no way of knowing this.

4   The word 'pass' has the meaning 'to adjudicate or make judgement'. However, the phrase 'pass water' has a very specific meaning that presents a trap to both the fluent and the inexperienced user of the language.

Idioms are useful devices. They provide users of language with ready-made phrases that communicate a clear, agreed meaning. They add colour and variety to the language. Because of the fixed structure and lexis of most idioms, they function more like words than phrases, and in any discussion or analysis of words and meanings, it is useful to treat idioms as words.

COMPUTER ANALYSIS OF WORDS

This section explores how computers can help us to study words and frequent patterns of words.

Activity

Look at the following table of words. The lists are taken from a corpus of language. A corpus (plural corpora) is a collection of texts from various sources. These corpora consist of texts which have been typed or scanned into a computer so that large quantities of information about the English language can be collected and analysed. The table shows the 50 most frequent words from a corpus of half-a-million words of written data and half-a-million words of spoken data.

What do you notice about the most frequent written words and the most frequent spoken words? Does the presence of any spoken words in particular surprise you? Why do you think some words are much more frequent in spoken than in written English?

Text: Spoken and written

	WRITTEN	SPOKEN		WRITTEN	SPOKEN
1	THE	THE	26	BY	WE
2	TO	I	27	ME	HE
3	OF	YOU	28	HER	DO
4	A	AND	29	THEY	GOT
5	AND	TO	30	NOT	THAT'S
6	IN	IT	31	ARE	FOR
7	I	A	32	AN	THIS
8	WAS	YEAH	33	THIS	JUST
9	FOR	THAT	34	HAS	ALL
10	THAT	OF	35	BEEN	THERE
11	IT	IN	36	UP	LIKE
12	ON	WAS	37	WERE	ONE
13	HE	IS	38	OUT	BE
14	IS	IT'S	39	WHEN	RIGHT
15	WITH	KNOW	40	ONE	NOT
16	YOU	NO	41	THEIR	DON'T
17	BUT	OH	42	SHE	SHE
18	AT	SO	43	WHO	THINK
19	HIS	BUT	44	IF	IF
20	AS	ON	45	HIM	WITH
21	BE	THEY	46	WE	THEN
22	MY	WELL	47	ABOUT	AT
23	HAVE	WHAT	48	WILL	ABOUT
24	FROM	YES	49	ALL	ARE
25	HAD	HAVE	50	WOULD	AS

The written sample – mostly newspapers and magazines – is taken from the Cambridge International Corpus (CIC, copyright Cambridge University Press 1996); the spoken data is taken from a corpus of spoken English (CANCODE, copyright Cambridge University Press, 1999).

Commentary

Particularly noticeable in both the written and the spoken list are lots of *grammatical words*. Grammatical words are words which play a mainly grammatical role such as pronouns (*I, you, we he*), determiners *(that)*, prepositions (*of, in, for, at*), auxiliary verbs (*have, do*) and conjunctions (*and, so*), and don't seem to have any lexical meaning or content which can be pointed to. As we might expect, these words dominate the top frequencies of both lists, and, indeed, one of the defining criteria of grammatical words is their high frequency. Grammatical words provide a kind of grammatical glue which holds language together.

On closer examination, some of the 'lexical' words which appear in the high-frequency grammatical word list prove to be elements in phrases which indicate direct interaction between speakers (e.g. *you know, I think*) or words which seem to organise stages in a spoken exchange (*well, right*). Other words such as *kind* or *sort* appear in phrases which we use when speaking to others (e.g. *kind of/sort of*). Such words are called **hedges**, and they allow us to avoid saying what we say too directly and possibly giving offence in the process. *Well* occurs approximately nine times more frequently in spoken than in written discourse. The hedging-word *just* ranks as 33 in the spoken; in the written it ranks at 61 and is two-and-a-half times less frequent. The computer shows us how frequent some of these interactive, interpersonal words are in everyday spoken English.

Activity

Are there any other words in the list which indicate the ways we communicate with each other in speech and in writing? Do you agree with the following observations? What would you add to them?

- The pronouns *I* and *you* are common because conversation is face-to-face.
- Spoken communication is mainly informal and this explains why *yeah* is more frequent than *yes*.
- *It's*, *that's* and *don't* are common in the spoken list because we use these contractions rather than the full forms (*it is*, *that is* and *do not*) all the time when we speak.
- *Do* and *don't* and *it* and *it's* are so frequent that they appear within a few places of each other.

95

Other items in the table call for closer scrutiny too. What are the commonest functions of the extremely frequent spoken uses of *got*? Is *got* used differently in spoken and written language? Let us consider some statistics. *Got* occurs approximately five-and-a-half times more frequently in our spoken sample than in the written. By far the most frequent use of *got* in spoken is in the construction *have got* as the basic verb of possession or personal association with something. But frequency statistics alone do not tell us everything and Carter and McCarthy (1997) observe that structures such as 'I've got so many birthdays in July' and 'I've got you' are typical spoken uses. In the first case the speaker is referring to the responsibility of sending birthday cards to members of the family: 'I've got' seems to mean something like 'I have to deal with'. In the second case the utterance means roughly 'I understand you'. Neither meaning would crop up in formal, written texts.

The words in the spoken corpus also bring us back to our definitions of what a word is. Not included in the top 50 above are **fillers** transcribed in the corpus such as *mm, er, erm*, and so on, some of which would merit being in the top 20 in terms of frequency of occurrence. They are not commonly thought of as words but like *oh*, which is included simply because it is so frequent, they express great affective and interpersonal meaning. They also occur with, or mark, pauses and thinking time. Perhaps it is right to call *oh* a word?

Activity

What do you think are some of the main problems when people transcribe words from tape recorders in ways which enable computers to read the data? What do you see as the advantages and disadvantages of collecting corpora of spoken and written language and then sorting the texts in a computer so that different types of words can be counted?

There are problems. Are *cos* and *because* to be recorded and counted as two different word forms? If *going to* is transcribed as *gonna* when it is uttered as such, should *got to* become *godda* and *have to* become *hafta* when they are uttered informally? Such decisions can greatly affect the count for these basic, everyday spoken word forms and there is no simple criterion that can always be followed.

Computational analysis of language corpora can reveal many interesting differences between spoken and written vocabulary use. But computers are less useful when it comes to understanding the way vocabulary is used as a communicative resource by individual speakers in individual situations, and a discourse- or conversation-analysis approach may be the best way of getting at how vocabulary is used in everyday spoken interaction (see Unit 5, especially p. 265 ff). (For example, the most common occurrence of *see* in the spoken corpus is in the unit *you see* (i.e. meaning 'understand'). Does this necessarily mean that the meaning of 'perceive with the eyes' should be relegated to second place?) However, conversation analysis of itself (especially of just one textual fragment) may mean we can't generalise easily and subsequent checking in a large corpus would always be advisable to see if insights from the individual text hold good across a wide range of samples. Corpus- and conversation-analysis of spoken and written words need to be looked at together.

Note: see satellite text: *The Language of Speech and Writing*

As we look further into word lists or even just notice words as we read and speak we see that the following lists of lexical words are very common in both spoken and written English. Why are they frequent?

Text: Idioms and frequent words

1   Hand, arm, finger, thumb, leg, feet, eye, hair

2   Cat, dog, mouse, spider, fly, bee, bird, horse

3   Ball, bat, goal, net, save, hit, tackle, score

4   Air, sun, rain, cloud, moon, water

5   Red, green, blue, yellow, white, black

6   Hat, shoes, shirt, belt, trousers, skirt, collar

7   Bread, egg, milk, meat, salt, butter, water

Commentary

These words are very frequent because they are used as part of everyday life. They are also frequent because such words are also widely used in idioms. We saw in the section on idiomatic language that idioms are words and phrases which don't carry a precise literal meaning. Several of these very frequent words can appear as individual words or in phrases which have both literal and non-literal meanings.

Idioms are common because they figure regularly in everyday life and in the way we regularly see the world and participate in it. We are surrounded by domestic animals; our bodies are basic to our everyday activities; the world is full of colours; sport figures prominently in the lives of many people; we can't manage without clothes and we have to eat and drink.

Take two of the lists and collect up to five idiomatic phrases from everyday language using the words in each list. (For example, list 1 *I'm all fingers and thumbs; he's always getting under my feet; can't you give them a hand?;* or from list 7 *It's their bread and butter; don't cry over spilt milk; butter wouldn't melt in her mouth; she's got lots of meaty proposals.*

Activity

Now look at Text: *Horoscopes*. How many idiomatic phases can you find? Why are they used? What kind of things are they describing?

Text: Horoscopes

CAPRICORN Dec 21 – Jan 20

You probably won't end the year with all your problems resolved. The 20th century may be nearly over, but many of the dramas it has brought around you will trundle on into the 21st. The good news, though, is that you will get a clear break from all this in the next couple of weeks. Right now, you're wrestling with something that seems to be posing a threat to all your seasonal celebrations. Once the Full Moon in your opposite sign has taken place, the pressure will reduce. Someone who is proving hard to communicate with will alter their attitude in a helpful (if somewhat surprising) way. Other important relationships will also improve. It will be a happy holiday — and, by the time you return to business as usual, you'll be feeling far more qualified to cope with it.

TAURUS April 21 – May 21

The picture on the card shows a family gathered by a tree, next to a cosy, crackling hearth. Usually, we see them through the window of an olde worlde house, glowing on to a cobbled street, covered in a dusting of snow. It is not just Australians who find this image wildly incongruous. Even in cold countries, you're more likely to find a hard-working central heating system. And as for a happy family? Well, there's a classic oxymoron if ever there was one. So be of good cheer. What lies in store for you is a real Christmas, not a cardboard cut-out celebration. It will be happy and magical. But it won't be predictable, and nor, most definitely, will it be peaceful. Expect to be rushed off your feet.

VIRGO Aug 24 – Sep 23

Le Père Noël, as the French call him, has many facets to his personality. Elsewhere in the world he is known as Father Christmas — or Santa Claus. Back in the Thirties, he enjoyed a major makeover. Prior to that, he always dressed in green. Then, in one of history's most successful advertising campaigns, Coca-Cola had him painted in their company colours. The new image stuck like Superglue. It is to be hoped that, in the next Millennium, he will abandon his sponsor and return to a more traditional look. Meanwhile, he stands as a scary example of how commerce can hijack culture. It can't, though, steal the spirit of your celebration this year. You have one precious prayer, one heartfelt hope, one very deep, pure and noble wish. Over the next two weeks, you will get much closer to what you want.

AQUARIUS Jan 21 – Feb 19

Some people are truly dreading the holiday season, while some have reasonably good reason to feel apprehensive. A lot of intense, emotional conflict can come to a head at this time of year. The longer the normal routine is disturbed, the more opportunity there is for abnormal drama to emerge. However, your own misgivings about the festivities are sorely misplaced. You'll be surprised how much you enjoy yourself and by how well most things pan out. Expect, among many other golden moments, conversations which reshape your expectation of the future. You're about to learn something valuable — about yourself and your prospects. This will fill you with enthusiasm for Christmas, and the new century which follows it.

GEMINI May 22 – June 22

'Peace on earth and goodwill to all men.' Hmmm. I wonder why the age-old saying makes no mention of women. Perhaps it is simply an example of the sexist culture that our ancestors perpetuated. Or perhaps there is a little more to it than that. Maybe the implication is that women don't need extra seasonal goodwill. For them, the spirit of this season is not so alien and unusual. There certainly seems, in your life now, to be a battle of the sexes taking place. The feminine influence in your world has one idea of how to celebrate the holiday. The masculine impulse has another. Both ideas — or sets of ideas — are based, to some extent, on a fantasy. They contain an unrealistic expectation. Neptune suggests some intense negotiations will take place soon. And in the end? All will go the way that the strongest woman wants it to.

LIBRA Sep 24 – Oct 23

How much are you seriously hoping to accomplish between now and the end of the year? Come on. Be realistic. You may as well concede that it's not all going to prove possible. You have set yourself one objective too many. Even if you can, by some superhuman effort, tick off every item on your list, you are going to be in no shape to enjoy the holiday. Revisit the plan. Reconsider the big idea. Tone it down, just a little. Leave more room in your schedule for spontaneity and for real relaxation. Your life is due to be busy enough, just dealing with all the unexpected, sudden demands on your time and energy that crop up naturally over the coming days. Save some strength for these and have some faith in serendipity. You don't have to control everything and everyone. Many things will work out well, automatically.

PISCES Feb 20 – Mar 20

It is time to do a deal. The only trouble is, you don't really want to. End of the century or no end of the century, you are feeling unusually stubborn at the moment. There is a point on which you do not wish to give way. You can see the sense in trying to establish a compromise, but your emotions are not at all inclined to follow your intellect down the road of give and take. Why should you? Because it's Christmas, that's why. Mellow a bit. You won't melt. Or rather, you will! Once you lose that strange rigidity of attitude now dominating your mood, you will soften and bubble away through one of the most pleasing fortnights you can ever remember.

CANCER Jun 23 – July 23

This coming Full Moon in Cancer will clear the air, change the atmosphere — and chase away that sense of foreboding which is hanging over you like a storm cloud. Maybe, just maybe, before it blows away, it will deliver a little rain. It could even produce a thunderbolt or two. Despite the imminence of the holiday and the desire, at this time of year, to be as bright and cheerful as possible, there is a gloomy, problematic factor in your world which seems determined not to budge. You are 'working round it', attempting to ignore it or to psychologically fence it off, so that it doesn't spoil your celebration. Actually, a real solution is possible — sooner than you think. It may well, though, require a sharp exchange and a strong decision.

SCORPIO Oct 24 – Nov 22

Those poignant Christmas tunes bring a tear to the eye of the most hardened cynic. We hear them warbling out of the speakers at the supermarket and we ignore them. We may even hear them on the radio and say, 'Oh, that's just so soppy and so singing.' But there comes a moment, in every week before Christmas, when a seasonal song suddenly makes its way into our mind, and before we know it we've gone all gooey. You've got some practical plans for the holiday designed to get you in one end and out the other with the minimum of fuss. Joy is not on your agenda. Survival is all you're bothered about. Fear not. You will get through it, and, well, too. But guess what. Twixt now and New Year, you're going to have a heartwarming moment or three as well.

ARIES Mar 21 – April 20

Rules get broken at this time of year. People make a real effort to be nice to one another. They say and do things which they might normally consider preposterous. We all let our hair down, or we try to. Other things, too, tell us that life is not 'normal'. Shop assistants smile. TV stations put on shows that are worth watching. All this is jolly fine, but it leads us to believe that we have become superhuman. We feel able to eat as much rich food as we can swallow and drink far more than we should. Venus forms a right angle to your ruler soon. You've got a fine festive season in store. But do, please, pace yourself. Moderation is more than just a virtue this year, it's the only way to stay sane.

LEO Jul 24 – Aug 23

This is not always your favourite time of year. You don't like to dwell, too long and hard, on your reasons for feeling doubtful about December — and you live in hope, each time the holiday comes around, that a minor miracle will enable you to enjoy it as much as everyone else seems to do. Sometimes, this happens. Indeed, every year, to some extent, it does. None of your Christmases are miserable. It's just that they don't quite always seem to match that 'great expectation' which you can feel yourself being encouraged to nurture. A part of you can't wait for the whole thing to be over. I won't promise you a total escape from that mood in the next couple of weeks, but I can (and will) assure you that the last celebration of the Millennium is going to be one that you truly enjoy in a way that you have never done before.

SAGITTARIUS Nov 23–Dec 21

Expect an intense couple of weeks. The world may be planning for a lot of time off, but the sky does not seem to have any such destiny in mind for Sagittarians. In the break from the usual routine that soon ensues, you will find yourself dealing with a pile of hot domestic, family or personal issues which you have been postponing or avoiding. There will also be some cold financial facts to face up to. Don't, though, assume that all is dire. You have needed this chance to get to grips with certain pressing matters. After some initial discomfort, as you realise that there's much more to think about than you expected, you'll get into your stride. You'll see marvellous movement in areas where, for too long, all has been stale. And yo can also expect to cook up som delightfully easy new solutions to aggravating old problems between now and New Year's Eve.

Commentary

It's interesting to see that quite a few of the idiomatic phrases in these horo-scopes involve some kind of judgement or evaluation of behaviour. The astrologer is talking in general terms that appeal to most people under that star sign and is evaluating aspects of character, situations and general behav-iour towards others. The idioms are used to mark out attitudes, emotions and predicted reactions to these things. The idioms used or the main words used to form the idiom involve basic things.

> rushed off your feet
> down the road
> give way
> clear the air
> hanging over you like a storm cloud

In each case the astrologer writes in an intimate and confiding manner. The use of idioms helps to create a simplicity and informality of tone and makes it seem as if the writer is simply engaged in an intimate conversation with the reader. Idioms play a key part in giving texts a more spoken or written character and it is worth looking at horoscopes in both popular and broad-sheet newspapers to see if you can find any differences in their use in more formal contexts. Notice, too, how idioms and metaphors can often keep each other company. In the horoscopes metaphoric phrases like 'mellow a bit' and 'melt' are used in creative blends alongside idiomatic phrases such as 'down the road of give and take'.

Of course, it is easier to work out the meaning of some idioms rather than others. For example, some people may find the following headline and the following notice in an office more difficult to work out.

> **Local Clubs play cat and mouse**
>
> **Keep the Office Tidy: Don't make your office
> a dog's dinner**

Or to say of someone that they '*have green fingers*' or that things are going well but there's '*a fly in the ointment*' and that you can '*smell a rat*' may make things more difficult for people less familiar with this aspect of the language, such as some foreign speakers of English, where the idioms do not translate directly into other languages.

Now examine Text: Keegan. Look at the first two paragraphs and the last paragraph of this sports report. What idioms do you notice? How and why are they being used? Are there any words which you would say are simply metaphors rather than idioms? (Note: there is no commentary on this activity.)

Text: Keegan

Keegan must throw the art of passing into the mixer

England need to play keep-ball to check the Romanian counter-attack

Martin Thorpe in Maastricht

Kevin Keegan, in his tactical approach to England's games so far, has looked like a DIY novice trying to mix his own cement. Against Portugal he poured too much water into the mix and England ended up with no solidity.

Against Germany Keegan tried to firm things up but overdid the cement powder and England ended up so rigid as to be incapable of creative movement. Before tonight's game against Romania the coach will be laying it on with a trowel to his players that this time they must get the mix right or hopes of a quarter-final place will collapse.

All this wasted possession simply invited Germany back on to England, prompting the defence to drop deeper, searching for what the England coach Les Reed calls "the comfort zone that comes with knowing there is no space behind you". As a result, Martin Keown was constantly exhorting the back line to push out.

"We definitely need to start passing the ball better," admitted Keegan on Sunday. "We pass it well in training, we just need to do it on the pitch." England have done it on the pitch already in this tournament, in the first 20 minutes against Portugal. Now they need to repeat that virtuosity against Romania while retaining the solidity of the Germany match.

Thankfully England need only a draw to qualify for the quarter-finals, though Paul Ince insists: "You know the English mentality. We never play for a draw." Either way, it must be hoped that Keegan the cement mixer has sorted out the right ingredients.

Note: see satellite texts: *The Language of Sport, The Language of Newspapers*

Summary

Idioms often involve very frequent words. Idioms can also involve words which are used metaphorically and once more the most frequent everyday words are used in blends between metaphors and idioms. It's also worth noting how idioms are used to indicate attitudes and emotions and, in particular, to **evaluate** things. When requests are made to keep an office tidy or when behaviour is commented upon (see p. 100), an idiom is often chosen to describe things. Idioms often accompany positive or negative statements.

DENOTATION AND CONNOTATION: WHAT ARE WORDS WORTH?

This section looks at the way words can carry value judgements with them. Each word will have its straightforward dictionary definition, but a large number of words will also carry extra associations, often personal or emotional, that the use of the word brings to mind. The dictionary definition of a word is its **denotation**. The denotation of the word 'dog' (noun) is 'carnivorous quadruped of the genus *Canis*'. The personal or emotional meaning that a word may carry is its **connotation**. The connotations of the word 'dog' will vary from individual to individual. To one person, 'dog' may connote loyalty, bravery, faithfulness, love; to another person, it may connote noise, nuisance, filth, danger.

Some words carry strong connotations, and those connotations are generally agreed on by users of the language. Such words are often described as 'loaded'. Loaded words have strong negative or positive connotations, and can have a powerful emotional impact.

Activity

Look at the following words. Decide whether they have (a) no particular connotations, (b) strong negative connotations, (c) strong positive connotations.

> vehicle, slavery, democracy, was, photosynthesis, torture,
> the, brat, morphophonemics, Rolls Royce, fascism, building,
> freedom, hovel, a

Compare your analysis of the list with someone else's. Do you agree on which words are loaded, and whether they are positive or negative in their connotations?

Commentary

As discussed above, connotation depends to a certain extent on individual response. However, certain words do tend to evoke similar responses from individuals. Here is an analysis of the list produced by a group of students who did the activity collectively:

No connotations	vehicle, was, photosynthesis, the, morphophonemics, building, a
Negative	slavery, torture, brat, fascism, hovel
Positive	democracy, Rolls Royce, freedom

There was some disagreement about Rolls Royce, fascism and democracy. The group felt that Rolls Royce had connotations of wealth and luxury that could be used in either a negative or a positive way. They agreed in their response to fascism and democracy, but decided that people with different political beliefs might think differently.

What characterises the words that are not loaded? Grammatical words such as articles and auxiliary verbs are less likely to carry connotations, as their meaning is grammatical rather than lexical. Therefore 'was', 'a', 'the' carry no connotations.

Words that are highly specialised and are restricted to a particular area of meaning are less likely to be loaded. 'Morphophonemics' and 'photosynthesis' are probably too restricted and specialised in their use to carry any emotional loading. The majority of English speakers will not have 'morphophonemics' in their vocabulary, and though 'photosynthesis' is more widely known, it still has a restricted range.

Words that are highly general are also less likely to be loaded. There are a lot of words that have a classification function, in that they are general terms that encompass more specific terms.

103

'Vehicle' is a general term that encompasses car, bus, bicycle, lorry, truck, van, etc. 'Car' encompasses sports car, saloon, hatchback, and a whole range of specific names such as BMW, Rolls Royce, Lamborghini, that have a wide range of cultural connotations.

Words that have this classification function are called **hypernyms**. Examples of hypernyms are:

fruit, animal, bird, flower

The words with a more specific meaning that can be classified by the hypernyms are called **hyponyms**. Examples of hyponyms are:

apple, orange, banana

dog, cat, buffalo, warthog

robin, vulture, eagle

Hyponyms are more likely to carry strong connotations than hypernyms, though this is not an invariable rule. The word 'animal' can carry negative connotations in metaphors such as 'He behaved like an animal.' However, more specific connotations can be carried by the use of more specific words. 'He ate like a pig.' 'You rat!' 'She's a bitch.'

The section on synonyms above looked at the way the English language often has a range of words that focus around the same area of meaning. There are historical reasons for this that the next section will discuss, but often this wealth of synonyms allows speakers or writers to express an opinion by choosing a synonym that is loaded in a negative or positive way.

Activity

Look at Text: Amnesty. Identify words used for feelings and emotions, words used to name individuals, and words used to name groups of people. How does the word choice work to make the text effective?

Rewrite the text, substituting proper names for the nouns relating to groups of people (e.g. for 'soldiers' substitute a person's name). Has this changed the impact of the text? How?

What is the effect of the use of personal pronouns 'we' and 'you'?

104

Text: Amnesty

The reason you join Amnesty is not words, but pain.

It's the pain of children like 16 year old Sevki Akinci, literally barbecued alive by Turkish soldiers who came to his village looking for guns which they didn't find.

It's the tears of 17 year old Ravi Sundaralingam, tortured by Indian troops in Sri Lanka – tied upside down with a fire lit beneath his head and electrodes sparking at his genitals.

It's the anguish of Angelica Mandoza de Ascarza, whose teenaged son was taken from home by the security forces in Peru, never to be heard from again. He joined the hundreds who have simply 'disappeared.'

It's the terror of a 23 year old Tibetan nun, raped by Chinese soldiers with an electric cattle prod.

It's the agony of children like Walter Villatoro and Salvadore Sandoval, street children in Guatemala City, whose eyes were burned out by police cigars, their tongues ripped from their heads with pliers.

Maybe you simply don't realise that such vile things go on.

But for two years now, we have been running appeals in this newspaper. With one exception, all of these cases were mentioned in previous appeals.

Amnesty International

Commentary

Most of the words used for feelings and emotions are abstract nouns with connotations of great suffering. The suffering is closely linked to the people whose proper names are given. The text does not, therefore, talk about pain and agony in an abstract way, but about the pain and agony of named individuals. The perpetrators, however, are anonymous groups: soldiers, troops and police.

These are comments made by students who carried out this task:

The anonymous groups are more sinister, more frightening.

The groups make it sound official, as though the people in charge wanted it to happen. Names could just be criminal killers, and that's different.

The groups are all employed by governments. They are supposed to protect people, not torture them. That makes it worse.

The use of 'we' and 'you' helps to establish a sense of exclusion in the reader. The function of the text is to persuade people to join Amnesty International, and the initial exclusion, in this context, makes the reader feel guilty and in some way responsible. If you, as a reader, feel this, then it is likely that you will want to become included, one of the 'we' not one of the 'you'.

Note: see satellite text: *The Language of Newspapers*

Activity

Look at the Amnesty text again, and the word 'barbecued' in line 3. Make a list of the connotations of this word (as it stands alone, not as it is used in the text).

(For commentary on this activity, see p. 122.)

Summary: words and meanings

The term 'word' is, therefore, not as easy to define as it first seems. Any analysis of text that is looking at word level needs to be done with an awareness of the complicated relationship that exists between words and meanings, the patterns words create with other words, how frequently the words occur, whether they are primarily spoken or written, and whether they can be interpreted literally or not.

Words and histories

This section looks at the origins of the English word stock, and the ways in which the language gains new words through the processes of borrowing, changing the use of existing words and creating new words.

GOT ANY SPARE WORDS?

English has often been described as having a very rich and extensive word stock. For political and historical reasons, it has borrowed from other languages all over the world, and still does. For example, Chinese food became popular in this country towards the middle of the twentieth century. This brought a whole range of new words into the language, many of them borrowed directly from one of the many dialects of Chinese. The word for the deep round-based pan used for stir frying, 'wok', is one of these.

Activity

For this activity, you will need an up-to-date dictionary that gives etymological information (information about the origins of a word).

Using a dictionary

| 1 | 2 | 3 | 4 |

CAMEL (kæməl). [Late Old English, adapted from Latin camelus

| 5 | 6 |

adoption of Greek adopted from Semitic]

The section of a dictionary entry in square brackets gives information about the origin of a word. In the example above, 1 is the word itself, 2 is the phonological representation, 3 is the period it first arrived in English, 4, 5 and 6 show the route this word followed to arrive in the English language.

107

A full etymological dictionary, such as the *Oxford English Dictionary,* will give all the meanings a particular word has had since it came into English.

Look up the words in the following lists, and locate them on a world map according to their country and language of origin. Some words may not be located in a specific country, but a more general area such as North America, e.g. Wampum, N. American, from Algonquin, wampumpeag.

List 1 contains words that are comparatively recent additions to the language. You may not be able to find them if your dictionary is not a very recent one, but you should be able to identify the place of origin.

List 1

balti, barbie (barbecue), couch potato, fatwah, glasnost, internet, intifada, karaoke, macho, tandoori, tuckus

---

List 2 contains words that have been in the language for a relatively long time, and therefore should be in any comprehensive dictionary.

List 2

attorney, banjo, barbecue, brogue, budgerigar, bungalow, butter, cartoon, coleslaw, concerto, dilemma, dirge, dragon, geisha, gorilla, junta, kettle, kimono, knapsack, macaroni, mediator, moccasin, mosquito, paprika, pound, samovar, scot (as in scot-free), sinecure, scorch

---

Commentary

A short dictionary investigation of this kind shows how widely the English language has borrowed from other languages. The borrowing is worldwide; in fact, there are very few languages English has not borrowed from at one time or another. The reason for this lies in the history of both the language and the country. The earliest borrowed words, or **loan words**, are from Latin, with a very small number from the original Celtic languages of Britain.

The Viking invasion introduced Scandinavian words. The Norman conquest introduced a massive number of French loan words. Later contact with other European languages through cultural exchange, trade, political contacts and exploration gave the language Portuguese, Dutch, Spanish and Italian loan words. Languages from the Near East – Arabic, Turkish, Persian, Hindustani, Indic, Tamil – came via trade, exploration, colonisation and, sadly, the slave trade.

How long has this pick 'n' mix approach to our lexicon existed? The English language has always borrowed from other languages, so are there any words that are 'truly' English?

This concept, 'truly English', is a difficult one to define. The earliest language spoken in Britain was the ancestor of modern Welsh. The earliest words that are identifiably English come from the Germanic languages from which English developed. It is probably reasonable to say that these earliest words from the Old English period are 'truly English'.

Activity

Read Text: *Beowulf*; an extract from the Old English poem *Beowulf*, in which the monster, Grendel, comes to the King's hall in darkness and kills one of the warriors.

Text: *Beowulf*

```
710  Ðā cōm of mōre under misthleoþum
     Grendel gongan, Godes yrre bær; . . .
     . . . Nē þæt se āglǣca yldan þōhte,
740  ac hē gefēng hraðe forman sīðe
     slǣpendne rinc, slāt unwearnum,
     bāt bānlocan, blōd ēdrum dranc,
     synsnǣdum swealh; sōna hæfde
     unlyfigendes eal gefeormod,
745  fēt ond folma.
```

Obviously, to the modern reader this looks like, and in many ways is, a foreign language. It is made more complicated by the fact that some of the letters have changed, the spellings are very different and the grammar of Old English required a lot of word endings (and some beginnings) that we no longer use. Can you identify any of the words? Try modernising the spelling and the word structure. Remove -e, -es, -a, -an, -um. Break the words into syllables to see if you can recognise parts of a word. Change the letters <Ð>, <ð>, <þ>, to <th>, and <ǣ> to <a>. Do any words now look familiar, even if you can't give them a precise meaning? Do any look completely strange?

Text: Translation (1) is a translation that is, as far as possible, word for word. How many words from the Old English text are still in use today?

Text: Translation (1)

> Then came over the moor under the mist bank
> Grendel going God's ire bore; . . .
> . . . Not that the fiend of delay thought
> but he seized quickly at the first opportunity
> the sleeping man slit greedily
> bit the bone-lock blood from the veins drank
> huge pieces swallowed soon had
> the unliving eaten completely
> feet and hands.

Text: Translation (2) is a translation into good modern English. You may also want to consult Seamus Heaney's translation of *Beowulf* which won the Whitbread Book of the Year award in 1999.

Text: Translation (2)

The Grendel came across the moors under the cover of darkness. The anger of God was upon him. . . . He didn't hesitate, but at the first chance, grabbed the sleeping man and greedily tore him apart, biting into the muscles, swallowing huge pieces and drinking the blood from the veins. Almost at once he had devoured the dead man completely, feet and hands.

Commentary

English has clearly lost a lot of words since the Old English period, but a large number have come down to the present day, particularly grammatical words such as articles and prepositions. There are also lexical words from this period in Modern English; commonly used verbs: come, go, think, drink, swallow, sleep; nouns to do with the body, weather and landscape, emotion and religion.

It is interesting to find frequent everyday words in a passage that certainly doesn't relate to everyday experience. Modern English contains a lot of words from the Old English period, and interestingly the hundred most frequently used words are almost all Old English. See also p. 94.

Even in this early period, English was borrowing from Latin and Greek, and this process continues to the present day. For historical reasons, Latin has been associated with learning and **formality**; words of Latin and Greek origin have become associated with a formal register. Look at the activity relating to levels of formality in Unit 4 (p. 177 ff.), and look up the origins of the words used in the texts. How many of them are of Latin or Greek origin?

Activity

The two extracts in Text: Speeches are taken from speeches made by Ronald Reagan (Text 1) and Martin Luther King (Text 2). Look up the origins of the underlined words. Which speech uses more Latin or Greek loan words? Which text uses frequent everyday words? What is the overall effect? Which, in your view, is the most effective text?

(For commentary on this activity, see p. 122.)

111

Text: Speeches

Text 1
We're <u>approaching</u> the end of a <u>bloody</u> <u>century</u>, <u>plagued</u> by a <u>terrible</u> <u>invention</u> – <u>totalitarianism</u>. <u>Optimism</u> comes less easily today, not because <u>democracy</u> is less <u>vigorous</u>, but because democracy's <u>enemies</u> have <u>refined</u> their <u>instruments</u> of <u>repression</u>. Yet optimism is in order because day by day, democracy is proving itself to be not at all a <u>fragile flower</u>.

Text 2
I have a <u>dream</u> that one <u>day</u> on the <u>red</u> <u>hills</u> of Georgia the <u>sons</u> of <u>former</u> <u>slaves</u> and the sons of former slave owners will be able to <u>sit</u> down <u>together</u> at the <u>table</u> of <u>brotherhood.</u> . . . I have a dream that my four <u>little</u> <u>children</u> will one day live in a <u>nation</u> where they will not be <u>judged</u> by the <u>colour</u> of their <u>skin</u> . . .

Activity

Using a thesaurus and a dictionary, replace the Old English and Old Norse words in King's speech with Latinate ones (e.g. I have a fantasy . . .). How has the impact of the text changed? Is it more or less effective in your view?

The origins of a word can often, therefore, be reflected in its use. It is not just a matter of formality. After the Norman conquest in 1066, the French language became associated with the court, the aristocracy, the wealthy and sophisticated. Our later contacts with and perceptions of French culture mean that English has often acquired words from the French language that relate to concepts of fashion, wealth and sophistication.

Text: Chanel is from the fashion pages of the *Observer*. Identify the origins of the underlined words. How do the origins of the words reflect the topic and the function of the text?

Text: Chanel

Coco Chanel first introduced the <u>androgynous</u> look to <u>womenswear</u> back in 1930s Paris; her pioneering appropriation of <u>masculine tailoring</u> for <u>female attire</u> has since become a staple of the working <u>woman's</u> <u>wardrobe</u>. This summer, city-boy <u>chic</u> looks good in or out of the office, with <u>briefcase</u> or <u>mobile</u> phone as optional <u>accessories</u>

113

Commentary

Many of the underlined words, words relating to the specialism of fashion, are loan words from French. Most of these are very much part of the day-to-day vocabulary. 'Fashion', 'attire', 'tailoring' may all be from a specialist field, but cause no problems to the reader.

As noted above, as early as the eleventh century, French words became associated with sophistication and fashion, and it is interesting that new words for artifacts that are not immediately associated with fashion but have clear connotations of 'style' to the modern reader have been taken from French. For example, why 'mobile' (French) phone, rather than 'portable' (Latin) phone?

Continued borrowing from French means that we tend to go to the French language when a word for a fashion concept is needed. 'Chic', for example, has its first recorded usage in 1856. Its status as a more recent arrival can be identified by its pronunciation, which has not become anglicised: /ʃik/ rather than /tʃik/.

French loan words came into English in great numbers as the language of a successful invader, and are well assimilated into the language. Loan words from other languages can often reflect the cultural contact that resulted in the borrowing. Thus, for example, words to do with music, particularly classical music, are often Italian in origin – aria, concerto, duet, opera, piano, violin – reflecting the interest that English culture had in Italian music.

Later borrowings from Italian reflect a recent interest in Italian cuisine ('cuisine' is a French loan word): lasagna, pizza, scampi are all recent arrivals, though spaghetti and gorgonzola have been in the language since the nineteenth century.

Dutch loan words have given English nautical terms and words to do with cloth (buoy, cruise, skipper; cambric, duffel).

Loan words from Eastern languages relate to science and trading goods (particularly fruits and spices): algebra, almanac, amber, camphor, orange, saffron, syrup.

English is often described as a language that has a very rich and versatile vocabulary. One of the reasons for this is the extent of the borrowing from other languages. English has probably more loan words in its word stock than any other language, and this gives the language a lot of scope for subtle shades of formality, tone and meaning.

Note: see satellite texts: *The Language of Advertising, The Language of Magazines*

WORDS MEAN WHAT I WANT THEM TO MEAN

The English language doesn't only acquire words by borrowing from other languages, though as the previous section demonstrates, many new words came into the language via that route. Another route is that of **semantic change**, or a change in the meaning of a word over time. A fairly recent example is the word 'gay', which used to have the primary meaning of happy or carefree, but now has the primary meaning of homosexual.

Activity

The following text appears puzzling at first. This is because the underlined words have been used with their original or earlier meaning. Look up the original meanings of the words, and rewrite the text into modern English.

> The <u>girl</u> wore his best <u>frock</u> to the dinner-party. He was a healthy young man with a healthy appetite, and he was in danger of eating so much he would <u>starve</u>. There was plenty of <u>meat</u> to suit his vegetarian tastes. After the meal, his <u>disease</u> was so bad he had to go and lie down.

Commentary

This text demonstrates the extent to which the meaning of a word can change. The problem faced by language purists who object to change of this kind is that many of the words that are commonly used have undergone the process they are objecting to, and unless they demand that the language should be subjected to some kind of 'purification' process in which all words were restored to their original meanings, the purists' position is a bit illogical.

There are patterned and recognised ways in which the meanings of words can change.

Generalisation and specialisation

A very common way for semantic change to occur is where a word either expands its meaning to include a wider range (generalisation) or narrows its meaning to become more specific (specialisation). Examples of this include 'wife', a word that used to mean woman in the general sense. The word gradually specialised to mean 'a woman of humble rank or low employment', giving the language constructions such as ale-wife or fish-wife. The word now means married woman. The word 'tail', on the other hand, has generalised in meaning. It used to mean a hairy tail, as that of a horse or a fox. It has come to mean any tail.

Activity

Look at the text from the last activity again. Say whether the underlined words have generalised or specialised in meaning. (Note: there is no commentary on this activity.)

Beware of the word! Taboo and euphemism

An important influence in the semantic change of words is the change of meaning brought about by the associations a word may have. There are certain concepts a culture may be uneasy about, and words associated with these concepts may attract censure. When this happens, such words can develop negative connotations. They may then be replaced by other words that are seen as a better or 'nicer' way of expressing the concept. Unfortunately, once the new word becomes associated with the concept, it too begins to attract negative connotations and needs to be replaced in turn. This process is known as **pejoration**. The reverse process, whereby a word acquires a 'better' meaning, is known as **amelioration**.

The following words refer to the act of human excretion, and the place where this should take place. Classify the words into groups under the following headings: casual/slang, technical/medical, formal/polite.

> pee, piss, urine, shit, crap, faeces, wee, pass water, urinate, defecate, go to the toilet/lavatory/bathroom, powder my nose, rest room, comfort station, w.c., ladies, gents, loo, lavatory, bog

Which words or phrases would be acceptable in a fairly formal situation?

A quick analysis of this word list suggests that excretion is a social minefield in the English-speaking world (or parts of it). A group of students doing this activity decided that in informal, peer-group situations, English is well equipped with words (though there are many groups who would not find these terms acceptable, even in very informal situations).

Interestingly, 'crap', a word that is mildly taboo, is probably a euphemism in origin. Its original meanings were husk, weeds and residue. 'Shit' has not changed its meaning over time, but is described in the *Oxford English Dictionary* as 'not in decent use'. 'Piss' is also an old form that has become mildly taboo.

Therefore, one word associated with a socially difficult concept began as a euphemism and has become taboo, while words that carry the original meaning have been considered taboo for some time. Presumably, newer euphemisms will also become taboo in turn.

'Piss' and 'shit' also seem to be acquiring new, non-taboo meanings. 'Pissed' is a well-known English slang term for drunkenness, and more recently American English has developed the meaning of 'belongings', detritus, the rest, etc., for 'shit', as in the following examples:

'Bring all your shit with you.'

(part of an invitation from a New Yorker)

Cornelius looked at me. 'That means I'm getting an A. Now that I know the difference between ain't and aren't and shit.'

(Susannah Moore, *In the Cut*)

117

Technical and medical terms, urinate and defecate, would appear to be clear and direct in meaning. Urinate has just the meaning to pass urine, but defecate has the original meaning of to purify.

The formal terms are all euphemistic. The group noted that there is no polite way to say what you are going to do. In this context, the use of a technical term will not help. 'I am going to urinate' would not be seen as socially acceptable. There are only polite ways of saying where you are going or asking directions. Even the most apparently direct words for the place are euphemisms.

'Toilet' originally meant a piece of cloth in which clothes were wrapped, then a cloth cover for a dressing table, then the dressing table itself. Its current meaning is fairly recent and is American in origin.

'Lavatory' used to mean a place to wash yourself (compare with current use of bathroom). Both 'toilet' and 'lavatory' have become socially a bit difficult, and the language has acquired a newer range of euphemisms: ladies, gents, powder room, bathroom, rest room, etc.

Semantic change, as with borrowing, is a continuous process, and far more complex than the brief outline above suggests. An awareness of the capacity of words to shift and change their meaning helps the receiver of text to be aware of change as it has occurred, or as it is occurring.

GET YOUR NEW WORDS HERE! CREATING NEW WORDS

A third way in which English acquires new words is by word creation, either through invention following existing word patterns, or through the direct creation of new words. As with semantic change, this is a massive area, and this section will only address aspects of it.

Activity

Text: Invented words lists words that don't actually exist in the English language, but could do according to existing routes for word creation. Even though the words don't exist, discuss the ways in which these words may have developed. Can you identify any words that do exist in the language and that may have arrived via similar routes?

Text: Invented words

Word	Definition
Spide (verb)	To move like a spider
Bookaholic (noun)	Someone who is addicted to reading
Pimad (noun)	A personally identified multiple aerial device
Buscar (noun)	A car that is used as part of a car pool
Busc (verb)	To drive a buscar
Gummer (noun)	Someone who makes children eat food they don't want (reference to the then Minister of Agriculture, John Gummer, who fed his daughter a burger on TV in an attempt to allay fears about BSE)

Commentary

Spide

Words follow patterns (see section on morphemes p. 76). Many words in English follow the pattern verb, verb + -er (noun of agency). For example, there are pairs like dance (verb) and dancer (noun), play and player, sing and singer. Some nouns have the -er agency ending but have no corresponding verb. Hammer is a good example. It is conceivable, then, that such words might at some time generate their own verb. So 'spider' might generate 'spide', or 'hammer' might generate 'ham', as in 'Can you ham this nail there for me?'

Bookaholic

A common way in which new words are created is by adding affixes (prefixes or suffixes) to existing words. Prefixes such as after-, be-, un-, under-; suffixes such as -er, -like, -hood, -ing, are just a few of the possibilities. All of these affixes go back to the earliest days of the language. However, the language is developing new affixes. The suffix -aholic/-oholic is an interesting one. The original source of this is the word alcoholic, from alcohol, the Latin adapta-

119

tion of an Arabic word for a powder used to stain the eyes, from which we also get kohl; and -ic, a suffix used usually for forming adjectives, as in artistic, neurotic. However, for some reason modern users of English have seen the word structure as alc-oholic, and created a new suffix meaning 'addicted to'. A similar process has occurred with 'marathon', a word of Greek origin that came into the language as a single morpheme (see p. 76), but has given English the new suffix -thon, thus telethon, slimathon, etc.

Pimad

Another fairly recent way of forming new words is via initials. Words created this way are called acronyms. Examples are scuba (self-contained underwater breathing apparatus), AWOL (absent without leave). A very recent example is twoc, to take a car, usually for joy-riding. This word comes from the charge, taken without owner's consent.

Buscar

Existing words are often combined to create new words. This can be done as with the example above, by combining whole words (though bus is an example of another method of word formation, shortening; the original word was omnibus). Examples in the language are doorman, greenhouse. Joy-riding (see above) is another example, its recent status marked by the use of a hyphen. It can also be done by combining parts of existing words. 'Daisy' is a combination of 'day's' and 'eye', the day's eye.

Busc

This kind of formation, back formation, is similar to the way spide might be formed. The word 'buscar' sounds as though it is a noun of agency, and should have a verb: busc. In fact, this would be to mistake the origin and structure of the word. This doesn't prevent such a process from happening. 'Burgle' is a back formation from burglar, for example.

Gummer

New words are often formed from a proper noun, the name of the inventor or of a person particularly associated with a concept or idea. The word hoover, for example, was originally a brand name for a particular make of vacuum cleaner. It has become an alternative term for vacuum cleaner, and has also become a verb (interestingly, despite the patterns identified above for nouns of agency, we hoover the carpet, not hoove it). If the original vacuum cleaner had been invented by Mitsubishi or Hotpoint, would we hotpoint or mitsubishi the carpet?

Summary: words and histories

The English language is over a thousand years old. Its word stock is wide and varied, with immense capacity for expressing subtle shades and wide ranges of meaning. As a living language, English will continue to develop and expand its word stock in response to social change and development, technological change, changes in cultural and religious beliefs, and all those other factors that operate to make a language a tool that its users need.

Answer to activity

Identification of morphemes (p. 77)

pig s, bark ed, un like ly, mother hood, salt y, cherry, tall er, hammer, dis please, hard ship, super hero es, play er.

Commentaries on activities

Shop names (p. 82)

All of these names are playing games with the language, and exploiting its capacity to produce ambiguous meanings, in many cases by using the capacity of the language to develop synonyms and polysemes.

Another cause of ambiguity arises in the use of words that are spelled differently, have different meanings, but have the same pronunciation. These words are homophones (see also p. 62). Some examples in the data are dye, die; wee, we; manor, manner.

The creators of these names are playing on our ability as users of language to create a meaning link where, strictly speaking, none should exist. The effect of this is to entertain the recipient, and to make the names memorable, whilst using words that give a positive view of the product or service on offer. There are some words that are close to homophones placed in a context where the reader or hearer would expect another word. For example, plumbing rhymes with coming. Placed in the phrase 'Plumbing your way', the language draws on both meanings, giving the effect of an identified service that is close at hand.

121

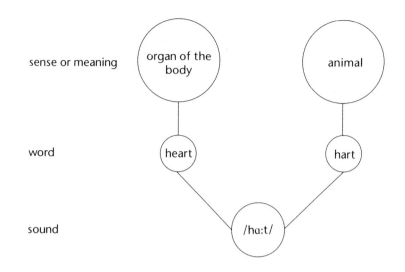

Connotations of 'barbecued' (p. 106)

'Barbecue' has connotations of pleasure. Barbecues usually take place in good weather, often occur in party or celebratory situations, and are good fun. The object of the action is an item of food, often meat, and the effect of barbecuing is to brown and sear.

To talk about a person being barbecued gives them the status of a piece of meat. This emphasises the contempt the perpetrators have for their victim. It is only too easy to visualise the effects implied by the use of this verb. The celebratory context that we associate with barbecues emphasises the shock the word creates, and also further dehumanises the perpetrators who could perform such an act.

The meaning of a text can, therefore, be strongly influenced by the connotations of the words that the producer of the text has chosen to use.

Speeches (p. 111)

There is a very clear difference between the two texts. Reagan's speech has a high proportion of Latin or Greek loan words, or words that came into English from Latin via French.

King's speech, on the other hand, though it does contain some Latinate words, draws very much on the older forms that come from Old English or Old Norse.

Reagan's speech seems in some way more elaborate, perhaps more difficult to follow than King's speech, which draws on the language of everyday usage.

This does not mean that King's speech is more simple or less complex. It has a complex pattern of metaphor and of rhetorical devices that help to give it its impact. King, however, choosing to select words from the day-to-day vocabulary of his audience, has produced one of the most famous and memorable speeches of the twentieth century.

Sentences and structures

The main aim of this unit is to introduce you to some of the most significant patterns of English grammar. It is, of course, impossible to introduce all the patterns, but those selected here are generally likely to be significant in the organisation of texts. Knowing about these patterns and understanding how they function will help you to see how meanings are made in texts and can provide a basis for interpreting what the texts mean to you.

Grammar is only one level of linguistic analysis, and interpreting the use of grammar in the text is not the same as interpreting the text. To do this we need to consider other patterns of language too, such as vocabulary, phonology and discourse. But grammar is a central resource for making and communicating meaning, and the more you understand how it works the more systematically you can work with texts that interest you.

Many students are frightened of grammar and of the terminology used to discuss it. Some consider that its study is no more than a mechanical exercise. The aim in this unit is to show how interesting and useful grammatical knowledge can be. The specific aim is to teach you some grammar by showing you how it works in different texts and contexts of use, not simply to name individual parts and forms out of context. To do this we need some language to talk about grammar, and part of that language will involve words and terms which are new and are explained in the 'Index of terms' at the end of the book. Most of these terms will be discussed and explained but some are emboldened. We aim to give you regular practice in using those terms so that you will feel comfortable and confident in talking and writing about grammar and working with grammar in texts.

Contents

In this unit you will learn about the following grammatical forms:

NOUNS AND PATTERNS
nouns and noun phrases; modifiers; main verbs; tense; pronouns; simple and complex noun phrases.

VERBS AND PATTERNS
tense; the verb 'to be'; modal verbs and modality.

SENTENCES AND PATTERNS
sentence and clause structure; deictics; active and passive voice; the get-passive.

Texts used include

- Poems, prose extracts
- Newspaper news reports
- A note from your milkman
- A campaign leaflet from an environmental organisation
- Advertisements
- An official notice
- An office memo

Activity

Grammar and patterns

The following sentence does not make sense. It is not grammatical. Put all the words in an order so that it does make sense overall. Then ask yourself how you did it.

weekend going am to I next disco the.

126

One way to do it is to look for groups of words which belong together in a pattern and then to put all the groups of words together. For example:

going am I   =   I am going (or am I going?)

the to disco   =   to the disco

weekend next =   next weekend

Sentences are made up of individual groups of words which form *patterns* with other groups of words. The patterns can be fixed; that is, they must follow a certain order. Or the patterns can follow different orders (though if they do, the meaning is normally changed).

For example, *to the disco* is a fixed pattern; but *I am going* can also be formed as *Am I going?* which turns a statement into a question. *I am going to the disco next weekend* can also be written as *Next weekend I am going to the disco*, which, by putting the reference to the time at the beginning, stresses *next weekend*.

Nouns and patterns

Activity

Write out a shopping list for shopping for your family at your local super-market. List the ten items which you think your family would judge to be the most essential items. Look at the list you have produced and consider what the words have in common. The words will be mostly consumable or usable items but try to identify what they have in common as words. What does the list look like on the page?

Commentary

In this section we will examine **nouns** and patterns involving nouns. Nouns are one of the most prominent of forms in a language. In fact, quite a few texts can be made up just of nouns; for example, 'London' is a noun and can stand quite meaningfully on its own on a signpost, or in answer to a question or on a train or air ticket or as the title to a book. 'School' is a noun and can stand on its own on a road sign, for example. 'Apples' is a noun and can stand quite independently on a shop ticket or shop sign. Take any word from the first sentence in this paragraph and try to make a meaningful text. You will see that it is difficult to make a meaningful list with words like *we* or *this* or *in* or *involving* when they occur on their own.

The shopping list you wrote probably consisted of nouns such as

milk
bread
tea bags
oven-ready chips.

As we have seen, nouns are not just single words; they form patterns with other words to form **noun phrases**. Again such phrases can stand on their own: for example, as titles to a book or story such as 'The Man with a Scar', or on a menu in a phrase such as 'Home-made celery soup', or on a shopfront name such as 'The Body Shop' or 'The Vegetarian Restaurant'. Or on a shopping list such as 'oven-ready chips' or 'semi-skimmed milk'. Writers of all kinds of different texts regularly make creative and communicative use of nouns and noun patterns. A good example is the poem 'Off Course' (1966) by Edwin Morgan.

Text: 'Off Course'

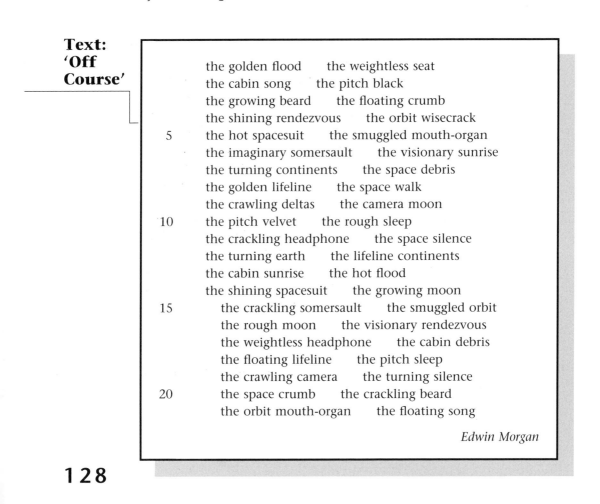

```
            the golden flood      the weightless seat
            the cabin song        the pitch black
            the growing beard      the floating crumb
            the shining rendezvous      the orbit wisecrack
    5       the hot spacesuit      the smuggled mouth-organ
            the imaginary somersault      the visionary sunrise
            the turning continents      the space debris
            the golden lifeline      the space walk
            the crawling deltas      the camera moon
   10       the pitch velvet      the rough sleep
            the crackling headphone      the space silence
            the turning earth      the lifeline continents
            the cabin sunrise      the hot flood
            the shining spacesuit      the growing moon
   15       the crackling somersault      the smuggled orbit
            the rough moon      the visionary rendezvous
            the weightless headphone      the cabin debris
            the floating lifeline      the pitch sleep
            the crawling camera      the turning silence
   20       the space crumb      the crackling beard
            the orbit mouth-organ      the floating song
```

Edwin Morgan

The most striking feature of the poem is its layout. The arrangement of the words on the page, or what is termed the 'graphology' of the poem, is especially distinctive and leaves the reader a little uncertain as to how it is to be read. For example, you could read across the page, which is the more conventional 'direction'; but you could also read down the page, reading the two columns one after the other almost as if the words were part of some inventory or list, rather like the shopping list which you created above. The layout of the lines is unusual and disorientating. The second column does not have the clear order and pattern of the first column, and at line 15 it looks as if a new paragraph begins. The lines move in a different direction and, as in the title of the poem perhaps, appear to go 'off course'.

Extension

1   Why do you think the writer has laid out the text as described above?
2   Why are there no punctuation marks used in the poem?

Commentary

The new direction appears to be a disturbing one for there is no obvious structure or ending to it. The movement of the second column of words is even more markedly laid out to suggest disorder, and this suggestion is reinforced by the fact that the poem has no real *punctuation*. There are no commas or colons or semi-colons or capital letters anywhere in the text. And the absence of full stops, especially at line 21, suggests that there is no ending to the text; it remains free-floating, searching for a pattern rather then clearly following an already existing one.

Yet closer inspection of the poem reveals that there are patterns. There are patterns of grammar across the whole text which are remarkably consistent and unchanging. Most striking is the pattern of **noun phrases**. In each case the structure is that of *d m n*, where *d* = definite article, *m* = modifier and *n* = noun. In fact, this structure is repeated in every line in the poem.

The most basic examples of this *d m n* pattern are in lines such as the following:

the hot flood

where 'flood' is the noun (*n*), 'hot' the modifier (*m*) and 'the' the definite article (*d*). Or:

the weightless headphone

129

where 'headphone' is the noun, 'weightless' the modifier and 'the' the definite article.

One reason why the term 'modifier' is preferred here to the more usual term 'adjective' is that 'modifier' is more inclusive. For example, nouns can be modified by other nouns as in 'the space silence' and the 'orbit wisecrack', where 'space' and 'orbit', which are both nouns, fill in these noun phrases the position of modifier, defining more precisely the nouns to which they are attached.

Activity

As we have seen, this basic structural pattern pervades the whole poem, and repetition of this pattern is a key feature of the poem. But there are variations within the repeated patterns. Take a basic pattern such as

the *pitch* black	(2)
the *pitch* velvet	(10)
the *pitch* sleep	(18)

and then find similar patterns in the poem in which a word is repeated with various partners. List as many of these patterns as you can. Why are there so many repetitions and what is suggested by the constant changes and variations?

Commentary

Here are some of the main patterns:

the floating *crumb*	(3)
the space *crumb*	(20)
the space *debris*	(7)
the cabin *debris*	(17)

the *space* debris	(7)
the *space* walk	(8)
the hot *space*suit	(5)
the *space* silence	(11)
the *space* crumb	(20)

These are fairly straightforward repetitions, involving the same word classes in each case (for example *crumb* is a noun and is still a noun when it is repeated with a different partner word). But some of the words are in different patterns when they are repeated. For example:

> the *orbit* wisecrack   (4)
> the *smuggled* orbit   (15)

– where *orbit* is both a noun (15) and a modifier (4). But we can notice how the repetitions are in effect no simple repetitions. The repetition of words helps to tell a story. The *space debris* referred to in line 7 has become the *cabin debris* in line 17. Bits and pieces floating in outer space are relatively normal but the presence of debris in a cabin works to suggest a kind of narrative in which events may have taken a turn for the worse.

In other words, the basic grammatical pattern provides a structural frame within and across which there are changing partnerships of words which in turn cumulatively create patterns of meaning. An increasingly prominent pattern is one in which there are suggestions of disaster or at least suggestions of things going seriously 'off course'. For example, headphones which crackle because of decreasing reception as the spacecraft moves further away from earth appear to become detached:

> the *crackling* headphone   (11)
> the *weightless* headphone   (17)

A *beard* which was *growing* normally (3) now collocates with *crackling* in an unusual and disturbing formation (20), possibly suggesting the movement of the hairs of a beard on the face of a dead body or on a body which has been subjected to electrical shocks or freezing air. The changing words within the same basic grammatical pattern enable the poet, Edwin Morgan, to embody changes to events and to perceptions of what is happening.

Note: see satellite text: *The Language of Poetry*

Activity

We should now consider other patterns which might go along with the noun phrases. For example, if we were to put the following nouns in a sentence, would you be able to make sense of the sentence?

> the tall man the black dog

What other words would you need to add to the sentence in order to make it make sense?

Take the verbs out of the following sentences. What are the results? Do the sentences make sense without the verbs?

> The girl kissed the boy.
> They lost the match 4–1.
> My friend's daughter has broken another vase.
> Paris is the capital of France.

Commentary

There are no main **verbs** in 'Off Course'. One effect of this omission of main verbs is that no clear relation seems to exist between the objects referred to in the noun phrases. Objects either seem not to act upon one another or have no particular 'action' of their own. Verbs create links. The links are usually between a grammatical 'subject' and a grammatical 'object'. In this example the subject 'man' is linked by a main verb 'walked' to the object 'dog':

> The man walked the dog

If the main verb is taken away, then the relationship between the noun 'man' and the noun 'dog' is no longer clear. Similarly, in the sentence

> My friend's daughter   has broken   another vase
> (subject)   (verb)   (object)

if the verb phrase 'has broken' is removed, we are left with 'My friend's daughter another vase', where we cannot work out the precise relationship between 'My friend's daughter' and the 'vase'.

So it is with the noun phrases in 'Off Course'. Verbs generally work to connect things, and so in this case the main effect is that of normal relations being suspended and disconnected. The poet has suspended the normal rules of grammar to create a world in which everything is turned upside down and suspended. In one sense this is appropriate to the conditions of outer space in which there is no gravity, but it may also suggest a space journey in which actions and events have become disturbingly abnormal.

The absence of main verbs in a text also removes any sense of time. Verbs are normally marked when something is taking place or took place. Thus, 'walked' tells you that the action is completed and is in the past tense. If there are no verbs in a text then there is no **tense**, and if there is no tense it is difficult to work out within what timescale things are happening. The poem 'Off Course' has as a result a certain timeless quality, as if normal temporal relations are suspended too.

However, it is not true to say that there are no verbs in the poem. There *are* verbs in the poem. For example, there is another distinct pattern in the text formed from the following groups of words:

the floating song
the growing beard
the shining rendezvous
the turning continents
the crackling headphone
the crawling deltas

and so on. The words ending in -ing are all what are termed present participles. The differences between the two verbal items in the following sentences:

the world turns
the turning world

underline that present participles function to create a sense of continuing, if suspended, action. In the poem they convey a feeling of things continuing endlessly or, at least, without any clear end. It may not be inappropriate, therefore, that the final line of the poem contains the group of words:

the floating song

which, with an absence of punctuation, possibly reinforces the idea of an endlessly drifting journey without a conclusion.

133

Notice, too, how many film titles contain present participles: for example, *Leaving Las Vegas*, *Boxing Helena*, *Being There*, *No Turning Back*. There are many more similar titles to check out in a local video shop, but consider why such forms are so common.

PRONOUNS AND PATTERNS

Although we interpreted the previous text 'Off Course' as being about a space journey which involved the lives of astronauts, there are, in fact, no actual references in the poem to people. The nouns refer to actions which we take to involve humans but the poem does *not* contain lines such as

> His rough sleep
> His growing beard
> Your hot spacesuit
> Her cabin song
> Our floating lifeline.

Words such as 'you', 'my', 'your', 'his', 'her' are **pronouns**. The main personal pronouns are: I, you, he, she, it, we, they. They are the main means of identifying speakers, addressees and others. The main possessive pronouns are: my, your, her, his, their, our. They indicate ownership. (Other types and functions of pronouns are explored in Unit 4 pp. 187 ff.) One possible effect of the absence of pronouns from 'Off Course' is to make the poem a little impersonal and cold, almost as if we are hearing a list of facts.

Activity

Text: Milk message also presents a number of facts but does it in a different way.

Find all the pronouns in this text and list them. Whom do they refer to? Why are so many pronouns used in the text?

134

Text: Milk message

Dear Valued Customer

A MESSAGE FROM YOUR CO-OP MILKMAN

You are probably aware of some of the major changes happening to the British Dairy Industry. I would like to take the opportunity to explain the action CWS Milk Group have taken to protect our service relationship with you, despite the increases in the cost of milk to us from the Milk Marketing Board (Milk Marque).

On the 1st July 1994 there was a rise in the price of milk charged to all dairies. Since this date we have held back on any increase to you, our valued doorstep customer.

Whilst we face still further increases in milk prices charged to us, *we are at present only increasing our price by 1p per pint. I hope that the action we have taken will give you confidence to continue to support us during these difficult times safeguarding our unique British service.*

The Co-op home delivery service performs a valuable social role within the community to all sectors, particularly to the aged, disabled and households with children. To all customers I offer on a daily basis a full range of milk types and a very competitively priced range of essential food items.

Please find enclosed coupons worth £2.00, as a special thank you for your continued support.

YOUR FRIENDLY CO-OP MILKMAN

Effective date Sunday 30th October 1994

Commentary

The strategy of the CWS Milk Group here is to address the customer directly and to show their sensitivity to their customers as individuals. In this message personal pronouns such as 'I', 'we' and, in particular, 'you' are extensively employed. A key sentence is:

> Since this date we have held back on any increase to you, our valued doorstep customer.

The message manages to describe the sale of milk to customers as if it were a collaborative venture. The use of the plural pronouns 'we', 'our', 'us' underlines the sense of the CWS group, the individual milkman and the customer as a 'team', and this is further emphasised by the description of the delivery of milk as an essential social and community service. At the same time the

135

message is still a subtly individualised message. The 'letter' is written as if it is from each individual milkman who uses the singular personal pronoun 'I' (complete with personal photograph) to personalise the relationship with 'you', the customer. It is an effective piece of writing and it is all the more effective for personalising a message which informs us that the price of milk is to go up. The resigned expression on the face of the milkman tells us that there is little anyone can do about this state of affairs but we can continue to look positive and good-humoured. Holding his milk crate like a trophy also establishes a clear pride in his job and in his relationship with his customers.

One other very obvious grammatical difference between the 'Milk message' and the poem 'Off Course' is that the message is written in complete sentences and makes use of much more familiar and conventional patterns of paragraphing and punctuation. The use of upper-case (capital) letters at the beginning and end of the message also emphasises the personal and individual nature of the relationship between the milkman and the customer.

Activity

Now read the 'Milk message' and see how many noun phrases you can find which have the same *d m n* pattern as those in 'Off Course'. If they are the same, consider why they are the same and, if the patterns are different, consider how and why they are different. It may help to list all the nouns that you can find in the text and then all the modifiers which occur in front of these nouns. Here are two examples to start you off:

> the CWS Milk Group
> the Milk Marketing Board.

Here the nouns are *Group* and *Board*; the modifiers are *CWS Milk* and *Milk Marketing*.

Commentary

In 'Off Course' the noun phrases are written, as we have seen, in the same pattern of *d* (definite article), *m* (modifier) and *n* (noun); in the 'Milk message' text the pattern is more complex. Here are some examples:

> the CWS Milk Group
> the Milk Marketing Board
> our valued doorstep customer
> the Co-op home delivery service
> a valuable social role
> a very competitively priced range of essential food items
> households with children.

These examples illustrate the much wider range of noun phrases which are possible in English, and they also illustrate that modifiers can occur after the main noun as well as in front of the main noun. The modifiers which occur before a main noun are called **pre-modifiers**, while the modifiers which occur after a main noun are called **post-modifiers**. In these examples 'with children' and 'of essential food items' are post-modifiers. On the surface they help to make the text a little more dense and complex to read than 'Off Course'.

Compared with 'Off Course' the 'Milk message' also employs more pre-modifiers in front of the main noun. This feature allows description to be a little more detailed and precise. Several of these pre-modifiers are also themselves nouns; and we should note that the pre-modifying nouns cluster in phrases which describe organisations or which provide a more technical definition of actions or entities (for example, the *Co-op home delivery* service). Normally, the more nouns which are used in a pre-modifying position the more technical or specialised the reference will be. You can often identify writing in science and engineering by the amount and density of this kind of pre-modification. For example, here are some terms from a car maintenance manual:

> metal hub-bearing outer race
> low-friction disc brakes
> aluminium precision dial gauge.

Although the letter to customers from their milkman is designed to be a personal letter, it nonetheless suggests that it is from a company which is in some way also specialised and efficient.

Text: Reebok trainers

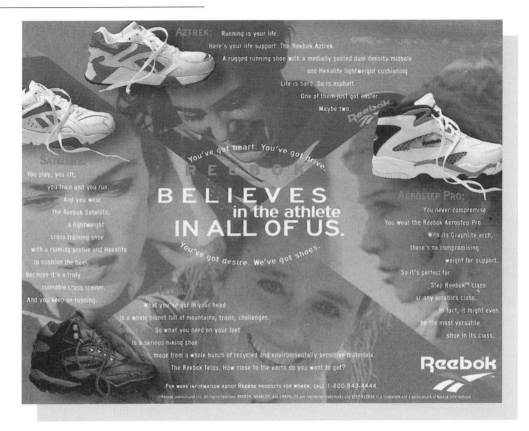

Extension

1   Text: Reebok trainers is an advertisement for training shoes. There are a number of interesting features of this text but your first task is to underline all the personal pronouns contained in it. How many pronouns are there? What kinds of pronouns are there? Are the pronouns singular or plural pronouns? What seems to be the purpose of the writer of the advertisement in using pronouns?

What is the shape of the advert? Why are capital letters in the centre and why does it seem as if the whole is like a wheel with spokes linking the centre and the perimeter? How many of the words at the centre are pronouns? Why?

2   Your second task is to underline the noun phrases in the text. When you have done this, write a short paragraph in which you say what you think the main effect is of noun phrases such as:

> Hexalite lightweight cushioning
> medially posted dual density midsole
> Graphlite arch.

3   Your third task is to write a brief advertisement yourself. You may choose the product for which you wish to write the advertisement but your text should make particular use of personal pronouns and of pre-modified noun phrases. Your choices of language should be appropriate to the product you wish to advertise.

Note: see satellite text: *The Language of Advertising*

Verbs and patterns

One of the most striking features of the poem 'Off Course' (see p. 128) is the absence of a main verb. In that poem one of the effects created by the omission of a main verb is a sense of suspension and disorientation as it becomes increasingly difficult to work out, grammatically, what are the objects and what are the subjects in the text (for discussion of 'subjects' and objects', see p. 132). Readers find it difficult to know where they are.

Activity

Text: *Bleak House* (1852–3) is the opening four paragraphs from Charles Dickens's novel. Dickens is one of the major English nineteenth-century novelists who saw the legal system of the country as a source of corruption and as a major obstacle to progress. Here the 'Lord Chancellor' is the head of the legal system.

One of the most striking features of Dickens's use of the language is that the opening three paragraphs do not contain a single main verb. Is the effect which is created for the reader the same as that created in the poem 'Off Course'?

139

London. Michaelmas Terms lately over, and the Lord Chancellor sitting in Lincoln's Inn Hall. Implacable November weather. As much mud in the streets, as if the waters had but newly retired from the face of the earth, and it would not be wonderful to meet a Megalosaurus, forty feet long or so, waddling like an elephantine lizard up Holborn Hill. Smoke lowering down from chimney-pots, making a soft black drizzle, with flakes of soot in it as big as full-grown snowflakes – gone into mourning, one might imagine, for the death of the sun. Dogs, undistinguishable in the mire. Horses, scarcely better; splashed to their very blinkers. Foot passengers, jostling one another's umbrellas, in a general infection of ill-temper, and losing their foot-hold at street-corners, where tens of thousands of other foot passengers have been slipping and sliding since the day broke (if this day ever broke), adding new deposits to the crust upon crust of mud, sticking at those points tenaciously to the pavement, and accumulating at compound interest.

Fog everywhere. Fog up the river, where it flows among green aits and meadows; fog down the river, where it rolls defiled among the tiers of shipping, and the waterside pollution of a great (and dirty) city. Fog on the Essex Marshes, fog on the Kentish heights. Fog creeping into the cabooses of collier-brigs; fog lying out on the yards, and hovering in the rigging of great ships; fog drooping on the gunwales of barges and small boats. Fog in the eyes and throats of ancient Greenwich pensioners, wheezing by the firesides of their wards; fog in the stem and bowl of the afternoon pipe of the wrathful skipper, down in his close cabin; fog cruelly pinching the toes and fingers of his shivering little 'prentice boy on deck. Chance of people on the bridges peeping over the parapets into a nether sky of fog, with fog all round them, as if they were up in a balloon, and hanging in the misty clouds.

Gas looming through the fog in divers places in the street, much as the sun may, from the spongey fields, be soon to loom by husbandman and ploughboy. Most of the shops lighted two hours before their time – as the gas seems to know, for it has a haggard and unwilling look.

The raw afternoon is rawest, and the dense fog is densest, and the muddy streets are muddiest, near that leaden-headed old obstruction, appropriate ornament for the threshold of leaden-headed old corporation: Temple Bar. And hard by Temple Bar, in Lincoln's Inn Hall, at the very heart of the fog, sits the Lord High Chancellor in his High Court of Chancery.

There are, of course, verbs in this opening to the novel. It is, in fact, difficult to construct a text without verbs and this passage is no exception. In the opening paragraph alone there are verbs such as 'retired', 'waddling', 'splashed', 'jostling', 'slipping', 'sliding', and so on. The verbs all serve to create an atmosphere of constant action and movement in the big city. Yet there are no **finite verbs** in main **clauses** in the text. There is thus a difference between the following two sentences, the first of which (1) contains a main finite verb, the second of which (2) does not:

(1)   Foot passengers jostled one another's umbrellas and lost their foothold at street corners.

(2)   Foot passengers jostling one another's umbrellas and losing their foothold at street corners.

Main finite verbs provide, as it were, a kind of anchor for the action. You know clearly when something took place and that the action was completed. In the second sentence above you are left suspended, knowing that the action is ongoing, but awaiting a main verb to give you your bearings. A sentence such as the following provides that kind of 'anchor' for the action in the verb *arrived*, which is the finite verb in the sentence:

Foot passengers jostling one another's umbrellas and losing their foothold at street corners *arrived* at the bank.

A finite verb is thus a verb which tells you when something happened (past or present), how many were/are involved (singular or plural) and who the participants are ('you'/'we'/'I', etc.). By contrast, when a **non-finite** *-ing* form is used the verb can be referring to any number, or tense, or first, second or third person. For example:

She is singing.
They have been singing.
You might be singing.

In these examples, *singing*, *been* and *be* are the non-finite forms; *is*, *have* and *might* are the finite forms.

Sentence (2) above is a kind of model for many of the sentences in the first three paragraphs. Sentences such as the following therefore serve to create a sense of both disorientation and dislocation. We feel that all the activity of London is confused and directionless; and we do not know what timescale we are in. The present participles in particular convey a feeling of continuous action which could almost be timeless.

London.
Implacable November weather.
Smoke lowering down from chimney pots . . .
Dogs, undistinguishable in the mire.
Foot passengers, jostling one another's umbrellas
Fog in the eyes and throats of ancient Greenwich pensioners,
   wheezing by the firesides . . .
Gas looming through the fog in divers places . . .

Given the timeless character which is imparted to these descriptions it is perhaps not surprising that Dickens can suggest that London has an almost prehistoric feel to it – 'and it would not be wonderful to meet a Megalosaurus, forty feet long or so, waddling like an elephantine lizard up Holborn Hill'.

In the final paragraph of this opening to *Bleak House* main finite verbs are restored to the sentences of the text. In particular the main verb 'to be' is repeated: 'The raw afternoon is rawest, and the dense fog is densest, and the muddy streets are muddiest . . .'. The presence of a main verb is most noticeable in the final sentence:

And hard by Temple Bar, in Lincoln's Inn Hall, at the very heart of the fog, sits the Lord High Chancellor in his High Court of Chancery.

Here the main finite verb is *sits*. The action and location of the Lord High Chancellor is thus clearly situated. Indeed, the sentence is structured so that the location of the main subject of the sentence ('the Lord High Chancellor') comes first in the sentence. He sits:

hard by Temple Bar
in Lincoln's Inn Hall
at the very heart of the fog.

Structured differently, the sentence might have read:

The Lord High Chancellor sits hard by Temple Bar in Lincoln's Inn Hall at the very heart of the fog.

This structure would be more normal and would follow the conventional word order for sentences in English in which the subject ('The Lord High Chancellor') occurs first and is then followed by a main finite verb ('sits').

One of Dickens's purposes may be to delay the subject so that it has more impact as a result of its occurrence in an unusual position. It also has a very particular impact as a result of being in the simple present tense ('sits') when readers of a novel or of any kind of narrative might expect verbs to be in the simple past tense ('sat').

'Sits' suggests, however, that the Lord High Chancellor always sits there and is a permanent landmark in this landscape. The simple present tense in English carries this sense of a permanent, general, unchanging truth, as in scientific statements such as:

Oil floats on water.
Mice have long tails.
Two and two make four.

In this final paragraph one of the main effects which Dickens creates may be to imply that the legal system of the country is in a state of permanent confusion or creates states of confusion which cannot be changed. And both in these opening paragraphs and in the novel as a whole *fog* assumes symbolic importance, reinforcing a sense both of general confusion and of not being able to see clearly. The Lord High Chancellor is always 'at the very heart of the fog' and nothing will alter this position. For this reason perhaps choices of language and of the structure of the sentence position 'the Lord High Chancellor' and 'the heart of the fog' together.

Note: see satellite text: *The Language of Fiction*

MODALS AND MODALITY

Text: Severn Trent Water communicates information; in this case the information concerns an interruption to the water supply and is on behalf of a water company. Whenever instructions are given, a **modality** enters the relationship between the writer and reader of a text. Modality takes a number of different forms in English but the presence of **modal verbs** is particularly significant. Here are some of the main modal verbs in English:

can, could, will, would, must, should, shall, may

Activity

What is the function of modal verbs in Text: Severn Trent Water?

What other verb forms work, in particular, to establish a relationship between the water company and the customers to whom it has distributed this notice?

Text: Severn Trent Water

Severn Trent Water

Notice of interruption to supply

We are sorry to inform you that necessary mains repairs in the area may cause an interruption to your water supply between the hours overleaf.

1. Every effort will be made to keep inconvenience and the duration of the shut-off to a minimum.

2. Do not draw more water than your minimum requirements.

3. If the water does go off, do not leave taps open or flooding may result when the supply is restored.

4. You may use water from the hot water system but it must be boiled before drinking.

5. Even if the domestic hot water supply runs dry there will be no risk of damage to the system, but as a precaution keep a low fire where a back boiler is installed and turn or switch off other sources of heating the water by gas, oil or electricity.

6. Central heating systems can continue to be used at moderate temperatures.

7. The main will be flushed before the supply is restored but discolouration and or chlorine may persist for a short time. Allow your cold tap to run for a few minutes to clear this water from your service pipe.

8. Do not use your washing machine or other appliances during the discolouration.

We apologise again for any inconvenience this may cause you and request your patience and co-operation. In case of any difficulty please contact the Nottingham District Office on the telephone number 608161, extension 4012.

Please remember neighbours who may be older or disabled - they may need your help.

ST,6253

144

Commentary

This text is in a curiously mixed mode. The water company has to inform its customers that repairs are unavoidable. It has to give its customers instructions which they need to follow both in their own interests and in the interests of other consumers. At the same time the company needs to reassure its customers that a more or less normal service is still available, that, in spite of the interruption to supply, the company still provides a good service and, above all, that there are no safety or health risks involved for its customers so long as they comply with the guidelines and instructions issued with the notice. It is important therefore that the company is clearly seen to be in control. This 'mixed mode' is inscribed in the different modal verbs in the text along the following general lines:

◎   *Mode of reassurance/possibility*: *may* cause an interruption; *may* persist for a short time; they *may* need your help; every effort *will* be made; flooding *may* result; any inconvenience this *may* cause you.
◎   *Mode of control*: *must* be boiled before drinking; the main *will* be flushed; *can* continue to be used.

Notice that some modal verbs can signal possibility and control, depending on the other words which surround them as well as on the context in which they are used. For example, 'you may use water' (primarily control); 'they may need your help' (primarily possibility).

   'Control' is also established through an extensive use of imperative forms of the verb which unambiguously inform us what to do and what not to do. For example:

Do not leave taps open
Allow your cold tap to run
Do not use your washing machine
Please remember neighbours.

Activity

Collect examples of further texts in which you would expect modal verbs to be used quite extensively. For example:

◎   horoscopes
◎   weather forecasts
◎   problem pages
◎   school notices
◎   recipes
◎   legal texts.

What other examples can you find? Why are modal verbs concentrated in some texts but not others? (Note: there is no commentary on this activity.)

Sentences and patterns

In this section we explore the role of grammatical patterns within larger patterns of language. We will consider the role of individual grammatical words and phrases but will focus on complete sentences.

Activity

Read Text: Christian Aid, an advertisement for making a will. Make a list of the main patterns you can find in the text. For example, the patterns can consist of repeated words and phrases, grammatical patterns (same type of pronoun or verb or noun phrase) as well as typographic and other patterns of layout. What do you think are the main effects produced on the reader by the patterns you have noticed? (Note: there is no commentary on this activity.)

Text: Christian Aid

Will your only legacy be upset, confusion and paperwork?

Without a Will, your wishes could count for nothing.

Without a Will, the State could take everything.

Without a Will, your family could lose out.

Without a Will, the taxman could easily benefit.

Without a Will, you can't remember your friends.

Without a Will, you can't remember Christian Aid.

Without a Will, life may be difficult for those closest to you.

Without a Will, life may be impossible for those far away.

- -

If you would like to find out how easy it is to make a Will, send for our free new booklet 'A Will to Care' to Christian Aid, Freepost, London SE1 7YY or phone Glenn McWatt 071-620 4444 ext 2226.

Name Mr./Mrs./Ms./Miss _____

Address _____

_____

Postcode _____ **Christian Aid**

Activity

The poem 'This is a Photograph of Me' is by the Canadian writer Margaret Atwood. As you read the poem and start to work out what it means to you, you might think about the following questions:

1　Who is the 'me' in the poem? Who is being shown the photograph?
2　Can you take the words of the poem literally?
3　Why is the speaker only 'just under the surface', if s/he has drowned the day before? Why can we 'eventually' see the subject of the poem if we 'look long enough'?

Text: 'This is a Photograph of Me'

It was taken some time ago.
At first it seems to be
a smeared
print: blurred lines and grey flecks
blended with the paper;

then, as you scan
it, you see in the left-hand corner
a thing that is like a branch: part of a tree
(balsam or spruce) emerging
and, to the right, halfway up
what ought to be a gentle
slope, a small frame house.

In the background there is a lake,
And beyond that, some low hills.
(The photograph was taken
the day after I drowned.

I am in the lake, in the center
of the picture, just under the surface.

It is difficult to say where
precisely, or to say
how large or small I am:
the effect of water
on light is a distortion
but if you look long enough,
eventually
you will be able to see me.)

Commentary

The title to this poem is intriguing. You might consider that its meaning is quite straightforward. You might consider that the line is spoken by somebody who is showing somebody else a photograph. You might consider that the poem is the photograph. Answers to these questions seem to be basic to our understanding of the poem. But it is not impossible that all the references in the poem to things being vague '(balsam or spruce)', 'a thing that is like a branch', and to outlines and shapes being 'blurred' and 'smeared' and 'blended' are deliberate, that everything is not as it at first seems and that we should perhaps not always assume that everything we see is obvious.

And in this connection you might also think about the word *drown*. Has the speaker literally drowned or are we invited to think of other meanings for the word drown? For example, we can 'drown' in a sea of paperwork or letters to be written or we can 'drown' in unsolved problems. However we choose to interpret the poem we cannot ignore such words; and we are likely to remain intrigued, in particular, by a word like *this* which is ambiguous. 'This' is a **deictic**. Words like *this, that, those, here, there* are all deictics. Deictics are directing or pointing words in so far as they direct our attention to particular points of reference. In this poem 'this' points to something which is near to us, maybe even to what is in front of our eyes, but it is not clear exactly what it refers to.

Several grammatical choices made in the poem by the writer also underline a tone of uncertainty and lack of clarity. For example, the poem refers twice to when the photograph 'was taken'. The choice of voice is that of the passive voice; and the subject, that is, *who* took the photograph, is not declared. In English a passive sentence allows actions to be described without the main agent of those actions needing to be mentioned; and sometimes the omission of the agent can be deliberate because we may not know the agent or because we choose not to mention by whom or by what means something is done. The use of the passive voice here in the sentences

It was taken some time ago.

The photograph was taken
the day after I drowned

adds to the apparent vagueness and indefiniteness of the experiences described.

References to time are also vague and not entirely logical and consistent. The tense of the poem, although mostly in the present, alternates

149

between past and present. For example, 'the day after I drowned' contrasts with 'I am in the lake'. The reader is consequently not sure of the temporal order or dimension in which they are placed by the poem.

This commentary continues after the next activity.

Activity

We have observed above that there are several means open to us in language to register certainty and uncertainty, definiteness and indefiniteness. Before looking at the extract below from a conversation between university students, look back to the activity on p. 144 and to the commentary on p. 145 where there is discussion of different degrees of certainty in language use. Now read the extract below and underline all those words and phrases which allow the speakers to sound deliberately vague, tentative and 'politely' indefinite (students are discussing how they've changed since coming to university).

> *A:* But you don't notice so much in yourself, do you? I don't think so, on the whole.
> *B:* I don't know, I definitely feel different from the first year. I don't think I look any different or anything.
> *A:* You're bound to keep changing, really, all your whole life hopefully.
> *B:* I don't know, I think it's probably a change coming away, I suppose . . .

Commentary

Likewise, what is certain and what is less certain is written into contrasts in modality in the poem. Modality in language underlines our subjective assessments of things; for example, adverbs like *probably*, *perhaps*, *generally*, *apparently*, *definitely* and phrases like *it is certain*, *I am sure* or *I don't know*, verbs such as *it seems* or *it appears* or the use of the present tense (e.g. Oil *floats* on water) encode different degrees of subjective response in the viewpoint of a speaker or writer. More specifically too there are modal verbs and modal expressions such as *must, will, can, ought to, should, be bound to.*

In 'This is a photograph of me' there are contrasts between a viewpoint in which everything is definite ('... you *will* be able to see me'; '... there *is* a lake') and a way of seeing where there is greater vagueness and unclarity ('... it seems to be'; 'It is difficult to say where precisely'). The speaker in the poem knows what 'ought to be' but things do not seem straightforward.

A note of strangeness and uncertainty is also created by the poet by putting the conclusion to the poem in brackets. And after the definiteness and confidence of the short penultimate sentence

> I am in the lake, in the center
> of the picture, just under the surface.

the final sentence is in distinct contrast. It is longer, more complex in structure and mixes subordinate and main clauses (the 'if' conditional clause is a subordinate clause), so that the grammar meanders as if 'it is difficult to say' where things are going and what they might mean.

We perhaps need to ask why the poet is making so much of uncertainty of viewpoint and the difficulty and unreliability of seeing clearly. (Notice by the way the number of times that there are references to 'seeing' ('see', 'scan', 'look').) We also perhaps need to ask who the speaker is and who is being spoken to. And in so doing we need to accept the seemingly improbable situation of someone who has already drowned showing us a picture of him/herself.

A basic interpretation of this poem might begin by saying that the 'I' in the poem is appealing for help and, in particular, for another person who will take the trouble to look closely at his/her situation. To do this requires another person prepared to see beneath the material surface of things and to adopt a more spiritual perspective. Only then might the identity and problems of the 'I' emerge more clearly.

The above analysis should not suggest, of course, that there are no other significant patterns or that they do not have a part to play. What is, however, evident is that a skilful and careful use of grammatical patterns is a key starting point for recognising significant meanings in the poem and that such analysis can provide a basis for further exploration and interpretation.

For a further discussion of main and subordinate clauses see p. 156.

Note: see satellite text: *The Language of Poetry*

Activity

Write a couple of paragraphs about Text: Friends of the Earth, a campaign leaflet inviting people to join this environmental group. In your paragraphs say what effect the leaflet has on you. Pay particular attention to the choices of language. For example, you may like to comment on some or all of these features: present tense; noun phrases; present participles; modal verbs; pronouns. (Note: there is no commentary on this activity.)

Text: Friends of the Earth

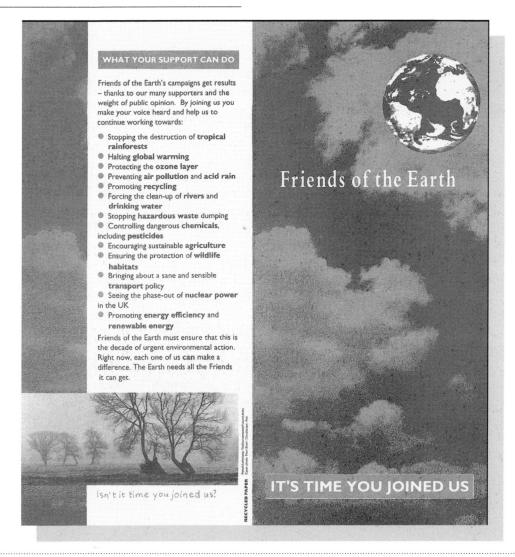

WHAT YOUR SUPPORT CAN DO

Friends of the Earth's campaigns get results – thanks to our many supporters and the weight of public opinion. By joining us you make your voice heard and help us to continue working towards:

- Stopping the destruction of **tropical rainforests**
- Halting **global warming**
- Protecting the **ozone layer**
- Preventing **air pollution** and **acid rain**
- Promoting **recycling**
- Forcing the clean-up of **rivers** and **drinking water**
- Stopping **hazardous waste** dumping
- Controlling dangerous **chemicals**, including **pesticides**
- Encouraging sustainable **agriculture**
- Ensuring the protection of **wildlife habitats**
- Bringing about a sane and sensible **transport** policy
- Seeing the phase-out of **nuclear power** in the UK
- Promoting **energy efficiency** and **renewable energy**

Friends of the Earth must ensure that this is the decade of urgent environmental action. Right now, each one of us **can make a difference**. The Earth needs all the Friends it can get.

Isn't it time you joined us?

Friends of the Earth

IT'S TIME YOU JOINED US

152

Write a page for a book which is designed to be read by children who are learning to read in the very early years of primary school. Your text should have the topic of family and family life. Twenty to thirty words should be sufficient.

After you have written a page consider what kinds of words you have selected? What are your most typical sentence patterns? Did you repeat these words and sentence patterns?

Read Text: Boys and girls and consider the accompanying illustration. Have you read this kind of text before? If so, where? What is the connection between the text and the illustration? What do you notice about the sentence patterns in this text?

Text: Boys and girls

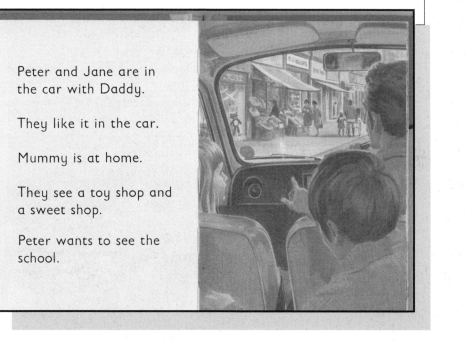

Peter and Jane are in the car with Daddy.

They like it in the car.

Mummy is at home.

They see a toy shop and a sweet shop.

Peter wants to see the school.

Commentary

Texts similar to this are often found in schools as part of reading schemes for children who are learning to read. Such texts are basic 'readers' with 'key words' which will help most in the early stages of learning to read. Are the patterns of words and sentences similar to the ones you wrote in the page of your book for infant school children?

This text is also laid out in a traditional typeface associated with many such readers, such as those produced in the Ladybird series (which can be found in the children's section of most libraries). Such texts also promote basic values with children often shown, as in the illustration here, as part of happy (usually white) families engaged with their parents, brothers and sisters, and often their pets, in simple and basic everyday pursuits such as gardening, picking and storing fruit, sailing toy boats, helping to build a rabbit pen (for Peter) and helping with the cooking (for Jane) or, as here, on a shopping trip and a visit to their new school.

The sentence structure is also very basic and is built on five sentences in which the same type of main clause is repeated. The sentence in each case is short and simple and readable. In each case the subject (S) comes first followed by a verb (V) and an object (O) or a phrase (here all the phrases are prepositional phrases – 'in the car', 'at home', 'in the car with Daddy'). Basic structures reinforce basic values.

This very basic structure can be varied (for example, an alternative pattern is to put an object first: 'Wine I like but I prefer beer', where the first clause here is OSV) but it is a fundamental sentence pattern in English and it is reinforced here by the repetition.

Compare the previous text with that for the promotion of a health drink
Text: Yakult. How many of the clauses in this text are similar to the Boys and
girls text? If the clause structure is different in the Yakult text, why is it
different?

Text: Yakult

ADVERTISEMENT PROMOTION

Back to your roots

Your digestive system must work efficiently for your body to function at its best. Lay the foundations for a healthy lifestyle by starting the day with Yakult.

A tree needs strong, healthy roots to gather vital nutrients from the soil. Likewise, you won't function at optimum level unless your body's equivalent to the roots – the digestive system – is in top form. When your digestive system is working well and in balance, it's far better at extracting vital nutrients from food to keep your body healthy.

What you may not realise is that we have trillions of bacteria (known as intestinal flora) helping out with the functioning of the digestive system. These bacteria can be divided into good guys and bad guys. As we get older the number of good bacteria goes down. Also, stress, antibiotics, or food poisoning can leave the baddies in charge. Yakult has long been aware of the importance of keeping the balance in favour of good bacteria in the intestines.

Drinking Yakult daily is a deliciously easy way of supplying friendly bacteria to the digestive system because it contains the good guy bacteria Lactobacillus casei Shirota. Worldwide, 23 million people drink Yakult every day. Now's the time to join them!

Although healthy digestion is vital for a healthy body, most people don't know their small intestine from their big toe! To help you find your way around your digestive system, Yakult has produced a jargon-free *Guide to the Gut*.

Just ring the Yakult Consumer Information Centre on **0345 697 069** for your free copy. (Local rate call.)

155

Commentary

This text contains a greater variety of clauses. The patterns include both main clauses and subordinate clauses. A subordinate clause relies grammatically on the main clause to which it is attached, usually in a dependent relationship so that the information in the subordinate or dependent clause contains information which is in the background compared to the main clause. Examples from this text are (the subordinate clause is underlined):

> <u>As we get older</u>, the number of good bacteria goes down.

> <u>Although healthy digestion is vital for a healthy body</u>, most people don't know their small intestine from their big toe!

> Drinking Yakult daily is a deliciously easy way of supplying friendly bacteria to the digestive system <u>because it contains the good guy bacteria</u> . . .

The text has a scientific character and seeks to impress the reader with references to research and by using technical vocabulary. The advertisement provides the reader with a lot of information and scientific explanation and the subordinate clauses, in particular, are used to elaborate the information contained in the main clause. The clauses are linked by conjunctions which signal the way in which the information in the main clause is elaborated. (The main conjunctions are 'as', 'although', 'because'.) Thus:

> AS introduces reference to a process.

> ALTHOUGH introduces a concession.

> BECAUSE introduces a reason.

Text: Yakult is explored further in Unit 4, p. 176, with particular reference to its metaphorical structure. Conjunctions are further explored in Unit 4, pp. 212 ff.

If you were writing an advertisement for a product, which products might you choose to promote using these very basic grammatical structures and why? Using the text: Boys and girls as a model, write an advert in the same style for one of the following products.

a mobile phone	a soap
organic food	a convertible car

(Note: there is no commentary on this activity.)

Now look at Text: Internal memo. The memo is chatty and informal. Rewrite the memo as a formal letter from Mark Tatchell as if he did not know the recipient of the memo. What have you changed? Are the structures of SVO any different? Are your clauses different? If so, why. If not, why not?

Text: Internal memo

From: Mark Tatchell, Smith Electronics
To: Alison Paulus, Customer Services
CC: Dan Ellis, Smith Electronics

Subject: Computer Purchase

5/5/1999

Hi, We're on our way to Caswell. The battery on the laptop's a bit low so we've stopped at a pub which is letting us use their fax. Just met Richard Haynes (MD at Wulfson) and, because he is spending so much with us on the refitting, agreed with him that we'd also supply a laptop.

He wants at least 6 Gb hard disk and 64 Mb RAM plus a portable printer. He'd prefer a machine which came with a nice carrying case.

Could you set this up with Kyle Barber and come up with a quote. Either Toshiba or Compaq. Fax back his quote to the hotel in Caswell. I'll be able to pick up e-mails there, I hope. Call the mobile, if I've missed something.

P.S. Tell David. Great deal. Worth the laptop. More in the pipeline.

Commentary

The fax is written in an informal style. Many faxes are written more formally and are closer to formal letters or memoranda. Here the sender and receiver know each other well and can use informal vocabulary choices such as 'Hi' and abbreviations such as 'quote' (for 'quotation'). Grammatically, there is a balance between main and subordinate clauses with subordinate clauses used as the writer elaborates, amplifies or qualifies information in more detail (for example, 'if I've missed something'; 'because he is spending so much with us on the refitting').

However, the clearest grammatical marker of informality is the use of **ellipsis**. Ellipsis is a grammatical structure in which key grammatical words are left out or are left for the reader or listener to fill in. Examples of ellipsis are *Good deal* for 'It was a good deal'; *Either Toshiba or Compaq* for 'It must be either Toshiba or Compaq'; *Just met Richard Haynes* for 'I've just met Richard Haynes'. In formal letters and memoranda ellipsis would not normally be appropriate. Ellipsis is very common in spoken language and is a key feature of spoken grammar. It occurs when it is obvious or when it can be taken for granted what speakers are referring to and there is no need to elaborate.

Extension

Collect two written texts which exhibit what are in your view different degrees of formality. One text should be more 'spoken' and informal and one should be a formal text with little or no elements of typical spokenness and informality. Make notes on the grammatical properties of the texts with particular reference to use of pronouns; modality; sentence structure and clause patterns; ellipsis.

Further guidance on the analysis of ellipsis is given in Unit 4, pp. 208 ff.

ACTIVES, PASSIVES AND MEANINGS

Sentences often express actions, and there are two main ways in which actions can be viewed. What are the contrasts in the way in which the action is expressed in the following sentences?

Two players chased the referee.
The referee was chased by two players.

The first sentence uses the **active voice**; the second sentence uses the **passive voice**, which is not as frequent overall. Which of the following sentences are passive and which are active? Write a description of how active sentences are turned into passive sentences.

1	The dog attacked the intruder.
2	The intruder was attacked by the dog.
3	The test tube was heated and the solution was prepared.
4	I was informed by the police.
5	The police informed me.
6	The two substances are mixed in equal proportions.
7	We can obtain both these books from the library.
8	Both these books can be obtained from the library.
9	It is accepted that there is no proper evidence.
10	It has been decided.

(Answers and commentary are on p. 164 at the end of this unit.)

159

COMPUTERS, PASSIVES AND MEANINGS

In the previous unit we looked at lists of frequently spoken and written words using evidence from a corpus – a computer-stored collection of texts which can be read by a concordance. A concordance is a computer program which enables you to work on texts, checking for which words are frequent, how words fit together and in some cases what patterns of words go together in what different kinds of text.

You can also study grammatical patterns using a computer corpus. An interesting pattern to study is the passive voice. As we have seen, in grammar the passive voice contrasts with the active voice.

Another form of the passive voice is the *get-passive*. As with many structures involving the word *get*, the get-passive is a structure which is more common in spoken English than in written English. Examples of this form of the passive are:

I got attacked by a wild dog

which can be chosen in preference to

I was attacked by a wild dog.

Or

He got suspended from school three times

which can be chosen instead of

He was suspended from school three times.

Activity

Now look at Text: Corpus Words from an analysis using a concordance of the get-passive as it occurs in texts in the CIC corpus (for CIC see Unit 2, p. 94). What do you notice about the grammatical patterns of the get-passive? Which words appear to the left of the key structure and which words appear to the right of the key structure? Do they have anything in common?

Text: Corpus words

```
 1    . He couldn't turn the water on. And he got badly burned. And it happened in Mar
 2   you heard of anybody any neighbours who got broken into recently? I know somebod
 3   ken any extra precautions since the car got broken into last time? Er well I cha
 4   d he jilted her at the altar. So so she got brought up by her grandmother not he
 5    she's been a bit nervous ever since we got burgled and and dark nights. Mm. Sin
 6   ou know of? They they got burgled. They got burgled once Yeah. that was a while
 7   ed by crime that you know of? They they got burgled. They got burgled once Yeah.
 8   ave done that so I suppose I could have got caned. Yeah. And as you've gone thro
 9    fool for being honest. Mm. You know he got called an idiot for being honest. An
10   know it didn't seem much point. No. All got deported I think. Every one of them
11    Yeah. Yeah. +to the machines. They all got deported in the end didn't they. Sen
12   road. Mm. And this chap actually he got got done for either the drugs. Cos it wa
13   p on that should have been white but it got dyed grey in the wash and my hair wa
14   ghs Yeah. Anyway tell us about when you got er picked up. About the hitchhiking.
15   randmother not her real mother then she got jilted at the altar by this fellow t
16   cently and she was saying that she they got kerb crawled her and her friend were
17   om the Social from the Job Centre. Em I got led up the garden path a fair few ti
18   I suppose and some do it you know. Em I got offered a job about three weeks befo
19   d then all of a sudden they em got they got raided by the police. Mm. And we wer
20    shop and told you about them. Mm. tuts Got ripped off didn't I. laughs laughs T
21   er say yes you are my daughter. She em got robbed in the will when she died. Em
22   entioned in October when your neighbour got robbed. Could you tell me what happe
23   y good like I just got there and I just got seen straight away. But then I think
24   eah. As did all the housewives who then got slapped in the face for it Mm. becau
25   ho's van got stolen. What about ? a van got stolen. Yeah. Where? My cousin . Yea
26    the on the the picture. Dear dear. And got sued by the owners because of it. Th
27   ve been there I don't know but we never got told about it you know. So. But trut
```

Commentary

◎   The lines from the corpus show that the get-passive is commonly used with personal pronouns. That is, we use it to describe things which have happened to us personally. It is not used much to describe what is done to impersonal things. For example:

> The Ministry of Finance was attacked by leading journalists at a meeting in London yesterday

is more common than

> The Ministry of Finance got criticised by leading journalists at a meeting in London yesterday

161

◎   When the get-passive is used, it is often used without reference to an agent. That is, the agent or source of responsibility for the action done to you is not mentioned. (In the sentence 'I was attacked by a wild dog' the agent is 'wild dog'.) The emphasis is on what happened to *you* and *me* and *him* and *them*.

◎   The get-passive form is more emotive. It seems to convey feelings about the action more directly than the standard passive found in most written texts.

◎   The words to the right of this passive structure frequently suggest things which are problematic or which describe adverse circumstances. For example,

> got burgled
> got deported
> got led up the garden path
> got ripped off
> got robbed
> got sued

The get-passive can, of course, be chosen to describe positive things. For example, *She got promoted, He got made captain.* However, the standard passive is used to describe circumstances which are positive as well as negative, is more neutral overall and makes a speaker or (more normally) a writer appear a bit more detached.

So a computer can help us to analyse patterns which we may not otherwise notice. The patterns can be significant for understanding how we choose to express meanings. We can see differences between spoken and written words. And we can see that certain grammatical choices entail certain vocabulary choices. Although we have looked at grammar and vocabulary separately so far, it is worth underlining that grammatical patterns and lexical patterns are more closely interrelated than is often assumed.

Extension

Now look at the following concordance lines for the verbs *provide* and *cause*. What do you notice about the patterns of meaning they create? Are the patterns similar? Are they different? If so, how?

have searched for a single	cause of aging – a critical gene, hor
s in property lending will	cause a a serious credit crunch – compa
lit second nobody moves?	Cause we're looking at the dolly-bird
ith in the fas lane is no	cause for driving without due care and
ion so far available gives	cause for concern about the circumstan
of 70–90 mph expected to	cause structural damage. The forecaste
aming. If untreated it can	cause permanent damage to heart. "
urder came not from any	cause worth the name but from the very
e in prison without good	cause, he says. The Foreign Office has
es of martyrdom in a noble	cause. He said they had been granted "
South West Water] did not	cause the problem is no defence at all
obviously bleeding, could	cause blood to seep from veins and art
justice is the Palestinian	cause and the right of the Palestinian
d the relevant details may	cause an underpayment and perhaps resu
onous toxins which could	cause kidneys to fail. This could happ
e of information liable to	cause serious injury to the nation wi
ity and its strength gives	cause for optimism for the prospects
ng legislation which could	cause considerable problems for compan
t in a situation likely to	cause unnecessary suffering, and permi
on of schools is likely to	cause ministers more problems than it
ffice staff, said the main	cause of recruitment problems was low
inspectors as the biggest	cause of poor reading standards. "Some
mmit criminal damage, and	cause public disorder, yesterday were
dence in you is total. Our	cause is just. Now you must be the thu
in 1987 for conspiracy to	cause explosions, was yesterday refuse

e opportunity, rather than	provide it. The House of Lords amended
and Outdoor World might	provide the breath of fresh air that i
t horrendous, a swap can	provide a route into areas where there
and the venues which can	provide such facilities will not doubt
major car-hire companies	provide cars with mounted phones. Amer
ed out. The motion was to	provide an access gate into the city
show is being prepared to	provide training throughout England an
he said. The bill aims to	provide the first coherent framework
said: "What we earn and	provide for ourselves is only one part
er international action to	provide places of safety for refugees
BARCLAYS Bank is to	provide a year's paid materinity leave,
s to encourage people to	provide their own pensions, by offerin
Plans to	provide power for the south-west of
mming pool operations, to	provide lifeguards or any other
any occasion declined to	provide the resources that are require
st time in British history	provide statutory guarantees for the
tish Constitution does not	provide for an Act of War to be approv
0 vehicles. We have had to	provide a site for them. It has just
a litre would be needed to	provide enormous killing power."
oops, the specialists will	provide support to medical and nursing
ns are run by BR staff to	provide tourist trips and do not compe
hedules will be cleared to	provide continuous news coverage for
(1,770–2,017m), which can	provide skiing from December until ear
says. The Government will	provide extra hostel beds if necessary
million every two years to	provide safe storage facilities for th

One way in which you can continue to explore for yourself how words are used using a very large number of words as your database is to obtain the sampler disk for the BNC (the British National Corpus). The BNC is a collection of 100 million words (90 million written and 10 million spoken). The sampler CD disk contains one million words from spoken texts and one million words from written texts. The CD comes with customised software systems which can be used to do different kinds of analysis, including frequency analysis, word counts, collocations (which words commonly keep company with one another) and concordances of lexico-grammatical patterns of the kind we have just examined in the above activity. The CD can be obtained from the Humantities Computing Unit of Oxford University, Oxford, England. More information, including details of an online free browse facility is available from <http://info.ox.ac.uk/bnc>.

For further analysis of the use of the passive voice in texts see Unit 4, p. 222. For further analysis of concordance lines see Schmitt (2000) to whom we are indebted for the above lines.

....

Answer and commentary on activity

Passives and actives (p. 159)

Answers

1	active	6	passive
2	passive	7	active
3	passive	8	passive
4	passive	9	passive
5	active	10	passive

Crystal (1995: 225) describes the following steps in making the basic form of the passive voice:

1   Move the subject of the active verb to the end of the sentence, making it the passive agent. Add *by*.
2   Move the object of the active verb to the front of the sentence, making it the passive subject.
3   Replace the active verb phrase by a passive one – usually a form of the auxiliary verb *be* followed by the -ed participle.

Text and context
Written discourse

The aim of this unit is to explore some of the language devices which enable whole written texts to work.

In linguistics, the phrase **discourse analysis** is used to refer to the analysis of both spoken and written texts. In each case, the aim is to analyse the way texts work across the boundaries of single sentences or utterances to form whole stretches of language.

This sounds very simple, but actually the word 'discourse' has had quite a long and complicated history. The situation now is that it means slightly different things inside and outside the academic world; it can also mean different things in different academic subject areas. For these reasons, it's worth spending a bit of time thinking about its variant meanings.

The basic meaning of 'discourse', in modern ordinary usage, is 'talk'. Originally, the term 'discourse' came from Latin, *discursus*, meaning 'to run', 'to run on', 'to run to and fro'. Historically, it has been applied more to rehearsed forms of spoken language – like speeches, where people 'run on' about a topic – than to spontaneous speech. The modern meaning of 'discourse' as encompassing all forms of talk has evolved because conversations, like formal speeches, 'run'. This means that speakers make an effort to give their interactions shape and coherence – not consciously, but as an integral part of co-operating with another speaker to make meaning. So when people refer to *talk as discourse* they are drawing attention to *the way talk is a crafted medium*. While it has long been understood that this was true of

165

speeches and other aspects of formal oratory, it has only recently been recognised that casual conversation is subtly and skilfully fashioned by speakers as they go along, often at rapid speed. The way different types of talk work will be explored in Unit 5.

Another way of looking at talk-as-discourse is to use the metaphor of weaving. In fact, we use this metaphor very often in our own talk about talk: for example, we talk about 'losing the thread of the conversation', 'cottoning on' to what people mean when they 'spin us a yarn'; teachers often close their lessons by referring to 'tying up loose ends'. We clearly see speakers as engaged together in discourse in the way a group of weavers would be to create a pattern in some fabric.

But it's not only spoken language that 'runs' or gets woven into patterns. This is also true of written language; and the modern use of the word 'discourse' can also be used to refer to aspects of written texts. This tends to be used much more within the academic world than outside it.

The word **text** itself originally meant 'something woven' (Latin *texere*, *textum* – 'to weave'), and you can see a relationship between text, textile ('capable of being woven') and texture ('having the quality of woven cloth'). Written language is also often referred to as 'material'.

Like speakers, then, writers manipulate different aspects of language in order to weave their texts and give their material 'texture'. So to talk about discourse in written texts is to focus on the way written texts are constructed. This is what this unit is all about.

Contents

MAKE AND MEND

This section involves practical activities of reassembling and writing material in order to show you what you already know about the way texts work.

TRACING THE PATTERNS

In this section, you will be exploring how you knew what to do in the first section. You will be looking at how texts work in a number of different ways:

Lexical cohesion
This looks at the way aspects of vocabulary link parts of texts together.

Grammatical cohesion
Here you will be exploring some of the important ways that grammar holds texts together across sentence boundaries.

Information structure
This focuses on the role of grammatical features in the ordering and presentation of information within texts.

THE TEXTILE INDUSTRY
In this section, the focus is on the way texts operate within contexts. This involves thinking about aspects of culture and representation.

Texts used include

◎ Advertisements
◎ Information leaflets
◎ Extracts from novels and short stories
◎ Poems
◎ Some children's writing
◎ A range of notes and memos

If the metaphor of text as weaving is true, then it must be possible to see how the various threads are woven together within written material.

The activities that follow aim to show how some important aspects of language act as the threads that give texts a particular texture.

167

Make and mend

Activity

Stitching it back together

Our constant and powerful need to understand what's around us leads us to try to make sense of anything that's presented to us as a text. To illustrate this idea, read through Text: Statements.

Text: Statements

Allow the fruit to steam in its own juice for a further 15 minutes.

So she hated it when that infuriating Keith Scott seemed to go out of his way to suggest that her heart wasn't in the affair.

That's why we created 'Portfolio', a brand new concept in saving.

Put them into a fireproof dish with the water, and a tablespoon of the sugar.

She knew that he loved her – in a calm settled way rather than any grand passion – and that he would make her a good, kind husband.

Ensuring that the lid is tightly sealed, put the dish into a preheated oven, Gas Regulo 6.

So that way, you can have your cake and eat it too.

Pour over the top, and serve with double cream.

Melodie Neil and Jed Martin were old friends.

Mix juice with the brandy, mulled wine, and rest of the sugar.

We do, too.

Wash and core the apples, taking care to remove all pips.

In short, when she became engaged to him she knew exactly what she was doing.

Spoon out the cooked apples and arrange them attractively in rounds on a serving plate.

Do you feel that you never get a fair slice of the capital cake?

Slice finely.

Portfolio is a high interest investment account that makes your money work for you, while still giving you instant access to your capital.

Reduce temperature to 3 after 10 minutes.

Could you read any of it in any way that worked and made sense?

If you could, that proves that you were already looking for patterns within the text.

In fact, the text you have just read contains statements in random order from three completely different sources. With your knowledge of this, use any strategies you have in order to put the original texts back together.

Divide up the statements; then, within each text, arrange the statements in order, so that they read naturally.

When you have finished your sorting, check your answers by turning to p. 241.

Look particularly at where you didn't get the order right. Can you see what led you astray? (Note: there is no commentary on this activity.)

Activity

Discourse consequences

This activity can only be done in groups.

Text: Starter lines consists of the first lines for six different types of writing – different genres.

Each group should take a different line, and add a second line to it in the same genre. They should then fold the paper over so that only the second line is visible, and pass it on to the next group. When all the groups have contributed a line, open up the folded page and read it aloud to the whole group.

As a whole group, assess how far the six different texts follow rules for the various genres (even if the writers have chosen to parody the text, they will be still be using the rules). (Note: there is no commentary on this activity.)

Text: Starter lines

1	Once upon a time there was a beautiful princess who lived in a castle high up on a mountainside.
2	Cricket is a game which involves as much psychological nerve as physical strength and dexterity.
3	This week you will need to have your wits about you, as Saturn's influence could lead you to be off guard at a crucial moment.
4	Male, 42, home-owner, recently relocated to Bristol.
5	'Spacegrazer to Hyperpod, come in.' Zhata feared the worst. The asteroid storm had passed just too close for comfort.
6	To make watercress soup, first sauté a finely chopped onion by melting a knob of butter in a saucepan over a medium heat.

Activity

Twenty-minute texts

Working in groups, each group should write a short text in one of the genres listed below. Each piece of writing must contain the following words:

figure   leaves   dusk

Don't spend any more than twenty minutes on your piece of writing.

Genres
◎   Epitaph
◎   Maths textbook
◎   Tabloid newspaper article
◎   Romantic fiction
◎   Advert
◎   Menu
◎   Set of instructions
◎   Estate agent's blurb

When you have finished all your texts, pin them up and read them out. How has each piece of writing followed the rules for its particular genre? (Note: there is no commentary on this activity.)

The sections that follow aim to show you some of the linguistic strategies you have just been using in working with texts.

Tracing the patterns

If a speaker or hearer of English hears or reads a passage of the language which is more than one sentence in length, he or she can normally decide without difficulty whether it forms a unified whole or is just a collection of unrelated sentences. **Cohesion** (or its absence) is what makes the difference between the two.

Cohesion is what gives a text texture.

(Halliday and Hasan, 1976)

One of the strategies you used was your understanding of words and phrases in the English language – the vocabulary system. In particular, you used your awareness of *relationships between words*: this is called **lexical cohesion**. There are many different kinds of relationship that could be involved.

Activity

In Text: Links, some of the links that are commonly used between words are outlined, with an example, where possible, from the sorting exercise you did previously (Text: Statements). As you read through these notes, see if you can add to the lists by finding examples from the texts you yourselves have written. (Note: there is no commentary on this activity.)

Text: Links

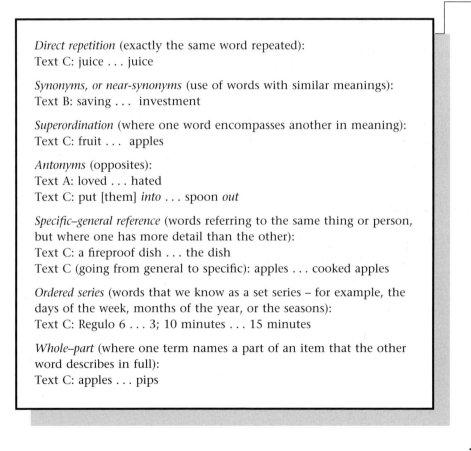

Direct repetition (exactly the same word repeated):
Text C: juice . . . juice

Synonyms, or near-synonyms (use of words with similar meanings):
Text B: saving . . . investment

Superordination (where one word encompasses another in meaning):
Text C: fruit . . . apples

Antonyms (opposites):
Text A: loved . . . hated
Text C: put [them] *into* . . . spoon *out*

Specific–general reference (words referring to the same thing or person, but where one has more detail than the other):
Text C: a fireproof dish . . . the dish
Text C (going from general to specific): apples . . . cooked apples

Ordered series (words that we know as a set series – for example, the days of the week, months of the year, or the seasons):
Text C: Regulo 6 . . . 3; 10 minutes . . . 15 minutes

Whole–part (where one term names a part of an item that the other word describes in full):
Text C: apples . . . pips

A much more general aspect of lexical cohesion is the use by writers of particular semantic fields (see Unit 2, p. 89): this means referring to a specific area of experience or knowledge. The clearest examples of semantic fields occur in the specialist language of occupations.

Activity

Read through Text: Occupations, which contains the language of ten different occupations. Try to work out what the occupations are, and which particular words and phrases helped you to pinpoint them. Answers on p. 242. There is no commentary on this activity.

Text: Occupations

The vehicle was seen proceeding down the main street in a westerly direction leading to a spacious and well-appointed residence with considerable potential. She went to work, mixing up the six-ten with two parts of 425, and dabbing the mixture through 6 ezimeshes. 'This one has a fine shaggy nose and a fruity bouquet with a flowery head', she said. He managed to get into a good position, just kissing the cushion. He said 'Just pop up onto the couch and we'll see what we can do'. She pulled down the menu, chose the command by using the cursor, then quit. She said to knead well, roll into a ball and leave overnight to rise. Instead, he mulched well, turned over and left the beds to settle. Good progress made, but concentration sometimes rather poor; more effort required if success is to be expected in the important months ahead.

However, semantic fields do not have to contain technical language, or occupational terms. It may be simply that a text uses several words that all refer to the same subject matter, activity or experience: for example, the romantic fiction text in the sorting exercise at the beginning of this unit (p. 168) contained many words associated with love.

Activity

Go through each of the extracts you reassembled in the first activity, and write a list of words and phrases within each text that are in the same semantic field. Make up your own headings for the columns. If you find that you have more than one semantic field in a text, outline each field by listing them in separate columns. For example, for the romantic fiction you might decide on the headings 'words for feelings' and 'words for relationships', in order to make finer distinctions than would be possible with one heading of 'love'.

Text A: romantic fiction	words for feelings	words for relationships

When you have shared and discussed your headings, turn to the texts you wrote yourselves. Can you find any examples of semantic fields that you have employed, in order to construct a particular genre?

(Note: There is no commentary on this activity.)

Activity

Sometimes, writers deliberately weave together different semantic fields in order to foreground a particular idea. **Foregrounding** is a type of high-lighting – it means that the writer is drawing attention to something and making the reader view it in a certain way. Look again at Text B (p. 241). Why does the writer of this text use two very different semantic fields – what idea is being foregrounded? How does the writer's use of the two different semantic fields help to shape the text?

Now read through Text: 'The Good, the Bad and the Ugly', which uses vocabulary from two very different types of activity. After you have read it carefully, list the two semantic fields that are used, giving as many examples of the use of each as you can find. Put a ring round any terms that could be included in either field.

Why do you think the writer has chosen to weave together these two different types of vocabulary? Why does the advert not simply use farming terms?

(Note: there is no commentary on this activity. *The Good, the Bad and the Ugly* is the title of a famous Western film starring Clint Eastwood.)

THE GOOD

Sting CT® Herbicide applied in stubbles or onto land cultivated after harvest, eliminates the problem of volunteers and annual weeds in the following crop. But good stubble management is only part of the story. Sting CT biodegrades rapidly in the soil. In terms of operator safety, it isn't classified under COSHH. Also, it's much less expensive than paraquat*. So Sting CT doesn't cost the earth.

THE BAD

Sting CT is active on volunteer cereals, volunteer oilseed rape, annual grasses and broad-leaved weeds at all stages of growth. It penetrates right down to the roots to prevent regrowth. What's more it's rainfast from 1 hour after application, and thanks to this fast absorption it allows you to start drilling within 6 hours of stubble cleaning.

AND THE UGLY
PLUS A WHOLE CAST OF VOLUNTEERS

By removing the "green bridge" you prevent the carry-over of diseases and remove a haven for ugly pests, for instance BYDV carrying aphids, which could otherwise carry virus infection into your next crop.

The Good The Bad and The Ugly is an everyday story of stubble management. With Sting CT, the plot has a happy ending.

*Average rates

For more information on Sting CT and Stubble Management send to:
Monsanto, Freepost, PO Box 61, London NW1 1TH.
No stamp required.

Name:

Address:

Tel:

Sting CT

Fast, Thorough and Doesn't Cost the Earth

Monsanto

Read the label before you buy. Use pesticides safely. Sting CT contains glyphosate. Sting is a registered trade mark of Monsanto Company. © Monsanto PLC 1991 (JC).

Activity

Another option that a writer has, in using vocabulary from different semantic fields, is to entwine the words and phrases so closely that the two systems are difficult to disentangle. One way of bringing different systems of vocabulary together is to use metaphor: this is where one thing is described as if it were another (see Unit 2). Because metaphor tells us that one thing *is* another, it is a powerful factor in positioning the reader and constructing a particular viewpoint.

Look back to pp. 166 ff. On these pages, the metaphorical terms describe language as if it were cloth. To get some more understanding of how metaphor works, do the following:

◎ Imagine language as vegetation. What kinds of words and phrases might now be appropriate in describing language? Example: *he tended his language carefully, and it blossomed.*

◎ Imagine language as a building. What terms could be used now? Example: *my sentences need some scaffolding.*

◎ Imagine language as a person. What terms, normally applied to people, might you use? Example: *my essay wandered off the point, and failed.*

Now read Text: Yakult, p. 155.
What metaphors are used in this text to describe the human body?
(Note: there is no commentary on this activity.)

Activity

Another wide-ranging strategy which you used in writing and handling texts in the first part of this unit was an understanding of levels of formality in vocabulary (see also Unit 2).

We talk about language being more or less formal as a way of describing how we vary our language according to the context we are in: for example, we will all use a relatively informal type of language when we are in the pub, relaxing with friends, compared with the more formal style we are likely to produce in a court of law or in an interview for a job. Formality can also be a reflection of social-group membership, particularly occupation, where some types of occupational language have retained specialist words which can sound very formal in everyday discourse: for example, a financial consultant or solicitor might use the word 'remuneration' where the rest of us would use 'salary' or just 'wages'. Calling a type of language formal or informal refers to more than simply vocabulary, but vocabulary will be an important contributory factor in a reader's impression of the formality of a text. For example, although the words 'home', 'house', 'residence' and 'domicile' might refer to exactly the same building, they vary a great deal in formality and therefore to replace one with another in a text will create a very different effect.

To enable you to see what formality of vocabulary might mean in practical terms, read through Text: Levels of formality. In each text, the level of formality has been disrupted at various points by the insertion of inappropriate vocabulary. Can you pinpoint where this happens, and suggest some vocabulary in each case which would be more in keeping with the style of the passage? (Note: there is no commentary on this activity.)

Text: Levels of formality

Letter from a bank manager to a customer

Dear Ms Allen,

Thank you for your letter of 1st September, requesting overdraft facilities of £500. In order that this overdraft facility can be granted we would first need sight of your contract of employment. Would you therefore kindly inform us of the School at which you will now be earning your daily crust.

Yours sincerely,
A. Curtis

Teacher's report

James needs to realise that success is the result of hard work and consistent effort. At present, he is being a real pain because he is so bone idle in class. If he wishes to do well in the examination, and achieve a grade which will do justice to his considerable ability, he must pull his socks up – and sharpish.

Memo from a university professor to his staff

Can I remind you that travel claims must be submitted *promptly*. Other departments, I learn, are not paying claims which are more than two months late. In particular, please remember that the financial year-end is now 31st July. Claims not submitted by 15th August will be substantially delayed by year-end procedures, and screw up our budgeting. Please get your claims in ON TIME.

Biology exam paper

Q1 As they pass from testis to oviduct during and after mating, mammalian sperms will pass through each of the following structures except the:

(a) urethra
(b) vas deferens
(c) vagina
(d) bottom

Q2 When the water in which a certain species of frog is living contains $5cm^3$ of dissolved oxygen per litre the frogs remain totally submerged, but when the oxygen content falls to $3cm^3$ per litre they go up to the top for a breather.
    As a result of reading the information above, do you have any inkling about how frogs breathe in water?

Extract from a hotel brochure:

Reception of Guests
The Hotel endeavours to have rooms ready to receive guests by noon, and it is hoped that departing guests will courteously assist in making this possible by getting a move on and not hanging about in bedrooms on the day of departure.

The texts in the previous activity come from genres of writing which tend to have a particular level of formality associated with them (although changes in levels of formality can occur as part of the process of language change).

But the operation of formality is actually more complex and subtle than that: for example, a writer, group of writers or members of an occupational group may write about the same subject in different ways according to the audience they are aiming at, and the purpose of their text.

Texts A–D were found in the same local council city planning department. Each text has a different writer–reader relationship, and a different purpose. These differences are not accidental, but rather arise from the different types of communication expected of the city's professional planners. The texts are placed in the order in which they were written, during a specific process: this was the drawing up of a Development Plan for the city of Manchester, specifying the priorities and intentions for city planning over the decade leading up to the turn of the century.

Text A is a piece of national legislation – an extract from the Town and Country Planning Act, 1990. This text, written by lawyers, would be used most often by lawyers and professional planners. Text A is a reference document whose purpose is to establish clear rules and conditions for the planning of developments in any community. The extract here describes the powers of the Secretary of State to intervene if a local planning authority does not fulfil certain obligations.

Text B is part of a free newspaper – *City Planning News* – which was delivered to all Manchester households. There were three newspapers altogether; the aim of this one was to encourage members of the public to contribute ideas to the planning department about issues of concern in local communities around the city. It was written by the Head of the Planning and Environmental Health Department.

The two texts here are from different parts of the paper: 'Down Your Street' is an early attempt to summarise some of the material that follows, while 'Can I Extend My Home?' appears later on in the paper.

Text C is an extract from a statement written to support the public inquiry that accompanied the process of devising the Development Plan for Manchester. Written by the same person as Text B, this type of document is officially entitled a 'Proof of Evidence'. The statement was made available to anyone who attended the public inquiry, which was open to all members of the public, and which acted as a follow-up to the public consultation represented by the newspapers. Its purpose was to give readers an idea of the planners' thinking at that stage with regard to policies on city development.

179

Text D, also written by the city's Head of Planning and Environmental Health Department, is an extract from the final Development Plan for the city of Manchester. While Texts B and C were written as part of a process, this text acts as a reference document which would be expected to be understood by anyone making a planning application. Its purpose is to be an agreed statement of policy, to act as a framework within which planning applications can be judged and agreed or rejected. The extract given here sets out some of the rules for house extensions.

When you have read through all the material, try to answer the following questions:

◎   How are the variations in audience and purpose reflected in the *vocabulary* used in these texts? Which of these texts is the most formal, and which the most informal? Can you pick out some contrasting vocabulary, to show differences in formality?

◎   As well as differences in formality, are there variations in vocabulary which relate to an abstract/concrete dimension? If so, how do you explain these differences?

◎   To what extent are other factors (e.g. grammar, layout) responsible for readers' possible impressions of formality/informality in these texts? Find some examples of language features that are *not* related to vocabulary.

(Note: there is no commentary on this activity.)

Text A: Town and Country Planning Act, 1990

Default powers
25 - (1) Where, by virtue of any of the previous provisions of this Chapter, any unitary development plan or proposals for the alteration or replacement of such a plan are required to be prepared, or steps are required to be taken for the adoption of any such plan or proposals, then –

(a) if at any time the Secretary of State is satisfied, after holding a local inquiry or other hearing, that the local planning authority are not taking the steps necessary to enable them to prepare or adopt such a plan or proposals within a reasonable period; or

(b) in a case where a period is specified for the preparation or adoption of any such plan or proposals, if no such plan or proposals have been prepared or adopted by the local planning authority within that period,

the Secretary of State may prepare and make the plan or any part of it or, as the case may be, alter or replace it, as he thinks fit.

Down Your Street

This is the part of the Plan for Manchester which gets down to the detail. But all we can do in this newspaper is give you an idea of the most important points for your part of the City – we hope it's enough to make you want to find out more.

■ The Plan for Manchester isn't about everything the Council does. It's only really about the way land is used throughout the City – should it be for housing? offices? shops? open space? It has a lot to say about making Manchester a safer and more accessible City for everyone to live, move about and work in – and much to say about transport, too. But you won't find much about education, or street cleaning or libraries and all the rest of the Council's many services.

■ We haven't tried to decide the future of every piece of land and every block of property in the City. That would be an impossible task. Anyway, because we're trying to look ahead till the end of the century, things are bound to change, and the plan would quickly become out of date if there was too much detail in it.

■ Instead, the plan tries to pick out the most important local issues and then makes clear statements ('policies') about them. You may agree or disagree with these policies. Of course, you might also think we've left something out altogether – whatever your view, tell us.

■ Don't forget the City-wide policies summarised on pages 2 and 3 which will be a guide for everyone – residents, landowners, developers, business people and the Council itself. So you must keep them in mind when reading about your own neighbourhood.

■ On page 15 you'll also find another list of suggested policies which are important. They deal with the Council's attitude to a whole range of more detailed things like house extensions, flat conversions, hot food takeaways, amusement arcades and taxi offices. These are matters on which the Council frequently receives applications for planning permission. They are often very controversial locally. The Council needs to make decisions in the light of this local reaction but also taking into account its broad policies for these kinds of activities. Because they are meant to apply throughout the City, we've put them in one place to save space.

■ Lastly – please remember we want everyone in the City to find out as much as they can about our ideas for the next 10 years. Come to the exhibitions. Tell the planners what you think!

1 Blackley, Charlestown and Moston
2 Cheetham and Crumpsall
3 Harpurhey and Lightbowne
4 Miles Platting, Newton Heath, Beswick, Clayton and Bradford
5 City Centre
6 Moss Side and Hulme
7 Ardwick and West Gorton
8 North and South Gorton

9 Whalley Range
10 Rusholme and Fallowfield
11 Longsight and Levenshulme
12 Chorlton and Barlow Moor
13 Withington and Burnage
14 Didsbury
15 Wythenshawe West of M56
16 Wythenshawe East of M56

CAN I EXTEND MY HOME?

The Council receives many hundreds of applications for quite small-scale proposals every year. To help deal with them in a consistent way, the Plan includes a set of 'development control policies', which cover the most common type of planning application. These are important, because when the Plan is approved, the Council will be able to point to these policies when deciding future applications – and they will also help the Secretary of State for the Environment come to a view if there is an appeal to him.

There's no room to go into any detail in this newspaper – so if you want to know more, ask to see the Plan itself. Copies of the individual policies can also be made available.

The City Council's current practice of consulting widely on planning applications that have a significant impact will not be affected by this and this remains important in helping the Council to reach a view about what local people think the impact of a proposal is going to be. At the same time, the whole point of having clear policies is that it helps everyone to know where they stand, and this means that the Council cannot lightly set aside these policies even where local opinion is strongly against a proposal that is consistent with them. This is why these policies are so important. So let's have a quick look at the most important ones.

House Extensions

These can often cause upset between neighbours, if not handled properly. The Plan sets down some 'groundrules' for dealing with extensions, to try and make sure that they don't cut off too much light, or cause problems of overlooking. They also have to 'fit in' with the rest of the Street – so, for example, two-storey extensions will usually have to have a pitched roof. And you won't usually be able to build a 2-storey extension right up to your neighbour's boundary, or a rear extension which is more than about 12 feet out from the back wall.

As with all kinds of planning application, your local area planner is there to give free advice (whether you are an applicant or a potential objector!).

Text C: 'Proof of Evidence'

8.6 The City's many *parks* are, of course, the responsibility of the City Council. I am aware of the concern which has been expressed in some quarters about the Council's intentions in relation to the future of the parks and am pleased to have this opportunity to provide some reassurance on that score. For the avoidance of doubt, the Council accepts, without reservation, that the City's parks are essential assets for the people of Manchester, and that their main value lies in their being quiet and safe places for informal recreation, particularly for young children and the elderly. They also have immense importance for nature conservation and for their landscape value. Nothing in the UDP seeks to disturb that analysis or that commitment.

Text D: City Development Plan

DC1.3 Notwithstanding the generality of the above policies, the Council will not normally approve:

(a)   rearward extensions greater than 3.65m (12 ft) in length;
(b)   2-storey extensions with a flat roof, particularly those which would be visible from the public highway;
(c)   2-storey extensions to terraced properties which occupy the full width of the house;
(d)   flat roofed extensions to bungalows;
(e)   extensions which conflict with the Council's guidelines on privacy distances (which are published as supplementary guidance).

Now look back at the texts you were working with in the sorting exercise at the start of this unit (p. 168). How far did the formality or informality of the vocabulary contribute to how the texts worked?

Choose one of the texts and examine the vocabulary closely, then write some notes to record your ideas. If you find it difficult to describe how formal or informal you find the vocabulary, try to think of synonyms for the term you are considering. This will help you to place the term as part of a set of alternative expressions in English to refer to the idea in question. (Note: there is no commentary on this activity.)

Sometimes, writers deliberately manipulate formal and informal styles in order to achieve certain effects.

Text: *Oranges Are Not the Only Fruit* (1987) is an extract from the novel by Jeanette Winterson. In it, the narrator is talking about her experiences as a child in a Lancashire primary school in the 1950s – particularly, the way that the boys and girls taunted and bullied each other.

Can you see how the writer interweaves more and less formal vocabulary in order to suggest two different voices – that of the adult narrator, and that of the child she originally was?

Pick out examples of language features which help to construct each voice.

Text: *Oranges Are Not the Only Fruit*

Country dancing was thirty-three rickety kids in black plimsolls and green knickers trying to keep up with Miss who always danced with Sir anyway and never looked at anybody else. They got engaged soon after, but it didn't do us any good because they started going in for ballroom competitions, which meant they spent all our lessons practising their footwork while we shuffled up and down to the recorded instructions on the gramophone. The threats were the worst; being forced to hold hands with somebody you hated. We flapped along twisting each others' fingers off and promising untold horrors as soon as the lesson was over. Tired of being bullied, I became adept at inventing the most fundamental tortures under the guise of sweet sainthood.

'What me Miss? No Miss. Oh *Miss*, I never did'. But I did, I always did. The most frightening for the girls was the offer of total immersion in the cesspit round the back of Rathbone's Wrought Iron. For the boys, anything that involved their willies. And so, three terms later, I squatted down in the shoebags and got depressed. The shoebag room was dark and smelly, it was always smelly, even at the beginning of terms.

Commentary

The child's voice is suggested by certain vocabulary items, such as 'knickers', 'shoebag', 'willies', 'smelly', 'Miss', 'Sir', as well as by the direct speech, 'What me Miss? No Miss. Oh *Miss*, I never did'. In contrast, the adult's language is considerably more complex and abstract: 'untold horrors', 'adept', 'fundamental tortures', 'sweet sainthood', 'total immersion'. The two styles are woven together very cleverly, with subtle shifts occurring within a short space; this can create humorous effects, as in the anti-climax of lines 'The most frightening . . . their willies'.

GRAMMATICAL COHESION

So far, you have been looking at how you used your lexical knowledge – your knowledge of vocabulary – as a strategy to help you reorganise and write the texts in the first part of this unit. The way lexical items are woven together through a text was referred to as lexical cohesion.

But in working on those texts, you also used your understanding of grammatical structures, and this forms the focus for what follows. The way that grammatical features are woven together across sentence boundaries is called **grammatical cohesion**.

Anyone who can speak and/or write a language knows grammar, as these structural patterns are learnt very early in life as an integral part of learning language; knowing grammar is different from knowing how to label parts of sentences, however. The knowledge you were using in the early part of this unit was your knowledge of grammar in use, and that was all the equipment you needed to do the tasks. But in order to see what you did, this part of the unit will need to go into a bit of detail about some of the structures you were using and matching. This will mean labelling some of the most commonly used grammatical principles and patterns. You may well be looking again at some of the aspects of grammar you studied in Unit 3; the focus here, however, is how grammar works across sentences rather than within them.

Reference

The Penguin *Concise English Dictionary* defines 'to refer' as 'to send for information', 'to seek information'. The principle of **reference** within texts is exactly that: it tells the reader that they can only make complete sense of the word or structure they are looking at if they look elsewhere in the text to get a fuller picture.

There are particular words that are often used for reference purposes. Some details are given below.

Personal pronoun reference

Personal pronouns are words that can substitute for nouns, and are as follows:

I   you (singular)   he   she   it   we   you (plural)   they   one

Note that some of these pronouns can occur in different forms, depending on the role of the word in a particular sentence. Below are the possible variants:

me   him   her   us   them

187

When one of these pronouns occurs in a text, the reader expects to have to link it with something – either an item that has already been mentioned or something that's coming up. The fact that these pronouns are called personal pronouns gives an indication of their reference function – they will mainly be referring to people; however, the words 'it' and 'they'/'them' can also be used to refer to non-human animates, inanimate objects and abstract ideas.

If the pronoun is referring back to something, this is called **anaphoric reference**; if the pronoun is referring to something coming later, this is called **cataphoric reference**. Here is an example of each:

Tom said that *he* was going home (anaphoric reference)

I couldn't believe *it – the house was a complete wreck* (cataphoric reference)

Much ambiguity is based on the workings of cohesion in a text – or rather, the lack of cohesion. In the example below (from a member of the public writing to his local council), can you see how the unintentional humour comes from the cohesion problems in the sentence?

> Our kitchen floor is very damp. We have two children and would like a third. Could you please send someone round to do something about it?

But lack of cohesion can also be very useful, in that it can throw reference wide open and make the reader work to locate the meaning. For example, what does the word 'it' refer to in the Coke slogan 'Coke is it', or in the Nike slogan 'Just do it'?

Making all the pronoun references link up is a skill that it takes children some time to learn. This is as true in speech as it is in writing.

Look at the two texts that follow.

The first consists of some speech which arose in the context of a teacher sending a 7-year-old pupil on an errand.

The second, The Quard, is a piece of writing by a 7-year-old. (Note: it's uncertain what a 'quard' is – perhaps a beach buggy vehicle?)

Both of these children are struggling with the cohesion demands of the communication. Go through the texts, pointing out where difficulties arise.

(Note: there is no commentary on this activity.)

Teacher A (Mrs Curtin): Go and ask Mrs Travis if she can give you the note that your mum wrote for her last week and bring it back here to me now.

Pupil (to Teacher B, Mrs Travis): Mrs Curtin says please can she give you the note for my mum?

My And Andrews Adventure

With a Quard.

One day Andrew Turner Came

To my house . My Dad

Took us to a beach race .

And my cousin Was raceing

but When He Went of

the jump you Could not

See him So We Went

to the hole and we

went down the hole

and First We Went

to a forest and

We could not find

the Quard. The next stop

Was at the Quard Shop.

and We found Him and He

won.

Activity

While pronoun reference can be a challenge for us as we learn language, sometimes writers deliberately disrupt pronoun cohesion in order to achieve certain effects.

Text: Rabbit's speech is a poem by Lewis Carroll. From *Alice in Wonderland*, the poem is a speech delivered by the Rabbit to the court, and is referred to in the book as a set of 'mysterious verses'.

How does Carroll use pronoun reference in order to create an air of mystery? (Note: there is no commentary on this activity.)

Text: Rabbit's speech

They told me you had been to her,
And mentioned me to him:
She gave me a good character,
But said I could not swim.

He sent them word I had not gone
(We know it to be true):
If she should push the matter on,
What would become of you?

I gave her one, they gave him two,
You gave us three or more:
They all returned from him to you,
Though they were mine before.

If I or she should chance to be
Involved in this affair,
He trusts to you to set them free,
Exactly as we were.

My notion was that you had been
(Before she had this fit)
An obstacle that came between
Him, and ourselves, and it.

Don't let them know she liked them best,
For this must ever be
A secret, kept from all the rest,
Between yourself and me.

A mysterious atmosphere is also the aim of Text: 'A Haunted House', which is the opening of a short story by Virginia Woolf, published in 1921. How does Woolf's use of personal pronouns help to create this atmosphere?:

Text: 'A Haunted House'

Whatever hour you woke there was a door shutting. From room to room they went, hand in hand, lifting here, opening there, making sure – a ghostly couple.

'Here we left it,' she said. And he added, 'Oh, but here too!' 'It's upstairs,' she murmured. 'And in the garden,' he whispered. 'Quietly,' they said, 'or we shall wake them.'

But it wasn't you that woke us. Oh, no. 'They're looking for it; they're drawing the curtain,' one might say, and so read on a page or two. 'Now they've found it,' one would be certain, stopping the pencil on the margin. And then, tired of reading, one might rise and see for oneself, the house all empty, the doors standing open, only the wood pigeons bubbling with content and the hum of the threshing machine sounding from the farm. 'What did I come in here for? What did I want to find?' My hands were empty. 'Perhaps it's upstairs then?' The apples were in the loft. And so down again, the garden still as ever, only the book had slipped into the grass.

Stevie Smith's poem 'Not Waving But Drowning' (1957) also uses a range of pronouns to refer to a number of different people, and to create specific effects. Map out how these pronouns work, thinking particularly about the following:

◎   Who are the various people in this poem?
◎   Why did Stevie Smith choose to use pronouns to refer to people rather than their names?

Text: 'Not Waving But Drowning'

Nobody heard him, the dead man,
But still he lay moaning:
I was much further out than you thought
And not waving but drowning

Poor chap, he always loved larking
And now he's dead
It must have been too cold for him his heart gave way,
They said

Oh no, no, no, it was too cold always
(Still the dead one lay moaning)
I was much too far out all my life
And not waving but drowning.

Commentary

Virginia Woolf extract

A sense of mystery is created in this text partly by the fact that the reader is unsure who is in the story, and this effect results from the range of pronouns used: you, they, we, it, she, he, one, I. At the beginning, it seems that 'you' means 'one' and that 'they' are 'a ghostly couple'. But then it's uncertain who is talking in direct speech in the second paragraph; also, the second use of 'you' (in the final paragraph) appears to mean, not 'one' as before, but 'they' (i.e. the ghosts). Throughout the whole text, it's unclear exactly what 'it' is that everyone seems to be searching for. The language makes the reader behave like the characters, in that it makes the act of reading an act of searching to locate the meaning.

Stevie Smith poem

The poem concerns a tragi-comic misunderstanding – a drowning man was ignored because onlookers thought he was cheerily waving at them, when he was really calling for help. This is taken beyond the literal level of a physical drowning to suggest another reading: that we explain away other

193

people's difficulties in rather simplistic ways because we can't face the impli-
cations – our own responsibilities, for example.

The misunderstanding is presented by the use of two sets of voices:
the 'I' of the dead man, and the 'they' of the onlookers; these voices are
presented by a third voice – that of the narrator, who, unlike the onlookers,
can hear the dead man speaking.

In using pronouns rather than individual names, the poem suggests
that its message has significance for all of us, whoever we are.

Activity

It should be clear by now that the type of cohesive link involving pronoun
reference is an important element in the way many texts work.

Now go back to the texts that you worked on in the 'Make and mend'
part of this unit. Find as many examples as you can of grammatical cohesion which uses pronoun reference. Trace how you might have used this
system as a supportive strategy in the texts you rearranged and wrote.

The politics of pronouns
Before leaving the personal pronoun system, there are one or two points to
note that relate to changes that have occurred through time. Grammar, like
other aspects of language, is subject to the processes of language change,
and although the personal pronoun system appears to be relatively fixed,
there have been important shifts in meaning and use. These shifts will be of
particular significance if you are studying older texts, or comparing older
texts with modern ones. It's important to realise that grammatical structures
are not simply neutral – they are intimately related to power: for example,
pronoun reference in a text is all about who is in the picture and how they're
being seen, as well as about helping to construct a particular kind of relationship between writer and reader. These are all issues of power, because
written texts are a powerful source of information for us about the nature of
our world – not just the physical world, but our social, political and emotional
'realities' too.

One difficulty with the personal pronoun system as it exists in English
is that there is no neutral way to refer simply to 'a person', without specifying a sex for them: 'one' can carry suggestions of pretension, and is hardly
a term in everyday use; 'it' sounds rude when used of a person (think how
insulting parents would find it if their newborn baby was referred to as 'it'
by a friend peering into the pram on the street). 'They' has had varied

fortunes in terms of its acceptability: while it was seen as correct in Shakespeare's time – for example, in *The Winter's Tale*:

God grant everyone their heart's desire

by the eighteenth century, prescriptive grammars were ruling this type of sentence as incorrect because singular and plural references were being used together. Eighteenth-century grammars ruled that if pieces of communication were intended to refer to people in general, or a person of unspecified sex, the terms 'man' and 'he' should be used, claiming that these uses were **generic** – i.e. referring in a general way. In fact, it is clear from research that we actually understand 'he' and 'man' to refer to 'male person' rather than simply 'person'. This means that the words are not capable of generic reference for modern readers.

Nowadays, in order to get round the clumsiness of using 'he or she' every time we want to refer to 'a person of either sex', we use 'they' very often in speech, and increasingly frequently in writing. For example, this sentence occurred earlier in this sub-section:

The principle of reference within texts is exactly that: it tells the reader that they can only make complete sense of the word or structure they are looking at if they look elsewhere in the text to get a fuller picture.

It's important to note, though, that people will disagree about whether the above sentence is correct, since eighteenth-century ideas about grammar were still current up to the 1960s. People's opinions about correctness will have been influenced by their age and the type of education they had.

Another personal pronoun that has had a directly political history is 'you'.

Originally, English had two forms of 'you': 'thou'/'thee' was used to one person, and 'ye'/'you' for group address. 'Thou' was used when the person was the subject of the sentence, and 'thee' for the object; similarly, 'ye' was used for the subject, 'you' for the object. An example of each is given below:

Thou hast my heart   (thou = singular = subject of sentence)

I love *thee*   (thee = singular = object of sentence)

Ye must go now   (ye = plural = subject of sentence)

I will follow *you*   (you = plural = object of sentence)

As well as denoting simply singular or plural address, however, these terms also came to mark relationships between people: if people who were social equals were addressing each other, the plural forms could be used between the individuals (i.e. as singular forms) to signal distance and formality, while the singular forms could signal closeness and intimacy when used reciprocally; if the people were not equals, however, the plural forms could be used in addressing the more powerful person, as a mark of respect and authority, while the singular forms could be used in addressing the less powerful person to mark low status. A diagrammatic representation of these possibilities is given below.

This pattern meant that speakers could signal meanings in a subtle way, simply by using a certain pronoun. While this distinction has been lost in modern usage (although the older forms are sometimes retained in dialect, and much can be expressed via personal names and titles), older texts can present patterns of pronoun reference that say much about social relationships.

The fact that 'thou' and 'thee' died out within standard English usage remains something of a mystery, although it has been put down to the fact that they became associated with the Quaker movement, who wanted the terms to become the universal address forms as markers of equality for all. As Quaker groups were seen as radical, establishment choice favoured 'you' instead.

Although the use of a plural term to denote respect to one individual has died out in the system above, we still have some residue of this idea in the royal 'we' to denote one powerful person in particular.

Stepping out of the text
At the beginning of this sub-section on grammatical cohesion, the idea of reference was defined as 'seeking information from elsewhere'.

Up to now, the focus has been on the reader searching various parts of the text for that information. But reference, particularly involving certain of the personal pronouns, can also involve moving outside the text to find the appropriate locus of information.

For example, the use of 'you' in a text as a direct address to the reader tells that reader to use himself/herself as the reference point; the use of 'I' in a text tells the reader that the writer (or the narrator) is being self-referential. In both these cases, the pronouns are functioning as signposts leading out of the text and making us focus on the human agents who are producing and receiving the text.

Where a reference item moves us outside a text, so that we can only make full sense of the text by referring to its context, this is called an **exophoric reference**; where we stay within the text, not needing any support from outside, this is called **endophoric reference**.

Activity

Go back to the texts you worked on in the first part of this unit, and find as many examples as you can of exophoric reference. Are there particular types or 'genres' of text that rely heavily on exophoric reference as part of their written conventions?

Commentary

There are certain types of text that are characterised by their use of exophoric references via the personal pronoun system: for example, many advertisements address the reader directly, using 'you', and companies refer to themselves as 'we'. An example of these pronouns can be seen in the 'Portfolio' advert you reassembled (p. 168), and you may well have found further examples of direct address in the texts you wrote yourselves. Also, note the use of 'your' in the hook line of the Yakult advert on p. 155.

Address forms which take us outside the text are also very characteristic of literature, particularly some types of prose fiction. For example, nineteenth-century novelists often addressed the reader directly: at the end of Charlotte Bronte's *Jane Eyre*, the narrator, Jane, talking of her relationship with Mr Rochester, says: 'Reader, I married him'.

The attraction of referring outside a text is that this can leave plenty of room for manoeuvre, as it is unclear who 'you', 'I' and 'we' actually are.

While this could suggest confusion, in fact there is much creative potential in not pinning down exactly who the creators and receivers of a text are, because that then means that readers have to construct their own versions of these figures: for writers of literature and adverts alike (and any other texts

197

that try to work in an interactive way), it means that many possible 'readings' can occur.

Because the type of communication that's described above is potentially very complex, it can be useful to represent diagrammatically how these layers of reference might work.

Look back at the Yakult advert on p. 155.

In this, the copywriters are the real writers of the advert, but there is an implied writer/speaker constructed through the language that's used to address the reader. The real readers are us, but there are some implied readers, too: ideas about what we might think of as important, ideas about how we live, what we know and the attitudes we have are all embedded in the text, constructing 'us' as certain types of people, and not necessarily the people we really are.

All this goes to show how a text can create a particular relationship between the real writer and the real reader by constructing a piece of fictional discourse between implied versions of themselves:

real writer	− implied writer	− TEXT −	implied reader	− real reader
advertising copywriter	narrator		assumptions made about us in the text	the real person
novelist	ditto		ditto	ditto

etc.

If you have difficulty understanding the difference between the real audience and the implied one, then think about the following analogies: TV adverts for washing powder show women ('implied readers') as people whose lives revolve around the quality of their washing. Is this a true reflection of how women really live their lives (the 'real readers')? TV adverts for aftershave show men ('implied readers') who only have to splash on a little of the product for hordes of women suddenly to appear and look at the men in an admiring and available way. Is this an accurate picture of the everyday lives of men (the 'real readers')?

Demonstrative reference (deictics)

Another type of reference which acts as a cohesive tie is carried by the following terms:

the, this, that, these, those, here, there.

These terms demonstrate where something is; they are **deictic** terms – they are 'verbal pointers'.

As with personal pronouns, demonstrative reference can work backwards (anaphoric) or forwards (cataphoric). Here is an example of each:

I went to *Italy* last year, and I want to go *there* again soon (anaphoric)

But the problem is *this: how can I afford it?* (cataphoric).

The terms above can be categorised according to how they position the writer and reader (or speaker and listener, since the terms are used frequently in speech, too).

'This', 'these' and 'here' all mean 'near the writer/speaker', while 'that', 'those' and 'there' all mean 'away from the writer/speaker'.

While in speech these terms are often used to refer to physical items in the environment, in writing physical proximity can stand metaphorically for attitude as well.

Activity

In Text: Dialogues are some examples of demonstrative reference in speech.
Read through the dialogues and trace how the demonstrative terms work within the conversations to refer to the physical context of the speakers.
(Note: there is no commentary on this activity.)

Text: Dialogues

Context 1: Speaker A is asking Speaker B to help her disentangle her earring from the telephone handset wire:

> A: Can you help me *here*? I've got my . . .
> B: What are you doing *there*?
>   (B moves closer to A)
> A: It's *this* stupid thing . . . it's all tangled up . . .
> B: Hold on. Keep still a minute. It's *this* clasp *here*.
>   Ah, got it . . .

Context 2: Speakers C and D are house decorators discussing the wallpapering of a room:

> C: If you finish off *that* roll in the corner . . .
> D: What about *this* end *here*, though?
> C: *That* will do the bit up by the beams over *there*.

Activity

As well as placing aspects of the physical speech context, deictic items can also refer to ideas in another speaker's utterance in order to make links with them. For example, imagine that the following speakers are having a discussion about their favourite meals, but that they are nowhere near any real food:

200

Speaker 1:   I really like fish and chips.
Speaker 2:   *That's* my favourite dinner, too.
Speaker 3:   What about pasta and pizza?
Speaker 4:   *Those* are nice, too.

In the utterances above, the words 'that' and 'those' point, not to any real dinner, but to the words that name the food.

Even more removed from any physical reference is the use that sometimes occurs of the word 'that' to mean 'the thing/person we all know about'. Here are some examples:

I've got *that* Friday feeling.

That Beethoven was a genius.

You've got *that* 'know-it-all' look on your face.

Because demonstrative reference is all about pointing out, this type of cohesion can be used to strike strong attitudes as well as physical positions. Advertisers, literary authors and writers of all kinds can use our knowledge of demonstrative terms to signal relationships and point of view.

Look at Text: Kellogg's Cornflakes, Text: Quaker Puffed Wheat, and Text: Ovaltine. What part do demonstrative and personal pronoun reference play in positioning the readers of the texts? (There is one commentary, on the 'Ovaltine' advert.)

It may be useful to know that Ovaltine was originally classified as a medical product, being sold in chemists' shops, rather than as a general foodstuff.

Hold on!

He needn't catch the early bus looking like *THIS*

"all awake and half starved—he's off to a bad start today! That's because he still hasn't really broken his night-long fast with a worthwhile breakfast. Yet he needn't miss the bus if he has Kellogg's with his breakfast!

Send him to work like *THIS*

He's on the beam all right today—he's had a quick, satisfying breakfast that included Kellogg's, top-of-the-milk, and sugar. No chance of indigestion even though he did eat it quickly. Straight from the pack, Kellogg's delicious deep-toasted Corn Flakes contain energy-giving carbohydrates.

Breakfast is the most important meal of the day—doctors and health-experts are agreed on this. They warn you that if you're going to do a hard day's work you've got to give your body the fuel it needs to keep going after a whole night without food.

But this is just what tens of thousands of men and women ignore. They demand too much of their bodies, think they can't prepare and eat breakfast *and* get to work on time—so they skip or skimp what should be the first, good meal of the day.

Get him there early—with breakfast inside him!
Do you have this problem, too? There's a simple and tasty solution! Give your man his usual breakfast plus a heaped bowlful of crisp, golden-toasted Kellogg's Corn Flakes with sugar, and cream or milk. Kellogg's is best and tastiest because this delicious cereal brings out the full goodness of the rich heart of the finest grains of corn.

A breakfast like this will get anyone to work on time and with a good supply of energy to keep him working happily and *well* till the first break.

There's no preparation, no cooking, no messy washing up of pots and pans. Kellogg's is a breakfast *everyone* can help themselves to in no time at all.

A natural source of energy

Health experts agree that Kellogg's, with milk and sugar, provides energy in a really digestible form. Partly because of the delicious crunchiness, partly because of the perfect, wafer-thin, oven-toasted flakes, Kellogg's "go down well" with everyone. Isn't it worth while ensuring that a man goes to work *on time* and feeling *up to it?*
Of course it is!
So just see that he goes to work on Kellogg's.

Go to work on *Kellogg's*
—*IT'S READY-TO-EAT!*

Kellogg's CORN FLAKES

Text: Ovaltine

Ovaltine advert

The authoritative voice of the text is immediately established by the phrase 'those children of yours': 'those' sets up a distance from the speaker, and 'yours' locates ownership and therefore responsibility for the potential problem raised by the speaker – that of children who may not grow normally.

The main body of the text uses scientific-sounding discourse in the form of many statements to further establish the expertise of the author of the 'open letter' in talking to the recipients – 'mothers of fast-growing children' (therefore all mothers, since few mothers would acknowledge that they had children who were slow-growing).

At the end, the power of authority is reinforced by a command which reminds the reader whose children are being discussed: 'Give *your* children "Ovaltine"'.

Rather than referring to the position of the speaker and hearer within a text, the term 'the' is often used to convey different levels of generality or specificity.

For example, it can be used generically in expressions such as the following:

> The snail is a fascinating creature.
> The family is a social institution.
> The heart is a large muscle.

In these examples, the reference is not to one particular animal, family or heart but to a whole species or type of item.

But 'the' can also refer to something very specific, with the suggestion that this item is the one and only example of its kind. In many types of discourse, we often use 'the' to refer anaphorically to something which has already been been introduced by using 'a'. For example, in this introduction to a fairy tale, 'a' becomes 'the' as the story proceeds:

> Once upon a time there was *a* king in *a* foreign land who had a great desire to marry. *The* king looked high and low in *the* land, but all in vain . . .

205

Now look at the use of 'the' in Text: Names. What message is this term conveying? (In the first example, it might be useful to know that there are two universities in Manchester – the other one is called 'The University of Manchester', and its logo is given here, for information.)

(Note: there is no commentary on this activity.)

Text: Names

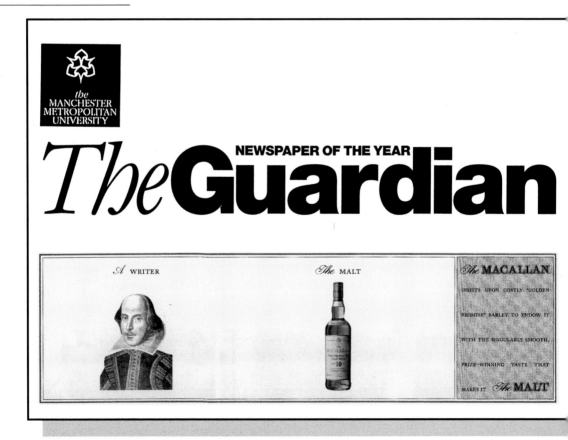

Comparative reference

Comparative reference tells the reader not just to 'look elsewhere for information', but to look elsewhere with a particular aim in mind – to *compare* the items that are being linked.

The most common way in English to mark grammatically that two items are being compared is to add 'er' to an adjective: for example, taller, nicer, healthier. It's also possible to suggest comparison with more than one item, by adding 'est': for example, tallest, nicest, healthiest.

Comparison can involve ideas about quantity and number: these meanings are carried by words like 'more', 'fewer', 'less', 'another'.

In many cases, we are given the reference point for the comparison being made, for example:

Annie is taller than Sue.

This sweater is nicer than that one.

Salad is healthier than fried bread.

But it is also possible to omit the reference point – leaving out the aspect that the mentioned item is being compared with.

Activity

Look at Text: Slogans, all of which have been taken from advertising texts. In each case, the comparative reference is incomplete. Try to explain in each case what the effect is of not completing the reference.

207

Text: Slogans

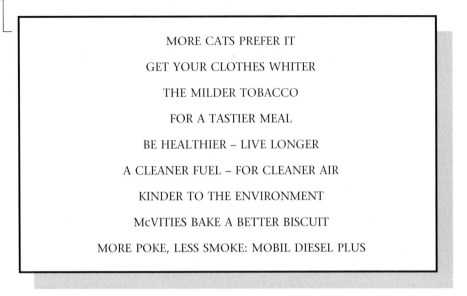

MORE CATS PREFER IT

GET YOUR CLOTHES WHITER

THE MILDER TOBACCO

FOR A TASTIER MEAL

BE HEALTHIER – LIVE LONGER

A CLEANER FUEL – FOR CLEANER AIR

KINDER TO THE ENVIRONMENT

McVITIES BAKE A BETTER BISCUIT

MORE POKE, LESS SMOKE: MOBIL DIESEL PLUS

When you have finished, read through the Quaker Puffed Wheat advert again (p. 203), locating the comparative references and explaining their effects. (Note: there is no commentary on this activity.)

Substitution and ellipsis

Alongside reference, substitution and ellipsis are also both powerful ingredients in textual cohesion.

Substitution means what it suggests – the writer or speaker has substituted one item for another in the text. This can often involve long phrases, replaced by useful smaller items such as the single words 'do' or 'so', and is very characteristic of spontaneous spoken discourse. One important function of this type of substitution is to make texts more economic by avoiding tedious repetition. The examples below show how, while 'do' is used to replace verbs, 'so' is more often used as a substitute for whole clauses. In each case, the phrase that is being substituted by 'do' or 'so' is in italics. The dialogue is between two friends, and they are discussing A's intended house sale.

> *A:* Has the agent for your house *put it in the local paper*?
>
> *B:* I think he must have *done*, because Terry saw it advertised around his chips from the chip shop.
>
> *A:* *That must have been a bit of a shock* if you hadn't told him.
>
> *B:* I think *so*.

Substitution can also involve nouns, and here we often make a substitution in order to redefine the original item. For example:

He looked at the potatoes, and picked out *the large ones*.

Please read through the contracts, and sign *the duplicate one*.

While substitution is about swapping elements, **ellipsis** involves omitting elements altogether. Speakers who know each other well often use ellipsis because they have many shared meanings and references that do not need stating explicitly. As a result, when measured against writing, speech can appear to have gaps and incompleteness: for example, minor sentences (sentences without a verb) are very common in speech (for a fuller treatment of ellipsis, see Unit 5).

In some types of written texts, ellipsis can be used deliberately in order to create an illusion of closeness between writer and reader. The reader is forced to adopt the same position towards the writer that a speaker would adopt to a close friend in conversation. Rather than obscuring meaning or loosening the cohesion in a text, ellipsis is a binding factor because ties between writer and reader are strengthened through the work that the reader has to do to fill the gaps.

Activity

Look at Text: Subaru, and identify places where there are omissions – ideas left incompletely stated, apparent gaps in sense or structure.

◎ To what extent does ellipsis contribute to the feel of this text as spoken language?
◎ What advantage do you think there might be for the advertiser in creating this illusion?

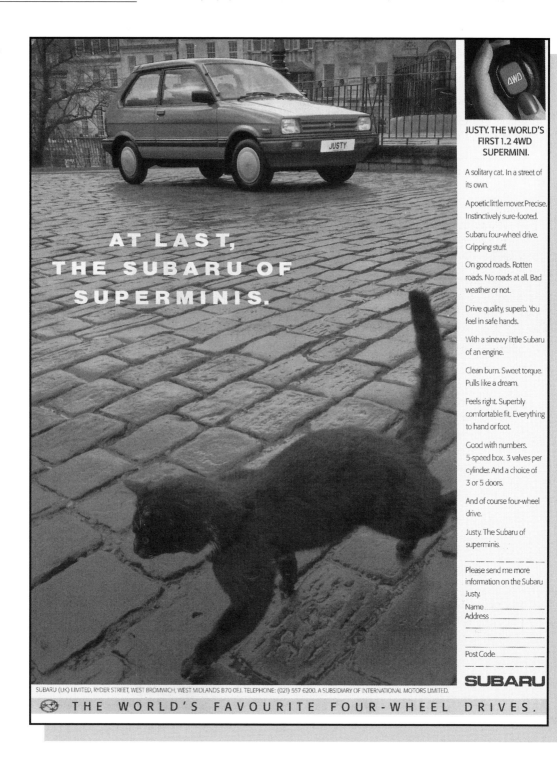

JUSTY. THE WORLD'S FIRST 1.2 4WD SUPERMINI.

A solitary cat. In a street of its own.

A poetic little mover. Precise. Instinctively sure-footed.

Subaru four-wheel drive. Gripping stuff.

On good roads. Rotten roads. No roads at all. Bad weather or not.

Drive quality, superb. You feel in safe hands.

With a sinewy little Subaru of an engine.

Clean burn. Sweet torque. Pulls like a dream.

Feels right. Superbly comfortable fit. Everything to hand or foot.

Good with numbers. 5-speed box. 3 valves per cylinder. And a choice of 3 or 5 doors.

And of course four-wheel drive.

Justy. The Subaru of superminis.

Please send me more information on the Subaru Justy.
Name
Address

Post Code

AT LAST, THE SUBARU OF SUPERMINIS.

SUBARU

SUBARU (UK) LIMITED, RYDER STREET, WEST BROMWICH, WEST MIDLANDS B70 0EJ. TELEPHONE: (021) 557 6200. A SUBSIDIARY OF INTERNATIONAL MOTORS LIMITED.

THE WORLD'S FAVOURITE FOUR-WHEEL DRIVES.

210

Commentary

The text uses ellipsis in the form of many minor sentences, including single words ('Justy', 'Precise'), two-word sequences ('Gripping stuff', 'Rotten roads', 'Clean burn', 'Sweet torque', 'Feels right'), and longer sentences where certain elements have been omitted: for example, verbs ('A solitary cat'), and nouns that stand for the subject ('Pulls like a dream'). This, along with other features – notably the fast turnover of items, as if imitating a person's unplanned thoughts, including afterthoughts signalled by 'and' – suggests spoken language rather than writing. On the other hand, the text is set out to resemble a poem visually, with the language arranged in 'stanza' form, fitting in with the idea of the car as 'a poetic little mover'. The text as a whole, including the visual aspects, calls up elements of the detective genre in its suggestions of the loneliness and threat of city meanstreets; the verbal commentary also has the staccato rhythm and dramatic tension of a detective film's narrator. The message of the text, though, is one of reassurance: the car is solid, reliable and secure. The hand in the picture inset is female, with carefully painted nails. This is a vehicle which will protect a genteel woman driver in a man's world: its engine, though little, will growl if necessary; the car is a comfortable outfit; 'Justy' is good with numbers even if its driver isn't.

The text's imitation of spoken language brings the narrator close to the reader, calling up a frisson of fear in order then to be able to dispel it.

Activity

Look back at the texts you worked with in the 'Make and mend' part of this unit (both those you reassembled and those you wrote), and try to find examples of substitution and ellipsis. Then, keeping the same focus, look again at any of the further texts you have studied in this unit. Where you find examples, assess how far the written texts you are looking at are trying to convey the feel of spoken language.

Conjunction

The term **conjunction** means 'joining'.

In a sense, all the aspects of cohesion are about joining or linking items together, but conjunction refers specifically to words and phrases which express *how* items should be linked. An example from the sentence you have just read is the word 'but': this tells the reader that what is to follow will revise, limit or re-focus the first part of the sentence.

Different types of writing tend to use different types of connecting word.

This is not just about conventions that have developed – it is often very much to do with the purpose of the piece of writing (see also 'Information structure', later in this unit). So, for example, a story may well concentrate on the way one event followed another in time. If this is so, then conjunctions such as 'first', 'then', 'after that', 'in the end' are likely to appear. On the other hand, an information text may be more interested in showing how an idea or theme is made up of different interrelating elements, and phrases such as 'on the other hand' may be more relevant here (as at the beginning of this sentence).

Activity

To look at this idea more practically, read through Text: High Peak, which is the front page of an information leaflet on conservation areas from the High Peak Borough Council.

In the text, the conjunctions have been underlined for you. Decide how they link together the various parts of the text – what instructions do they give the reader on how to put elements of the text together?

When you have finished, look for any more cohesive links, based on the types you have covered so far: for example, uses of 'this' and 'these'.

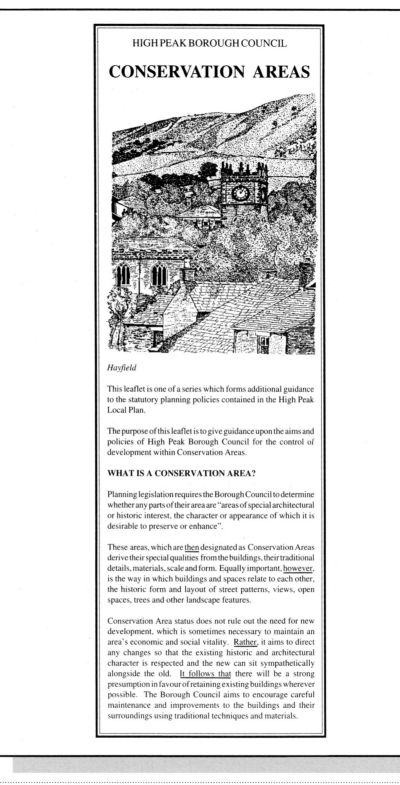

HIGH PEAK BOROUGH COUNCIL

CONSERVATION AREAS

Hayfield

This leaflet is one of a series which forms additional guidance to the statutory planning policies contained in the High Peak Local Plan.

The purpose of this leaflet is to give guidance upon the aims and policies of High Peak Borough Council for the control of development within Conservation Areas.

WHAT IS A CONSERVATION AREA?

Planning legislation requires the Borough Council to determine whether any parts of their area are "areas of special architectural or historic interest, the character or appearance of which it is desirable to preserve or enhance".

These areas, which are then designated as Conservation Areas derive their special qualities from the buildings, their traditional details, materials, scale and form. Equally important, however, is the way in which buildings and spaces relate to each other, the historic form and layout of street patterns, views, open spaces, trees and other landscape features.

Conservation Area status does not rule out the need for new development, which is sometimes necessary to maintain an area's economic and social vitality. Rather, it aims to direct any changes so that the existing historic and architectural character is respected and the new can sit sympathetically alongside the old. It follows that there will be a strong presumption in favour of retaining existing buildings wherever possible. The Borough Council aims to encourage careful maintenance and improvements to the buildings and their surroundings using traditional techniques and materials.

Activity

Here are some more conjunctions, with a brief explanation for each group of what they are telling the reader to do. (Note that some conjunctions can occur in more than one category.) Read through the notes, add any further examples you can think of, then specify the types of text (e.g. stories) that tend to use the various types of conjunction. (Note: there is no commentary for this activity.)

Type of conjunction	Meaning	Examples
additives/ alternatives	add/give an alternative	and, or, furthermore, in addition, likewise, in other words
adversative	contradict, concede	but, yet, though, however, on the contrary
causal	one idea/event causes another	so, then, for this reason, consequently, it follows that, as a result
temporal	one event follows another in time	one day, then, finally, up to now, the next day
continuatives	please continue to follow the text	well, now, of course, anyway, surely, after all

INFORMATION STRUCTURE

So far, attention has been focused on the way vocabulary and certain grammatical structures act as binding agents in texts. This sub-section looks at further aspects of both these areas, but with a focus on how particular types of text are connected with the internal ordering of information within them.

Different texts follow different rules which dictate to a certain extent the shape of the text produced: to return to the metaphor of weaving, you could say that texts come in different shapes in the same way that fabric is made into different garments.

But texts also have internal patterns in the same way that fabric has particular designs. The equivalent of a fabric design for a text is the pattern which results from how information and ideas are organised. For example, in the High Peak Borough Council leaflet, there are certain features that mark it out as belonging to the genre we might call 'information text', and some of these are to do with its directly visual shape: the title, in upper-case letters, the illustration, the boxed nature of the text, the way the text is broken up into spatially distinct sections. This is the equivalent of recognising a garment as a shirt or a dress. But there are also features of a more narrowly linguistic kind that relate to the way the text chooses to present its information and to foreground certain parts of it: this is more like the designs we see printed on a piece of material. These features are also part of the way we recognise and typify a genre, and they form the focus for the work that follows.

Sentence functions

Different sentences can perform very different functions, and, for this reason, the kind of sentence chosen often relates directly to what the text is trying to do.

Here are the four main functions sentences in English can perform:

- *Questioning:* Question sentences ask the reader to look for information.
- *Stating:* Statement sentences offer the reader a description of the state of things.
- *Commanding:* Command sentences (sometimes called 'imperatives') tell the reader to do something.
- *Exclaiming:* Exclamations express emotion directly.

To illustrate the differences in these functions, look at the High Peak Borough Council leaflet again.

The writers of this leaflet have chosen to use a question–answer format as a way of presenting information, so they have a question sentence as the heading:

WHAT IS A CONSERVATION AREA?

The effect of this is to justify the text that follows, in the sense that the text 'pretends' the reader has asked this question in the first place, so the writer is therefore doing the reader a favour by answering it. This in turn makes the text seem less authoritative than if the question had been a statement sentence:

CONSERVATION AREAS EXPLAINED

215

The other possible sentence functions – command and exclamation – would have had different effects again: a command sentence would increase the distance between writer and reader by giving the reader an order to be carried out:

FIND OUT ABOUT CONSERVATION AREAS –
READ THIS LEAFLET

while an exclamation would have suggested that the whole subject of conservation was highly emotive and controversial (which it may well be, but the council is unlikely to want to suggest this):

CONSERVATION AREAS!

To summarise: information texts are known to be difficult texts to read because they demand a lot of information-processing skills from the reader. They are also likely to seem remote and authoritative, since explaining something to someone suggests that the giver of information is more powerful (because more knowledgeable) than the receiver. In this particular leaflet, the writer has tried to remove this distance by using a question sentence to introduce the information.

Activity

Go back again to the texts you worked with in the 'Make and mend' part of this unit.

◎   Do the different genres of the texts use different kinds of sentences?
◎   What are the effects of the different kinds of sentence they use?

When you have finished, look at Text: Gap.
This illustrates how sentence functions can be manipulated in order to create multi-layered readings. The text is an advertisement for a chain store called 'The Gap'. The advert came out around Christmas time in a variety of forms – on flyers and cards in the shop itself, as well as on hoardings and buses. Explain how the advert uses the idea of different sentence functions to create more than one level of meaning. (You might also consider why the advertisers chose to use lower-case letters on the word 'what', and why they positioned the text in a certain way, used a variety of typefaces, and chose the term 'certificates'.)

216

what to give.

what to get.

Gap gift certificates.

Gap gift certificates are good at
all Gap and GapKids stores. They are
available in any denomination, and
come in a great little bag.

GAP

PATRICK DEMARCHELIER © GAP 1993

Commentary

The lines 'what to give', 'what to get' could be read as two different types of sentence structure: as questions, or as statements. The fact that question marks are missing doesn't stop us from reading a possible question structure into the text. We would perhaps have been more 'worried' about the lack of question marks if the sentences had been full ones, with main verbs, and if they had had capital letters at the beginning in each case. As they stand, the sentences suggest spoken language as much as written and, as such, we are likely to be more ambivalent about whether they need formal punctuation.

The advertisers are clearly hoping to call up both question and statement structure: readers will then understand the statements as answers to the questions:

Q: what shall I give? what shall I get (buy/receive)?
A: (Gap is) what to give and get.

There are gaps in the text in a number of ways: grammatically, as above, in the statement reading of the sentences; in the visual space left in the text as a result of moving the second sentence to the right; and at the bottom, where a large space has been filled by the word 'Gap' stretched out vertically.

In its italicised form and decorative typeface, the official answer – 'Gap gift certificates' – supplies a solution which appears speech-like, gentle and friendly. The text below this is laid out as if on a commemorative plaque – the kind of layout seen on a certificate, a word which connotes achievement and reward rather than the financial transaction suggested by the word 'voucher'.

Another way we learn to recognise different genres of writing is by looking at the verbs used, particularly **tense** and **voice** (see Unit 3).

Tense

Tense refers to the way verbs are used to signal time: for example, a verb can be marked to show that an action happened in the past. This is done mainly by adding 'ed', but a minority of verbs change their internal structure. Here is an example of each type of marking: talk → talked (regular verb); speak → spoke (irregular verb). Certain types of writing tend to use particular verb tenses as part of their convention, and this in turn is related to what the text is trying to do. As an illustration of possible differences in what texts are concerned with, it is useful to think in terms of broad categories – for example, prose fiction compared with non-fiction information texts. Because information texts are intended to tell the reader about 'the nature of things' or 'how things are', these types of text tend to use present-tense verb forms couched in statements about present 'reality'. While prose fiction may equally give messages about the nature of the world, it tends to do this by looking back and giving an account of a series of events that happened to a set of fictional characters. It is therefore more likely that prose fiction will employ past-tense verb forms. Note that these statements are referring to norms or tendencies, not absolutes – so exceptions are always possible. In particular, it can be a very useful scene-setting strategy in fiction to 'stop the clock' and give a description of a place or person which uses present-tense verbs to convey the idea 'this is how things usually are in this place/with this person'.

Compare the verb tenses in the High Peak Borough Council leaflet with those in Text: *K is for Killer*, which is from a detective novel by Sue Grafton. How far do the verb tenses bear out the picture given in these notes? (Note: there is no commentary on this activity.)

Text: *K is for Killer*

I drove east along Cabana, the wide boulevard that parallels the beach. When the moon is full, the darkness has the quality of a film scene shot day for night. The landscape is so highly illuminated that the trees actually cast shadows. Tonight the moon was in its final quarter, rising low in the sky. From the road I couldn't see the ocean, but I could hear the reverberating rumble of the tide rolling in. There was just enough wind to set the palm trees in motion, shaggy heads nodding together in some secret communication. A car passed me, going in the opposite direction, but there were no pedestrians in sight. I'm not often out at such an hour, and it was curiously exhilarating.

By day, Santa Teresa seems like any small southern California town. Churches and businesses hug the ground against the threat of earthquakes. The rooflines are low, and the architectural influence is largely Spanish. There's something solid and reassuring about all the white adobe and the red tile roofs. Lawns are manicured, and the shrubs are crisply trimmed. By night the same features seem stark and dramatic, full of black and white contrasts that lend intensity to the hardscape. The sky at night isn't really black at all. It's a soft charcoal gray, nearly chalky with light pollution, the trees like ink stains on a darkened carpet. Even the wind has a different feel to it, as light as a feather quilt against the skin.

The real name for CC's is the Caliente Cafe, a low rent establishment housed in an abandoned service station near the railroad tracks. The original gasoline pumps and the storage tanks below had been removed years before, and the contaminated soil had been paved over with asphalt. Now, on hot days the blacktop tends to soften and a toxic syrup seeps out, a tarry liquid quickly converted into wisps of smoke, suggesting that the tarmac is on the verge of bursting into flames. Winters, the pavement cracks from dry cold, and a sulfurous smell wafts across the parking lot. CC's is not the kind of place to encourage bare feet.

I parked out in front beneath a sizzling red neon sign. Outside, the air smelled like corn tortillas fried in lard; inside, like salsa and recirculated cigarette smoke. I could hear the high-pitched whine of a blender working overtime, whipping ice and tequila into the margarita mix.

Voice

Verb voice is also something that tends to vary according to the genre of the writing. Voice refers to the way different emphases can be given to sentences (see Unit 3, p. 160).

There are two types of voice: active and passive.

If a verb takes an object (a thing or person affected by the action of the verb) as well as a subject (the thing or person doing the action) then it can be changed from active to passive. In the sentences below, the elements in italics form the object of the verb in each case:

> She sold *the car.*
> He kept *the pictures.*

These sentences are in an active form at present. Each can be expressed in a different way, however:

> The car was sold by her.
> The pictures were kept by him.

Now the sentences are passive: the object of the previously active sentence has moved to the front, to subject position; the verb has changed its form (to the form that it would take with 'have') and has added the verb 'to be'; the previous subject has moved to the end of the sentence, becoming a phrase (called the 'agent phrase'). In fact, this phrase could be left out altogether:

> The car was sold.
> The pictures were kept.

The fact that this phrase could be left out is a crucial factor in why the passive construction is favoured in some types of writing. Passives are often a way of depersonalising a text, because in removing agent phrases, the people and forces behind actions can be downplayed, leaving the process itself as the major focus – above, the selling of the car, the keeping of the pictures. It follows that any written genre wanting to highlight, for example, institutional procedures rather than individual concerns – such as legal documents or scientific reports – will tend to choose passive structures rather than active ones. In the High Peak Borough Council leaflet, the italicised parts of the text below are passives:

> These areas, which *are* then *designated* as Conservation areas . . .

> Rather, it aims to direct any changes so that the existing historic and architectural character *is respected* . . .

Passives are not simply an alternative form of expression, however. The fact that the agent behind the process can be removed from a passive construction can also mean that a text can appear to have a veneer of neutrality, scientific 'truth' or newsworthy 'fact' when, expressed in another way, it seems to be nothing more than personal dogma or ideological bias.

Activity

In Text: Voice are three brief texts written entirely in the active voice. Turn them into the passive throughout, leaving out, wherever possible, the agent phrases. Possible rewrites are given on p. 242.

Text: Voice

They drove the car quickly away from the scene of the crime. They had blown open the safe, shot the security guard and left him for dead. A bystander called the emergency services and a passing motorist comforted the guard until they arrived.

I took a group of 40 people and surveyed their attitudes to alcohol. I found that most of the people surveyed drank more alcohol per week than the level that the government recommends.

If you take out a mortgage, the building society will repossess your house if you do not keep up the monthly payments. You must let the building society know if you are going to make late or reduced payments at any time.

When you have finished changing the texts around, think about the following:

◎ What differences in meaning or emphasis have resulted from your rewriting?
◎ What advantages might there be for writers, in using the passive voice?
◎ What types of text, in your experience, are likely to use passive structures?
◎ Are there valid reasons for using passives, as well as dubious reasons?

(Note: there is no commentary on this activity.)

Theme

Another important aspect of textual cohesion is the way in which the feature we call **theme** works across sentence boundaries.

Theme refers to the first part of a sentence, which is where the subject matter of the sentence is usually laid out for the reader. It covers all the material before the main verb. When sentences are woven tightly together, the end of one sentence (called the 'focus') can become the theme of the next. But themes have to have some continuity across sentences, otherwise a text that *looks* tightly knit can make complete nonsense.

Activity

The text below is tightly knit in that the end of each sentence (focus) is linked with the start of the next (theme). But there are no links between themes (which have been italicised). As a result, the text reads as somewhat bizarre.

> *I* got up early and fed my cat. *Cats* like cream. *Cream* is a popular colour for paint. *Famous painters* include Michelangelo, who painted the Sistine Chapel in the Vatican. *The Vatican* is where the Pope lives.

Do a short piece of writing like the one above, where there is no thematic continuity, but where the end of each sentence links with the start of the next. (Note: there is no commentary on this activity.)

Activity

Although the text you have just written would be considered faulty if judged by the rules of normal discourse, you might be able to find a text written in this way in some types of prose fiction – particularly where the writer is trying to imitate a kind of free-wheeling consciousness, where a character's thought process is being presented. Such texts are often described as using a 'stream of consciousness' technique. Text: Student's writing is an example. Can you see any cohesion in this text, or is it composed of entirely random sentences? (Note: there is no commentary on this activity.)

Text: Student's writing

> Must take the dog for a walk this morning. Washing waving about. Wonder what he might think of me if I don't phone. Blue sky, blue sky. Helen never said, did she? Bloke over there, sitting on the wall. Where's my coat? Thought I left it somewhere else. Funny how old towns speak about their past. To swim, or not to swim, that is the question. Nicer on a Greek beach, body brown and oily, cheap novels in abundance. Don't need many clothes in some parts of the world. On then.
>
> *Deborah Freeman*

Activity

Text: *The Shepherd* (an extract from the novel by Frederick Forsyth) shows how sentence themes can be controlled very carefully in order to give the reader a sense of place and time. Read it through and plot the way in which the themes construct a particular spatial and temporal orientation for the reader as the text proceeds.

224

Text: *The Shepherd*

For a brief moment, while waiting for the control tower to clear me for takeoff, I glanced out through the Perspex cockpit canopy at the surrounding German countryside. It lay white and crisp beneath the crackling December moon.

Behind me lay the boundary fence of the Royal Air Force base, and beyond the fence, as I had seen while swinging my little fighter into line with the takeoff runway, the sheet of snow covering the flat farmland stretched away to the line of the pine trees, two miles distant in the night yet so clear I could almost see the shapes of the trees themselves.

Ahead of me, as I waited for the voice of the controller to come through the headphones, was the runway itself, a slick black ribbon of tarmac, flanked by twin rows of bright-burning lights, illuminating the solid path cut earlier by the snowplows. Behind the lights were the humped banks of the morning's snow, frozen hard once again where the snowplow blades had pushed them. Far away to my right, the airfield tower stood up like a single glowing candle amid the brilliant hangars where the muffled aircraftmen were even now closing down the station for the night.

Inside the control tower, I knew, all was warmth and merriment, the staff waiting only for my departure to close down also, jump into the waiting cars, and head back to the parties in the mess. Within minutes of my going, the lights would die out, leaving only the huddled hangars, seeming hunched against the bitter night, the shrouded fighter planes, the sleeping fuel-bowser trucks, and, above them all, the single flickering station light, brilliant red above the black-and-white airfield, beating out in Morse code the name of the station – CELLE – to an unheeding sky. For tonight there would be no wandering aviators to look down and check their bearings; tonight was Christmas Eve, in the year of grace 1957, and I was a young pilot trying to get home to Blighty for his Christmas leave.

Commentary

This text gives an acute sense of a moment suspended in time as the pilot waits to take off; during this moment, he appears to have a heightened perception of his surroundings while looking out through the cockpit canopy. There are several sentence themes that specify spatial orientation: behind me; ahead of me; behind the lights; far away to my right; inside the control tower. At the end, we are brought back to the idea of time passing as the waiting pilot thinks ahead to 'within minutes of my going', at which point we view with him how the surroundings will appear as he takes off. We are brought back down to earth when we are told there would be no 'wandering aviators' that night; finally we are given factual details of time and direction – Christmas Eve 1957, a flight back to Britain. These details bring us back inside the plane, ready for take off.

The textile industry

The title of this whole unit is 'Text and context'.

So far, the focus has been on how texts work internally, in how they are put together. This section examines another level at which texts operate, in the sense of the context that surrounds them.

The word 'context' contains the word 'text': it refers to the factors that work alongside or with the text to create meaning. 'Con' means 'with', and in Latin, the verb *contexere* means 'to weave together with'; the word 'con' in contemporary Italian and Spanish still means 'with', and you can see its operation in phrases such as the Spanish 'chili con carne' ('chili with meat').

So the context for any text is the larger culture which surrounds it, and the reading of any text results from the interplay of the text itself and the cultural framework that the reader brings to it.

The word 'culture', however, is not a straightforward term to define.

One use of the term refers to being part of an elite group: when we say someone is 'cultured', the suggestion is that they know about such areas of artistic expression as classical literature and music, and that they go to such venues as the theatre or art galleries as part of their social life. This is also what is meant by 'high culture', which was a phrase coined by Matthew Arnold to describe, in his opinion, 'the best that has been thought and said in the world'. In contrast, Arnold would have considered such pastimes as going to football matches, watching TV, viewing mass-circulation films or reading popular fiction or magazines as examples of 'low culture'.

This elitist view of culture, however, is not the whole story.

In sociology, culture has a much wider meaning: it refers to all the factors that bind groups together in all aspects of social life:

> Culture refers to the ways of life of members of a society, or of groups within a society. It includes how they dress, their marriage customs and family life, their patterns of work, religious ceremonies and leisure pursuits. It also covers the goods they create and which become meaningful for them: bows and arrows, ploughs, factories and machines, computers, books, dwellings . . .
>
> (Giddens 1993)

Activity

In the quote above, culture is defined as *the ways of life of members of a society, or of groups within a society.*

Text: The Phone Book contains many references to aspects of culture, and assumes reader knowledge of at least the following:

◎ A popular science fiction character and series.
◎ What a phone book is and how it works, including its typeface conventions.
◎ Particular cultural conventions in personal names, house names and place names.

Imagine that you were talking or writing to someone who had no knowledge of any of the above. Try to lay out in as much detail as possible how these aspects of culture work, and how they are exploited in the advert.

To what extent would everyone within the culture that produced this advert (that is, UK-based, English-speaking) understand the references you have identified? For example, would the age, social class or ethnicity of the readers make any difference to how they understood this text?

(Note: there is no commentary on this activity.)

Boldly go.

```
Kirk D, 90 South St, Sandstone..........................................Ledbrooks 98689
Kirk B.A ,19 New Road, Bington........................................Wilkston 05792
Kirk C, 256 Lansdowne Pl................................................Ashtree 99892
Kirk C, 42 The Drive, Bascom..........................................Brandyarce 28990
KIRK CAPTAIN JAMES T, Spc Expir
              Trek Ho, High St..............Sherby 30106
Kirk Charles, 84 First Ave, Blandover.........................Padluck 71103
Kirk, Cyril, 29 Wilbury Rd, Spindleton.......................Bepen 21710
Kirl D, Caburn Road.......................................................Long Deaton 93678
Kirk D.P, 61 Palmeria Av, Lobyton.............................Kirksworth 42147
Kirk Emil, 88 High St, Balsover....................................Sherby 51883
```

Superboldly go.

```
Kirk A, 20 ... Rd, Balsover...........................................Padluck 43689
Kirk A, 22 Embankment Rd, Chadderton....................Bepen 50217
Kirk A, 68 Newbury Rd, Penbrook................................Long Deaton 99892
Kirk A.B, 84 Marine Dr..................................................Kirksworth 28990
KIRK ADMIRAL JAMES T,
     Astro Conslt—
     Dunbeamin, 16 Rivermeed Rd................Sherby 30106
Kirk Alan, 46 Goodwins Cres, Chellerham ...............Bepen 53689
Kirk, A.R, I, 61 Cambridge Rd, Horton.......................Padluck 24750
Kirl B, 88 Skipton Road................................................Sherby 01821
```

Every enterprise needs a little assistence. Because a business needs its customers and it's important to help them find you easily. A Simple solution is to beef up your entry in the Phone Book. For a small charge, we'll print your name, address and number in big bold type.

For just a little more, we'll make them even bigger and easier to find. The number of phone calls made every week in business after referring to Phone Books is a staggering twenty seven million.

It only takes one, though, to find out how to get your fair share of them. Just dial 100 and ask for Freefone Phone Books.

The better you stand out, the easier it will be for your customers to find you. And the more likely it is you'll grow where no business has grown before.

THE *phone* BOOK

British TELECOM

If society is made up of many groups, it follows that any text may encode the culture of one group but not another. More than that, a text may, in giving voice to one group's culture, misrepresent another group or depict it in a negative way. In other words, any text adopts a point of view or position as a result of whose culture is being represented and how this is done. Such decisions are very much bound up with what is meant by the 'textile industry' in the title of this section: texts in the public domain such as advertisements, newspapers and forms of literature serve purposes which are often to do with the commercial profit margins of the most powerful groups in society, and they form a system which constructs ways of thinking for all of us.

Look at Text: Iberia. What aspects of culture are embedded in this advert? Think about the following:

◎ What is the role of the black athlete in this text? What does he symbolise (represent, or stand for)?
◎ What kind of figure do you imagine would normally be sitting in the vacant airline seat?
◎ Think of other texts where non-white figures were depicted or described. Were they presented in particular ways?

Texts don't always appear to hide their own ideologies, however. Advertisements in particular can use ideas about representation as part of their persuasive message. This can make the advertised company appear to be very open and truthful.

Look at Text: Daewoo, which contains a message about how car companies have traditionally sold their products. In Unit 1, the way one text can refer to or base itself on another was called 'intertextuality'.

Explain how Text: Daewoo uses intertextuality and refers to the stereotyping of particular groups to construct its persuasive message.

(Note: there is no commentary on this activity.)

Text: Iberia

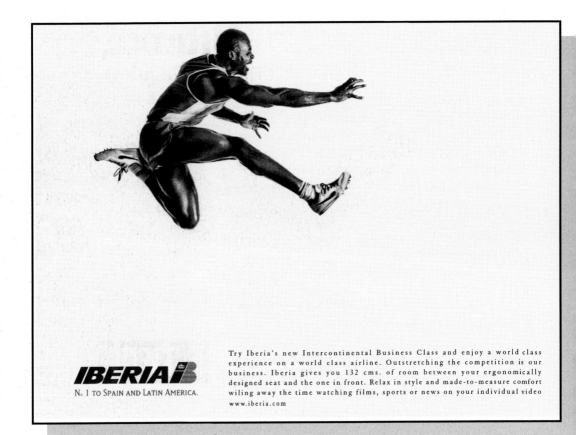

Try Iberia's new Intercontinental Business Class and enjoy a world class experience on a world class airline. Outstretching the competition is our business. Iberia gives you 132 cms. of room between your ergonomically designed seat and the one in front. Relax in style and made-to-measure comfort wiling away the time watching films, sports or news on your individual video www.iberia.com

IBERIA
N. 1 TO SPAIN AND LATIN AMERICA.

We've outstretched the competition.

Business
INTERCONTINENTAL

screen, make a call from your seat on your personal telephone or treat your palate to a Mediterranean Cuisine inspired choice of three menus, amongst many other possibilities. And when you've landed and had time to reflect, you'll have no doubt as to why Iberia is today one of the leading business airlines of the world.

Distance measured between rows.

231

**EVERY NEW DAEWOO COMES
WITH A RATHER ATTRACTIVE EXTRA.**

Tempted? So you should be because all our models come with three years free servicing. No small print, no disclaimers, just free servicing including all labour and parts. (Apart from the tyres that is, they come with their own guarantee.) Unlike other car manufacturers this offer isn't for a limited period, nor is it an extra, hidden in the hiked up cost of the car. Our offer is the same right across the Daewoo range and is included in the fixed price you see on the cars in the showroom. Those prices range from £8,445 to £12,895 for the 3, 4 and 5 door Nexia and the Espero saloon. As if this isn't enough of an offer, we'll even telephone and arrange your car's service, then collect it from your doorstep leaving you with a courtesy car until yours is returned, if you wish. But what happens in between servicing? That's covered too. Every new Daewoo comes with a three year comprehensive warranty, three years Daewoo Total AA Cover and a six year anti-corrosion warranty. In fact, the only thing you do pay for is insurance and petrol. Take a look at the list and see for yourself. 1). 3 year/60,000 mile free servicing including parts and labour. 2). 3 year/60,000 mile comprehensive warranty. 3). 3 year Total AA Cover. 4). 6 year anti-corrosion warranty.

5). 30 day/ 1,000 mile money back or exchange guarantee. 6). Free courtesy car. 7). Pick up and return of your car for service if needed. Mainland UK only. 8). Fixed purchase price with no hidden extras. 9). Delivery included. 10). Number plates included. 11). 12 months road tax included. 12). Full tank of fuel. 13). Metallic paint included. 14). Electronic ABS. 15). Driver's airbag. 16). Side impact protection. 17). Power steering. 18). Engine immobiliser. 19). Security glass etching. 20). Mobile phone. 21). Free customer helpline. If you were glad to hear all this we'd be glad to tell you more, so please call us on 0800 666 222.

A car where the extras aren't extra? That'll be the Daewoo.

DAEWOO

232

Extension

Collect some written texts in order to explore a particular dimension you have found interesting in this unit.

Here are some starting points, to get you thinking:

◎   intertextuality – texts that refer explicitly to other texts
◎   the representation of groups – e.g. gender, age, ethnicity, social class, region
◎   different types of writing on a common theme. These could include:

food:	recipes, menus, adverts, food labels, poems . . .
drink:	beer mats, wine labels, wine reviews, adverts . . .
relationships:	greetings cards, lonely hearts columns, fiction . . .
travel:	holiday brochures, travel writing, travel guides . . .

When you have collected a range of material, focus on an overall question for language analysis which will enable you to contrast a small number of texts for a specific reason. For example, within the area of food, the following contrasts might yield interesting results:

Language change: comparing an older text with a contemporary one from the same genre, what has changed, and why?

Spoken compared with written discourse: spoken (i.e. TV or radio) recipe compared with a written one. You could even compare texts from the same person, as several professional cooks have produced books to accompany their TV series.

The functions and features of different genres: how might the purposes of two types of writing – for example, a persuasive advert compared with an informative food label – be reflected in their language use? Are they more similar or more distinctive than we might think?

Texts specifically aimed at different audiences: how do recipes or menus aimed at children vary from those aimed at adults? Do adverts for food target male and female audiences differently? Do menus aimed at different regional and social-class groups encode ideas about the supposed audience?

233

Activity

To enable you to explore the usefulness of contrasting two different texts within the same genre, read through Text: Menu A and Text: Menu B. They are from very different establishments: A is from a roadside café in the Manchester area; B is from a large chain hotel in Newcastle.

What ideas about its target audience are suggested by each of the menus?

Text: Menu A

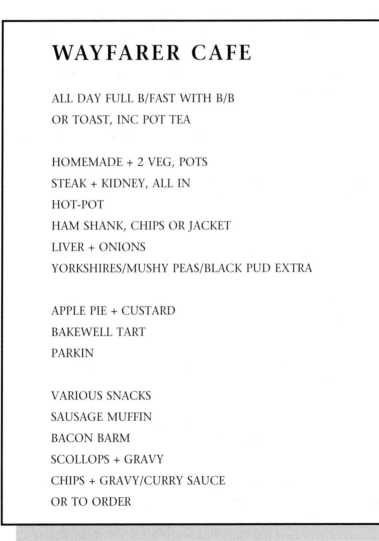

WAYFARER CAFE

ALL DAY FULL B/FAST WITH B/B
OR TOAST, INC POT TEA

HOMEMADE + 2 VEG, POTS
STEAK + KIDNEY, ALL IN
HOT-POT
HAM SHANK, CHIPS OR JACKET
LIVER + ONIONS
YORKSHIRES/MUSHY PEAS/BLACK PUD EXTRA

APPLE PIE + CUSTARD
BAKEWELL TART
PARKIN

VARIOUS SNACKS
SAUSAGE MUFFIN
BACON BARM
SCOLLOPS + GRAVY
CHIPS + GRAVY/CURRY SAUCE
OR TO ORDER

The Ravenscroft Suite:
GOURMET DINNER DANCE

*An interesting warm salad of smoked bacon, wild mushrooms and duck,
quickly cooked and abound with a melange of winter leaves sprinkled in a
walnut dressing*

*

*Peeled prawns bound in a tomato enhanced mayonnaise with diced
pineapple and walnuts, nestled on a meli-melo of lettuce served in a glass*

*

*A collection of cured meats and poultry, nestled on a rustic salad and
doused in a warm raspberry dressing*

*

A terrine of fresh vegetables, sliced onto a coulis of tomato and fresh herbs

***

*Supreme of fresh salmon attentively grilled, presented on a cushion of
homemade noodles with a champagne sauce*

***

*Fillets of fresh monkfish spread with a mousse of scampi caressed in
cabbage and poached, sliced onto a dry vermouth and avocado sauce*

***

*Medallions of pork pan-fried and masked in a pink peppercorn sauce
accompanied by caramelized kumquats*

***

*Escalope of turkey folded with cranberry sauce, dusted in breadcrumbs and
baked, escorted by a rich Madeira sauce*

***

*Rounds of venison quickly pan-fried and masked with a sharp
blackcurrant sauce with just a suspicion of Juniper berry*

***

*A tournedos of beef topped with a liver parfait, enrobed in crepinette and
oven-baked, served with a Madeira and truffle fondue*

Commentary

Graphology/phonology

These two texts represent variations within the menu genre in terms of their layout and organisation. Menu A groups its items in three sections, separated by space: the first section lists main meals, the second lists sweet dishes, while the third offers snacks. Menu B is laid out differently: all the items are equally spaced, but the number of asterisks denotes whether the food described is a starter or main course item. In each case, it is assumed that the reader knows about the organisation of the text as part of his/her reading skills within English-speaking cultural groups: a reader of Menu A would therefore not expect to have to select an item from each of the sections, while a reader of Menu B would not expect the items framed by three asterisks to be snacks.

Menu A uses upper-case letters in a plain typeface, suggesting clarity and straightforwardness, while the italic lower-case script of Menu B carries connotations of artistic purpose.

Menu A uses a range of abbreviations and symbols: b/fast, b/b, inc, veg, homemade, steak + kidney, pots, jacket, yorkshires, pud, 2, +, /. Again, there is an assumption here of shared understanding: there is no need for the text to spell out in any detail what is being referred to. The resulting economy of language suggests little use for the decorative, aesthetic aspect of communication. In contrast, the language of Menu B strives to expand rather than contract: for example, where Menu A uses a plus sign, Menu B renders additive meaning by phrases such as 'accompanied by' and 'escorted by'. Menu B also foregrounds its own language by imitating an artistic construct in its use of sound symbolism – peeled prawns, meli-melo, fillets of fresh monkfish, caressed in cabbage, pork pan-fried . . . pink peppercorn, accompanied . . . caramelized kumquats. The reader could be forgiven for thinking that some of the ingredients are included as much for their alliterative as for their culinary value.

Vocabulary

Menu A contains a large proportion of regional dialect terms, labelling regional food from the Lancashire/Yorkshire area: 'homemade' (a steak pie), 'hot-pot', 'ham shank' (leg of boiled ham), 'Yorkshires' (Yorkshire pudding), 'mushy peas' (baked marrowfat peas), 'black pudding', 'Bakewell tart' (from Bakewell, Derbyshire), 'parkin' (a cake made with black treacle), 'muffin' and 'barm' (both dialect terms for bread rolls), 'scollops' (potato slices dipped in batter and fried). While neither chips nor gravy are regional items, their combination on the same plate is much favoured in the North.

Menu B contains many terms derived from French, including some which are still given French pronunciation – for example: 'melange', 'coulis', 'mousse', 'parfait'. French terms are used to describe particular cuts of meat or fish – 'supreme', 'fillets', 'medallions', 'escalope', 'tournedos'; and the French-derived term 'poultry' is preferred to the Anglo-Saxon alternative, 'chicken'. Dressings and coverings of various kinds – 'mayonnaise', 'coulis', 'mousse', 'parfait', 'sauce' – are of French derivation. French terms also refer to arrangements of food – for example, 'melange', 'meli-melo' (French for 'topsy-turvy'), or particular dishes and items – 'terrine', 'fondue', 'crepinette'.

Beyond the terms related specifically to food, many other terms within the text are French/Latin-based, and have connotations of formality and high status: for example, 'enhanced', 'presented', 'accompanied'. Some terms also suggest sensuality – 'nestled', 'cushion', 'caressed' – while others almost raise the food items to a level of human animacy: the warm salad is 'interesting', the salmon is *attentively* grilled', the venison carries a 'suspicion' of Juniper, while the turkey is 'escorted', and the beef is 'enrobed'. The picture constructed is one where the food is a sensual experience, but of a high aesthetic level, unfolding within a world of good manners and delicacy, not within an animalistic world of base appetites.

The connotations of the names of the respective establishments provide revealing semantic contrasts: the 'Wayfarer' represents a transport-type cafe, appearing to suggest a travelling clientele, but offering a very localised fare which needs no explanation, therefore constructing readers who are known and familiar customers; the 'Ravenscroft', on the other hand, suggests ample provision in offering itself as a 'suite', and constructs an audience of sophisticated food experts – 'gourmets' – who have the leisure time to dance as well as eat. The food appears to be explained in some detail, but is couched in language which is not everyday and familiar, and which, in many cases, would need some knowledge in order to pronounce as well as under-stand.

Grammar

While both texts are lists of a kind, Menu A presents nouns with occasional modification: for example, 'full b/fast', 'ham shank', 'mushy peas', 'Bakewell tart', 'various snacks', 'sausage muffin', 'bacon barm'. In contrast, Menu B presents nouns or noun phrases which are heavily modified, with complex sets of dependencies: for example 'peeled prawns' is qualified by 'bound in a tomato enhanced mayonnaise', which is in turn qualified by 'with diced pineapple and walnuts'; the whole of this structure is then qualified by 'nestled on a meli-melo of lettuce', which is in turn qualified by 'served in a glass'. The effect is of layers of structure where the relationships between the parts of the utterance have to be unravelled; this effect is repeated in each description. The grammar is a linguistic simulation of the food it describes.

One or two aspects of the grammar of Menu B are deviant: for example, 'abound with', 'sprinkled in'. By the time the reader reaches the possibility of being 'caressed in cabbage', there is the distinct feeling that the writer has been overcome by the excesses of his/her own verbiage.

Discourse

The functions of the two texts are clearly different. Menu A offers information, while Menu B is more of a persuasive text resembling an advertisement. Menu A constructs an audience which is a known clientele who expect straightforward food with few trimmings; Menu B offers food which is dressed up via a text which simulates that elaboration. The audience constructed by Menu B is passing trade rather than regular patrons; such patrons may not actually be sophisticated, but the text suggests that they like to think they are – receptive to and impressed by the high-status connotations of French cuisine, rather than Anglo-Saxon cookery.

Activity

If your data is rich in interesting language features, then you don't need very much material in order to do a useful analysis. For example, Text: InterCity (an advert for British Rail's 'InterCity' service) itself sets up two contrasting texts as part of its message – one text basing itself on notions of speech, and the other on written language.

Explain how the two parts of this advert work. Note: the original advert included two images: above 'Flat out on the outside' was a drawing of a train rushing through landscape; in the middle of 'Laid back on the inside' was a drawing of a dozing female face.

There is no commentary on this activity, but working on this text will form a good bridge between this unit and the one on spoken discourse that follows.

238

Flat out on the outside.

London 2.55pm you've got to get to Edinburgh in a hurry so you board the new InterCity 225 at Kings Cross and Britain's fastest train races out of the station and the grey of North London becomes the green of Hertfordshire and surely this can't be Peterborough already but yes it is or rather yes it was because you're off again and this is your driver speaking we are now flying at a height of 6 feet above the ground at speeds up to 125 mph and countryside rushes past a blur of green and gold fast forward to York don't blink or you'll miss the historic Minster all aboard and once again you're going flat-out across Yorkshire's hills and dales with no roadworks radar-traps or flashing blue lights to stop you and the cars in the fast lane on a motorway race past you backwards coming soon to a window near you Newcastle phew its a wonder you don't need seat belts on this train and the Northumberland coast is clear and you sprint along beside the sea to picturesque Berwick and one day you decide you'd like to stay here longer but not today and you're in Scotland now don't take the high road or the low road take the railway and you'll be there before anyone because time waits for no man except you travelling on the InterCity 225 it's now three hours fifty nine minutes since you left today this must be a record welcome to Edinburgh.

Laid back on the inside.

London, 2.55pm.

You have to get to Edinburgh, but you want to enjoy travelling there as much as arriving there.

So you board the new InterCity 225 at Kings Cross.

The whistle goes and Britain's most comfortable train glides effortlessly out of the station.

(Do trains still run on rails, you wonder, or cushions of air?)

You sink slowly back into your seat (ahh bliss) and look around.

While the world rushes past outside, it feels unusually tranquil inside.

The effect of the soft lighting, muted colours and tinted glass.

Even the electronic doors at either end slide to and fro with a soothing shhhhhh.

What was it you were worrying about just a few minutes ago?

Funny, you can't remember.

Time to wander along to the buffet, perhaps.

Relax, the buffet comes to you, courtesy of a steward with a trolley.

Coffee? Tea? Orange Juice?

Sandwiches? Friendly repartee?

A sense of well-being now begins to fill you and you start to unwind, as if you were starting a holiday.

Here in the sanctuary of the InterCity 225, you have plenty of something that normally you have precious little of.

Time to yourself and peace and quiet in which to enjoy it.

You can read the paper from cover to cover, for once.

Compose a long overdue letter to Auntie Mary in New Zealand.

Practise transcendental meditation.

Or just sit back and enjoy the view, while we change the scenery.

Here, life seems wonderful indeed.

At some point you must have passed Peterborough, York, Newcastle and Berwick.

Because you arrive at your destination, three hours fifty nine minutes after you left Kings Cross.

Far too soon.

Oh, if only you were travelling further than Edinburgh.

INTERCITY

Answers to activities

Statements (p. 169)

Texts: A = romantic fiction book 'blurb'; B = advert; C = recipe.

A

Melodie Neil and Jed Martin were old friends.

She knew that he loved her – in a calm settled way rather than any grand passion – and that he would make her a good, kind husband.

In short, when she became engaged to him she knew exactly what she was doing.

So she hated it when that infuriating Keith Scott seemed to go out of his way to suggest that her heart wasn't in the affair.

B

Do you feel that you never get a fair slice of the capital cake?

We do, too.

That's why we created 'Portfolio', a brand new concept in saving.

Portfolio is a high interest investment account that makes your money work for you, while still giving you instant access to your capital.

So that way, you can have your cake and eat it too.

C

Wash and core the apples, taking care to remove all pips.

Slice finely.

Put them into a fireproof dish with the water, and a tablespoon of the sugar.

Ensuring that the lid is tightly sealed, put the dish into a preheated oven, Gas Regulo 6.

Reduce temperature to 3 after 10 minutes.

Allow the fruit to steam in its own juice for a further 15 minutes.

Spoon out the cooked apples and arrange them attractively in rounds on a serving plate.

Mix juice with the brandy, mulled wine, and rest of the sugar.

Pour over the top, and serve with double cream.

Occupations (p. 172)

The vehicle was seen proceeding down the main street in a westerly direction = police force

Leading to a spacious and well-appointed residence with considerable potential = estate agency

She went to work, mixing up the six-ten with two parts of 425, and dabbing the mixture through 6 ezimeshes = hairdressing

'This one has a fine shaggy nose and a fruity bouquet with a flowery head', she said = winetasting

He managed to get into a good position, just kissing the cushion = snooker

He said 'Just pop up onto the couch and we'll see what we can do' = medical profession

She pulled down the menu, chose the command by using the cursor, then quit = computers

She said to knead well, roll into a ball and leave overnight to rise = baking

Instead, he mulched well, turned over and left the beds to settle = gardening

Good progress made, but concentration sometimes rather poor; more effort required if success is to be expected in the important months ahead = teaching

Voice (p. 222)

Possible rewrites:

The car was driven quickly away from the scene of the crime. The safe had been blown open, the security guard had been shot and left for dead. Emergency services were called and the guard was comforted until their arrival.

A group of 40 people were surveyed on their attitudes to alcohol. Most of the people surveyed were found to drink more than the recommended level of alcohol per week.

If a mortgage is taken out, the house will be repossessed if monthly payments are not kept up. The building society must be informed if late or reduced payments are going to be made at any time.

Text and context
Spoken discourse

The aim of this unit is to demonstrate that, just as written discourse has rules which govern its form and help convey meaning, so too does spoken discourse. These rules have one major difference, however, from the rules which govern written texts, and that is that we are largely unaware of them. In fact in two-way conversations we are unconsciously taking part in a script which hasn't been written yet. As we improvise our way to sharing an experience, explaining ourselves, getting information, telling a joke or even spreading gossip we are negotiating time with our respondent in which to speak, knowing when we have a signal to take a turn in speaking and supporting the other speaker during his/her turn.

Spoken discourse exists within a social context, and this unit aims to use everyday **speech events** as a starting point from which to recognise that while we may not speak in words, sentences and paragraphs, we do have rules to follow, though they can be broken just as the rules of syntax can be. It's important to realise that spoken discourse should not be judged using the rules of written English: terms such as 'word', 'sentence' and 'paragraph' above, all come from the study of writing. The written form is not an appropriate medium for oral language but, of course, in order to properly analyse speech we need to see it on paper.

Having signposted some of the features of speech events, this unit will then consider one-way discourse such as storytelling and speeches; it will go on to explore the features of dialogue, and will conclude with an examination of how the speech of some social groups is represented on the page.

Contents

Texts used include

- ◎ Personal writing
- ◎ Oral narratives
- ◎ Public speeches
- ◎ Extract from a language work book
- ◎ Spontaneous face-to-face conversation
- ◎ Telephone conversations
- ◎ Computer chat-room logs

Speech events

Imagine how the conversation might go as you take your leave of someone after having had dinner at their house. You might signal your intention of leaving by some line such as 'I must be going', you might express gratitude for the meal, you might say thank you, you might praise the excellence of the food, you might suggest a return visit to your place, the conversation might drift back to an earlier topic or even start a completely new one, you might say thank you again, and then you embark on the 'goodbyes' and 'goodnights' before finally going. In such a situation or speech event as this English speakers will be unconsciously following rules whose purpose is to express thanks, reinforce relationships, leave on good terms and allow a suitable length of time between first suggesting you must go and actually going. Saying you must go and then immediately fleeing the house would be considered inappropriate and rude – certainly in British culture. Conversation, then, exists within a social context and this context determines the shape of the discourse.

Activity

Consider possible interactions in the following speech events. What do you think the rules are that govern discourse here? And what would break the rules?

- Customer–hairdresser conversation
- Introductions
- Answering the phone and signing off
- Recording answerphone messages – both outgoing and incoming
- Phoning for an appointment at the doctor's

Conversation, however, is not always clear-cut, and sometimes a breakdown in communication occurs because intention is misunderstood. What the speaker intends but what the listener hears has informed much of Deborah Tannen's work on gender and conversation (1992). She cites, for example, the case of the woman who had just undergone surgery to have a lump removed from her breast. She tells her female friends that she found it upsetting to have been cut into, and that the operation had left a scar and changed the shape of her breast. Her friends replied: 'I know. It's as if your body has been violated.' But when she told her husband, he replied: 'You can have plastic surgery to cover up the scar and restore the shape of your breast.'

She felt comforted by her friends' comments, but upset by what her husband said. Her friends gave her *understanding* but her husband reacted to her complaint by giving *advice*. His intention was to offer help, but what his wife heard was him telling her to undergo even more surgery.

Intention lies behind a range of specific utterances called **speech acts**. When someone says, for example:

I apologise
I promise
I do (at a wedding)

245

s/he is doing something *beyond* what's being said. By saying 'I apologise', for instance, s/he has performed an apology; there has been a change in the state of things, an act has been carried out. Speech acts are particularly prevalent and important in the language associated with ritual and ceremony. Here speech acts may contribute to the accepted rules or code of conduct or order that a ceremony has to follow; they often also have legal status. Saying 'I *do'* at the appropriate moment in a wedding ceremony – assuming you meet all the other criteria, being the bride or groom, for example; the choir boy or organist shouting out 'I do!' doesn't count – will get you married in the eyes of the law. The minister also confers legal status when s/he announces 'I *name* this child . . .'; the judge when s/he declares 'I *sentence* you to two years' imprisonment'.

Saying, then, is doing and doing is performing. Speech acts are involved in lots of everyday conversation and a simple test to check if an utterance *is* a speech act is to put the words 'I hereby' in front and see if it makes sense. So:

I hereby apologise
I hereby promise
I hereby do take

make sense, but 'I hereby know you' doesn't.

Several attempts have been made to classify the thousands of possible speech acts in everyday occurrence. Perhaps the most useful has been made by Searle (1969) who has suggested five groups:

Representatives: the speaker is committed, in varying degrees, to the truth of a proposition, e.g. 'affirm', 'believe', 'conclude', 'report'.
Directives: the speaker tries to get the hearer to do something, e.g. 'ask', 'challenge', 'command', 'request'.
Commissives: the speaker is committed, in varying degrees, to a certain course of action, e.g. 'bet', 'guarantee', 'pledge', 'promise', 'swear'.
Expressives: the speaker expresses an attitude about a state of affairs, e.g. 'apologise', 'deplore', 'thank', 'welcome'.
Declarations: the speaker alters the status quo by making the utterance, e.g. 'I resign', 'you're offside', 'I name this child', 'you're nicked', 'you're busted punk'.

(Note: there is no commentary on this activity.)

Activity

Look at the following examples: which group does each belong to?

insist
congratulate
I now pronounce you husband and wife
vow
deny

(For answer and commentary on this activity, see p. 305.)

Activity

Read the commentary on the previous activity on p. 305 and then try a similar gradient from direct to indirect speech act:

1   *Asking* someone out on a date
2   *Requesting* someone to stop talking in the cinema.

Extension

1   Exploring the style and pattern of everyday speech events can prove valuable, fruitful and interesting. Consider also whether different ethnic groups follow different rules in some situations. Also can gender or age play a part in what happens? How does gender play a part on the phone, for instance? These questions are taken up in the final section of this unit.
2   Alternatively consider examining the ritualistic language of ceremonies such as weddings, baptisms, funerals. Oscar, Britpop, Booker Prize or similar award-winning ceremonies or the language of the courts are also areas fertile for investigation.

(Note: there is no commentary on this activity.)

Storytelling

SPOKEN VERSUS WRITTEN

This section will draw on two real spoken stories in order to highlight some of the common features of the oral narrative. Jonathan's story is about a car crash on the M4; Esther's is about travelling in a plane which is struck by lightning. Text: Jonathan's story (1) gives the openings of his story, one the spoken version and the other a written version. Which is which? (To make them appear the same on the page slashes have been used instead of conventional punctuation.)

Activity

Having spotted which is the spoken version take a few minutes to jot down some of the ways it differs from the written one.

Text: Jonathan's story (1)

Extract 1

sometimes I think I'm lucky to be alive / I can't help enjoying really simple things because all the time I'm telling myself that I could be dead instead / once for instance I could have died on the motorway / it was the beginning of my second term of my second year at university / I had spent Christmas with my parents / dad took me to the railway station in Kidderminster / I had to go to Birmingham and then change for Reading / as he shook my hand a yellow Ford drew up / my friend Paul was in it / he smiled roundly and said he had the day off so he'd drive me back to university / I accepted

Extract 2

right well um the whole thing happened er as a result of going back to university one day / this was when I was about nineteen in January 1983 er a friend of mine suddenly turned up er at a railway station my best friend just as I was about to get on the train / back to Reading and said I'll drive you back er I was delighted er partly as it was company and an adventure through half the country / so we started driving back and got desperately lost / we were trying to get back to Reading from just above Worcester we ended up near Bristol

Jonathan Timbers

Commentary

You might have noted the use of words like 'um' and 'er' in the transcription of the spoken version. 'Ums', 'ers', 'erms' are **fillers**. Very common in spoken discourse, they act as pauses, or very often, as in extract 2, they accompany pauses and in effect lengthen the gap between words. In spontaneous speech we are 'thinking on our feet' and the use of fillers allows us to do some forward planning on what to say next. They help to cement ideas together in conversation. Also fillers are often added to the common conjunctions 'and' and 'but'; the pause is then effectively lengthened.

The spoken version seems unnecessarily repetitive, e.g. 'a friend of mine . . . my best friend' and 'I'll drive you back . . . we started driving back'.

The two extracts are reproduced in Text: Jonathan's story (2) in their punctuated and transcribed versions.

Text: Jonathan's story (2)

Extract 1

Sometimes I think I'm lucky to be alive. I can't help enjoying really simple things because all the time I'm telling myself that I could be dead instead. Once, for instance, I could have died on the motorway. It was the beginning of my second term of my second year at university. I had spent Christmas with my parents. Dad took me to the railway station in Kidderminster. I had to go to Birmingham and then change for Reading. As he shook my hand a yellow Ford drew up. My friend Paul was in it. He smiled roundly and said he had the day off, so he'd drive me back to university. I accepted.

Extract 2

right well um the whole thing happened er as a result of going back to university one day (.) this was when I was about nineteen in January 1983 er a friend of mine suddenly turned up er at a railway station my best friend just as I was about to get on the train (.) back to Reading and said I'll drive you back er I was delighted er partly as it was company and an adventure through half the country (.) so we started driving back and got desperately lost (.) we were trying to get back to Reading from just above Worcester we ended up near Bristol

249

The use of a full-stop, in brackets, in a transcription indicates a pause – conventionally of about a half-second duration. Longer pauses of one second, two seconds, three seconds, etc., would be conveyed as: (1), (2), (3), etc.

LABOV'S NARRATIVE CATEGORIES

A comparison of spoken and written forms of the same narrative can be very useful in highlighting some of the ways in which oral narratives work. We expect stories to have a beginning, a middle and an end. Oral stories, however, operate in a different context from that of written forms: attention may have to be attracted from potential listeners and, once attracted, kept. William Labov (1972), in an essay entitled 'The transformation of experience in narrative syntax', posited a six-part structure for a fully-formed oral narrative, based on work he had done on collecting real narratives from New York Black English vernacular culture.

Abstract: signals that a story is about to begin, gets the listener's attention, might ask for permission to tell a story, gives some indication of what the story is about.

Orientation: puts the story into a context, gives the time, place, person(s) involved and situation/activity; the 'when, where, who and what?' of the story.

Complicating action: the main narrative body providing the 'what happened' element of the story.

Resolution: the final events, the 'what finally happened' element.

Evaluation: makes the point of the story clear, suggests why it's worth being told, why it's of interest.

Coda: signals that the story has finished, can also link back to the beginning or return to the present time frame.

With the exception of evaluation, the categories are listed above in the order they would be expected in a typical fully formed narrative. Of course, though, many narratives may lack one or more components or may justifiably have elements which seem to do the work of two components. For example, non-fully-formed narratives may have openings which seem to be both abstract and orientation; or, where stories have been invited by the listener or interviewer, then an abstract would seem

250

to be irrelevant, or even silly. Evaluation can appear at any point in the story and this is represented graphically in the diagram below:

e	v	a	l	u	a	t	i	o	n

abstract	orientation	complicating action	resolution	coda

Activity

Now look back at the very start of each extract in Text: Jonathan's story (2). What do you think Extract 1 is doing that Extract 2 doesn't attempt?

Commentary

The opening of Extract 1 seems to be justifying its existence; it's saying why it's being written, why it's worth reading. Finally, it's giving some idea of what the story is going to be about: almost dying in a motorway crash. The oral narrative of Extract 2 jumps straight into the story and refers to the incident with no specific detail as 'the whole thing happened'. This is the abstract of the narrative.

   The next part of each Extract seeks to establish the *time* that the incident took place; e.g. Extract 1: 'the beginning of my second term of my second year at university . . . [at] Christmas'; and Extract 2: 'going back to university one day . . . when I was about nineteen in January 1983'. Also the *place*; Extract 1: 'the railway station in Kidderminster . . . had to go to Birmingham . . . then change for Reading'; Extract 2: 'a railway station . . . the train back to Reading'. We learn about the *persons* involved; Extract 1: 'parents . . . dad . . . my friend Paul'; Extract 2: 'a friend of mine . . . my best friend'. Finally we are told of the circumstances, the *situation*, i.e. being driven back to university. All these details help to place the story in context and can be labelled orientation.

   The story proper, the 'what happened' element, known as the complicating action, only gets going in Extract 2: 'so we started driving back . . . ', etc.

Activity

Now have a look at another oral narrative, Esther's story, and decide whether the elements in it could be labelled according to Labov's categories. (Note: there is no separate commentary on this text – both Esther's and Jonathon's stories are discussed on pp. 254–5.)

Text: Esther's story

Extract 3

I remember being on an aircraft (.) when I was about five (.) and I was with my parents coming back from a holiday in Greece (.) and would you believe I mean it sounds ridiculous now but the aeroplane was being hit by lightning and um there was an aircraft above and an aircraft below and we were coming back and it was a massive storm and I can't remember a lot of it (.) I was sat with my mum and my father was sat with my sister behind (.) the lights went off and the air hostesses went absolutely wild everyone was strapped in (.)

the pilot explained what was going on but don't panic and there was um a lot of Muslims coming back and they were all saying their prayers and going (.) aiee aiee and I remember a lady standing up and saying we're all gonna die we're all gonna die and this lady stood up and smacked her across the face and said if we're all gonna die we don't want to listen to you and um afterwards I mean 'cos I was really young I didn't realise (.) I realised there was panic going on in the plane and when we actually landed and the pilot came out and said you were very lucky um (.)

it was frightening though very frightening (.) but it doesn't (.) I think it was because I was so young that I've never been frightened of flying (.) never I mean even when I get on an aeroplane now I'm not bothered

Esther Gosnay

The rest of Jonathan's dicing with death is given in Text: Jonathan's story (3) with Labov's labels. A full discussion follows.

most of this is the main body of the story: the *complicating action*

on the way we managed to park for five minutes er it was a queue of traffic lights (.) and we also tested y'know one or two of the beers of the local area er y'know we found a really good one called Wadsworth Six erm

on the way on the M4 we eventually managed to find the M4 to drive up to Reading again having driven about 100 miles out of our way (.) er Paul managed to switch the heating on the car really high (.) er

and we were travelling about 70 and I suddenly noticed we were beginning to creep onto the hard shoulder (.) *and I couldn't actually believe that I mean I couldn't drive my dad had always driven me nearly everywhere basically apart from a couple of wild nights when I was 17* (.)

and the idea that cars weren't on rails somehow suddenly struck me as unbelievable (.) and er I suddenly realised we were coming off the road (.) and at that point Paul woke up and he then corrected but he over-corrected and so instead of going over the hard shoulder we headed towards the central barrier of the M4 at 70 miles per hour (.) er we hit that (.) er we then proceeded to flip over it (.) into the fast lane of the other carriageway (.) erm

I remember thinking (.) *oh shit and having this mental image of y'know steps up to heaven and I think I remember thinking oh shit this is really unoriginal* (.) and as we flipped over the central barrier my head went out to the side window and I wasn't wearing a seat belt *as the seat belt rules hadn't quite come in yet* er we then (.) the top of the car hit the fast lane of the other carriageway and I was sort of half way out and half way in the car (.)

it was really interesting when you go outside the window because the air pressure suddenly changes in your ears and I went through so hard it really didn't do too much damage to my face er but I managed to sort of bang the back of my head on the hard shoulder as we flipped over at 70 miles per hour (.)

I also recognised that the car was about to roll on top of me (.) and sort of sever my head (.) so I managed to push myself out and sort of my arms suddenly developed this incredible strength and just pushed myself out the side window (.)

erm I couldn't really see at all *and had there been any traffic coming immediately on the hard shoulder course I'd be knocked over and crushed but* erm er I was in a complete daze and started looking for my glasses which had

except: *evaluative commentary* = a comment by the speaker on the events

complicating action = series of narrative clauses, ordered chronologically, with verbs in the simple past

except: *embedded speech* = the classic form might be: 'this is it!'

been flung in the middle of the motorway (.) the first car that came was a staff nurse off duty and she bundled me into the back of the car and took me to the nearest hospital (.) which er turned out to be a sort of rather nice cottage hospital but I got put in the senile ward (.) so I kept on getting well the few times I managed to get to sleep getting woken up at like midnight by *somebody shouting bring the pisspot nurse or no not the injection I know what those injections are for* (.)

dramatized re-enctments = acting out a story, giving a performance

er I did actually manage to get to sleep for I think for about half an hour that night and as soon as more or less after half an hour some nurse came through and shone a bright light in my eyes to see y'know to see if my vision was working (.) *by that night it had come back* and a very strong image even now of being wheeled through on casualty not really being able to see anything but *thinking well at least I'm alive even if my eyesight's like this for the rest of my life*

resolution = the final event

coda = signals that the story has ended, may also include evaluation

Commentary

Evaluation covers anything which is not strictly narrative, anything above and beyond the 'blow-by-blow' account of what happened; it's anything which is not strictly necessary in relating the events, the 'we did this and then we did that and this happened and then that happened'. It is of course pervasive in most narratives (and sometimes the most interesting element) and it takes many forms. The two broad areas most useful for us to consider can be labelled evaluative commentary and embedded speech.

Perhaps the most common form, evaluative commentary, as the term suggests, is a comment by the speaker on the events. An example of this occurs early in Esther's narrative even before the story proper starts:

and would you believe I mean it sounds ridiculous now

where she takes momentary time off from the story proper to underline her assertion that the aeroplane she was travelling in was being hit by lightning and she also uses this comment to deflect any doubting listeners. It's as if she's saying 'Yes I know all this sounds a bit far-fetched or exaggerated, but it really happened!'

Jonathan does something similar in his car-crash story. With the car in which he was travelling drifting out of control, he offers the frank admission that

> the idea that cars weren't on rails suddenly struck me as unbelievable.

Evaluative commentary can also add extra interesting information. As Jonathan crashes and is forced through the car window, he comments:

> it was really interesting when you go outside the window because the air pressure suddenly changes in your ears.

Also under this heading you might find comments such as:

> I really thought my number was up

or any other idiomatic expression meaning impending death. Any comment, too, which aims to underline the seriousness of the situation, such as:

> we were very lucky; or
> two seconds later and it would have hit us

can be considered as evaluative commentary.

Another form of these 'time outs' from the bare bones of the story is embedded speech; this may well add interest too, and heighten the dramatic presentation of the story. The classic form would be:

> I said to myself, 'This is it!'

Of course in reality such clichéd responses are rare. But any words articulated as direct speech, indirect speech or even left as thoughts would count as evaluation. We find an example at the end of Esther's story:

> when we actually landed and the pilot came out and said you were very lucky,

and, on collision course at 70 miles per hour for the central barrier, Jonathan tells us:

I remember thinking (.) oh shit and having this mental image of y'know steps up to heaven and I think I remember thinking oh shit this is really unoriginal.

A further point on embedded speech is worth making. Labov does not regard speech as part of the narrative core; he only counts what is done rather than what is said. This may be problematic, however. It may well be difficult, if not impossible, to divorce some speech from the narrative flow as if it just doesn't contribute to 'what happens'. Obviously the pilot's comment above *is* outside of what is essentially happening: the plane being hit by lightning; the events would have happened anyway. But there will be cases when the speech *is* part of what happens and does precipitate events, bring things to a head, or whatever; we may be driven to action by what someone says. To take a well-known example from the world of film, surely Dirty Harry's taunt to the gunman he's facing of 'Make my day, punk!' *does* influence the action and cannot, therefore, be considered extraneous or unnecessary to the plot. It seems, then, sensible to differentiate between speech which is central to the core of the story and speech which is not. Dirty Harry's speech, therefore, would be complicating action, and the pilot's comment would be classed as evaluation.

Relevant to this, it seems sensible, too, to consider at this point the work done by Wolfson (1982) on storytelling as dramatised re-enactments. She writes:

> When a speaker acts out a story, as if to give his audience the opportunity to experience the event and his evaluation of it, he may be said to be giving a performance.

Wolfson also draws attention to dramatised categories which seek to provide a more vivid and involving experience of that story, while exploiting special performance features as resources for highlighting the story's main point. Further examples from Esther's story seem more accurately described as dramatised re-enactments rather than the more general term embedded speech:

> the pilot explained what was going on but don't panic; and

> a lady standing up and saying we're all gonna die we're all gonna die.

The highlight of her storytelling performance:

> they were all saying their prayers and going . . . aiee aiee

illustrates two more of Wolfson's categories: expressive sounds, and motions and gestures.

1   Write a linguistic analysis of the narrative in Text: Jessica's story. In the process consider how helpful Labov's categories are; and focus on the role of the embedded speech/dramatised re-enactments in the story.

2   The narratives given by Jonathan and Esther were in response to the question: 'Can you tell me of a time when you were in a life-threatening situation?' Jessica's story, on the other hand, centres around a friend's discomfiture. Collect a range of narratives – e.g. when someone's life was in danger, a story about someone you know, a funny story. Do they follow the same structure? Does the nature of the narrative influence the relative importance of each category?

3   Compare spoken and written versions of the same narratives. It's better to ask for a spoken version first; then having got that on tape ask your informant if s/he would give you a written version. It's also more interesting to choose informants from different backgrounds and of different ages.

Text: Jessica's story

well Gabriel (.) who's a little on the impulsive side (.) met this bloke when she was sixteen (.) moved in with him the next day but that's beside the point (.) she met this bloke on Saturday night (.) he said ooooh come out to the pub like on Sunday lunchtime (.) so she went out (.) started drinking with this sort of rugger-bugger type (.)

so eight pints later she was in the curry house like this (.) and she funnily enough she slumped over her chicken tikka or whatever (.) and erm what they did all these ten blokes hid round the corner like in the kitchen of the curry house and they got the manager to come and wake her up and say all your mates have gone (.) you've got a hundred quid bill (.) you've got to pay (1) she'd only met this bloke the night before (1)

and she was going like (.) oh my God I haven't got anything here (.) take my jewellery (.) take my watch (.) I'll (.) I'll come back with the money as soon as I've been to the bank later (.) he was going no no I'm not going to let you leave the premises (.) I'm going to call the police (.) all this sort of stuff (1)

anyway they waited till she was on the point of hysterics and they all came out going ha ha what a good joke (.) like this (.) it's not a very nice story is it (.) she's still with him (.) that's four years later (.) and that's his bloody nicest feature (.) that's the nicest story she can tell about him

Jessica Gardner

Speeches

Scripted speech, like the oral narrative, is normally 'one way', that is once the speaker has the floor s/he continues until the end of the speech is reached and the normal rules of co-operation in conversation don't apply or, at least, don't operate in the same way. Of course this is not to say that speakers aren't interrupted, supported or even heckled; indeed in some contexts audience response is expected or even encouraged. The stand-up comic may thrive on feedback or incorporate it into his/her routine; the Prime Minister needs to deal with it at Question Time. That notwithstanding, the scripted speech is composed before delivery and skilful speakers, or their speech writers, use certain rhetorical structures to help them in what is normally the prime aim of a speech and that is to convey a message and convince the audience of a point of view.

Activity

Look at these three examples. Try and say what makes them memorable.

> 1   that's one small step for man
> one giant leap for mankind
>
> 2   to be or not to be
> that is the question
>
> 3   I came
> I saw
> I conquered

Commentary

The quotability of a speech can be very important, and speakers may make great efforts to construct what we now term as 'soundbites', short, pithy, sometimes witty chunks of language which catch the ear and the imagination of the media and, through them, the attention and memory of the public.

1   Neil Armstrong's classic two-liner – 'that's one small step for man / one giant leap for mankind' – as he became the first human to walk on the moon has a balanced structure where the second line mirrors the first. There are three clear links between the lines: small–giant, step–leap, man–mankind. This rhetorical structure where two groups of words are closely related to each other – in meaning and form – is called a contrasting pair.

2   Hamlet's lines 'to be or not to be that is the question' are perhaps a more obvious example of another contrasting pair. Here the contrast is more black and white and the two key words 'to be' are actually repeated, giving almost total symmetry to the line.

3   The structure of 'I came, I saw, I conquered' is known as a three-part list.

Both contrastive structures and three-part lists are very common in public oratory. But note also that lists of three do seem to feature largely in popular sayings and folklore, at least in English-speaking culture:

as simple as ABC,
ready, steady, go
blah blah blah

Activity

Read the following excerpts from speeches, identify the structures being used, and comment on the way the utterances work:

1   Never in the field of human conflict has so much been owed by so many to so few (Winston Churchill, 1940, praising the Battle of Britain fighter pilots).

2   Ask not what your country can do for you. Ask what you can do for your country. (John F. Kennedy's inaugural address as US President, 1961).

3   Two thousand years ago the proudest boast was 'civis Romanus sum'. Today, in the world of freedom, the proudest boast is 'Ich bin ein Berliner' (speech made by John F. Kennedy in West Berlin, 1963).

4   I have a dream that one day my four little children will not be judged by the colour of their skin but by the content of their character (Martin Luther King's 'I have a dream' speech, Lincoln Memorial, 1963).

5   Government of the people by the people for the people (Abraham
     Lincoln's Gettysburg address, 1863).

(Note: there is no commentary on these extracts.)

Activity

Read the text below, which is an extract from the speech delivered by Tony
Blair to his party followers at the Royal Albert Hall after being assured of a
large Labour majority in the general election, May 1997.

How is language being constructed here in order to convey a political
message? Pay particular attention to the structures you have just been
studying, but also focus on any other aspects of language you have learned
about during the course of this book – for example, the use of pronouns,
metaphors, sound patterning.

(For commentary on this activity, see pp. 305–6.)

Text: Tony Blair

This vote tonight has been a vote for the future, for a new era of politics in
Britain, so that we can put behind us the battles of this past century and address
the battles of the new century. It will be a Britain renewed, where through
education, technology and enterprise we equip our country for the future in a
different and new economic world. And where we build a nation united. With
common purpose, shared values, with no one shut out, no one excluded, no
one told that they do not matter. In that society, tolerance and respect will be
the order of the day, as we watch our children grow in strength and our elderly
rest easy and secure in old age. That is the country we have wanted for so long.
A Britain whose politics start once again to live up to the finest ideals of public
service. And a Britain that stands tall in the world, whose sense of its future is
as certain as its sense of its own history.

Today, on the eve of this new millennium, the British people have ushered
in this new era of politics, and the great thing about it is that we have won
support in this election from all walks of life, from all classes of people, from
every single corner of our country. We are now today the people's party.

Just because speeches go through a process of careful planning and construction at the pre-delivery stage does not mean that, in delivery, they will seem consciously crafted and calculating. Indeed, the best speeches will appear to express, as if spontaneously, exactly what the speaker intends, in an honest and heartfelt way.

Read through the text below, which is the opening section of the speech made by Earl Spencer at Westminster Abbey in September 1997, as a memorial to his late sister, Diana, Princess of Wales. This speech was rated by many people as very effective and moving (see Montgomery, 1999). Obviously, it's difficult to estimate the effect of what is missing on the page, from the speaker's tone of voice and facial expression to the physical environment of Westminster Abbey itself. However, simply focusing on the words that were spoken, analyse how Earl Spencer uses different aspects of language to pay tribute to his sister.

The transcription markings here are as follows:

/   intonation boundary marker (that is, where the elements inside the slashes were given a particular intonation contour)

(0.7) times in brackets are seconds, or fractions of a second

(.)   indicates a normal length of pause – that is, nothing unusual

       underlined words or parts of words show where particular syllables were stressed

(Note: there is no commentary on this activity. For a detailed discussion of this text, see Montgomery, 1999.)

Text: Earl Spencer's speech

/ I stand before you today / (0.8) / the representative / of a family in grief / (1.0)
/ in a country / (.) / in mourning / (1.0)
/ I before a world / (.) / in shock / (2.0)

/ we are all united / (1.0)
/ not only in our desire / to pay our respects / to Diana / (0.8)
/ but rather / (.) / in our need / to do so / (1.0)
/ but such was her extraordinary appeal / (0.8)
/ that the tens / of millions / of people / (0.6)
/ taking part in this service / (0.5) / all over the world / (0.7)
/ via television / and radio / (0.7)
/ who never actually met her / (1.0)
/ feel that they too / (.) / lost / someone / (.) / close to them / (0.5)
/ in the early hours / (0.8) / of Sunday morning / (1.4)
/ it is a more remarkable / tribute to Diana / (0.7)
/ than I can ever hope / to offer her / (.) / today / (2.3)

/ Diana was the very essence / (0.7) / of compassion / (0.5)
/ of duty / (0.7) / of style / (.) / of beauty / (1.0)
/ all over the world / (.) / she was a symbol / (.) / of selfless humanity / (1.5)
/ a standard bearer ? (.) / for the rights / (.) / of the truly downtrodden / (1.0)
/ a very British girl / (.) / whose con – who transcended / (.) / nationality / (1.0)
/ someone with a natural nobility / (0.7) / who was classless / (1.0)
/ and who proved / in the last year / (0.5)
/ that she needed / no royal title / (.) / to continue to generate / (.) / her particular brand / of magic / (2.0)
/ today / (.) / is our chance / to say thank you / (0.5)
/ for the way in which you brightened our lives / (1.0)
/ even though God granted you / (.) / but half a life / (1.0)
/ we will all feel cheated / (.) / always / (0.5)
/ that you were taken from us / so young / (1.0)
/ and yet / we must learn to be grateful / (.) / that you came along at all / (1.0)
/ only now you are gone / (.) / do we truly appreciate / what we are now without / (1.0)
/ and we want you to know / (.5) / that life without you / (.) / is very / (.) / very / (.) / difficult

Extension

1   Earlier when discussing the structure called the 'three-part list' it was suggested that three as a number seemed an important aspect of folk-lore. Explore the concept of 'three' in a range of texts, for example, fairy stories, religious tales and jokes. If you are familiar with more than one set of cultural traditions, consider whether the number three is commonly referred to cross-culturally.

2   Although the idea of contrasting structures and three-part lists has been discussed with reference to spoken texts, can you find any evidence that these same structures are used in writing? If so, are they used in particular types of writing – for example, writing that is trying to be interactive rather than monologic?

3   Political speeches are readily available from political party headquarters. Analyse them from the page or, if they are being broadcast on radio or TV, consider the speaker's sense of timing and response to applause.

4   Consider how the audience affects the nature of the speech: for example, examine transcripts of speeches made just for broadcast. These include the Queen's Christmas message and party political broadcasts. Speeches given by authority figures forced into resignation can also be very interesting, mixing the personal with the public voice.

Conversation

The analysis of political speeches is part of a long-standing academic tradition termed 'rhetoric', which goes back to Ancient Greece. In contrast, analysing conversation, particularly the kind we might call 'casual', is a relatively recent enterprise. For one thing, the fleeting and transitory nature of much everyday dialogue has eluded our hitherto clunky pieces of recording equipment: it wasn't *that* long ago that tape recorders were heavyweight pieces of reel-to-reel technology that involved bringing the speakers to the machine instead of vice versa. And positioning speakers round a large machine with external microphones has always been a sure-fire way to kill the art of conversation.

Technical problems aside, there are perhaps further reasons why conversation does not have a long analytical tradition. Historically, it has not been considered as highly skilled as, say, delivering a political speech or composing a poem. We seem to have had the idea that 'chatting' was something anybody could do, whereas performing as an orator or poet was a skill possessed only by an elite few. As a result, conversation as a form has been relatively neglected and its practitioners downgraded.

There is now a growing interest in the analysis of so-called 'ordinary' language use, and contemporary research on everyday dialogues has revealed, as you would expect, considerable complexity in how conversation works: just because most people engage in conversational interactions in their daily lives does *not* mean that what they are doing is easy; it *does* mean that they have learned some complex skills that, as mentioned earlier, they are probably unaware of using.

263

When looking at conversation as a whole, the idea of complexity can be explored in a number of different ways. For example, as well as managing to collaborate with at least one other speaker on any one occasion to make meaning, speakers engage in different types of behaviour depending on which sub-genre of talk they are engaged in, and depending on whether the conversation is face to face or mediated by an aspect of technology, such as the phone or the computer. You can sense some of these potential differences just by looking back at this page and observing how many different words have been used to refer to types of talk: dialogue, conversation, casual conversation, chat. Some of these variations will be explored in this section. However, you need to realise that one section of a unit can only be a starting point. There is much more to say about talk than space in this book allows.

Activity

Make a list of all the spoken interactions you have been involved in during the past couple of days, then, working with a partner, try to come up with some categories to enable you to group your examples together. There is no set answer for this activity: its aim is to get you thinking about the various dimensions that affect the type of interaction you have, and also to get you to identify those types of interaction you might call 'conversation'.

Think about the following dimensions:

◎ Is *physical setting* a factor that determines the type of talk you engage in? For example, are there some places where casual conversation seems inappropriate?

◎ How far does the *purpose* of talk affect the way interactions work? For example, does gossip have a different 'shape' from, say, a service encounter in a shop? What about teaching–learning interactions? Would you call any of these 'conversation'?

◎ How far do your spoken interactions vary according to *medium*? For example, how would a face-to-face casual conversation with one of your friends compare with a phone conversation with the same person?

◎ How far does the *relationship between the participants* determine the nature of talk? For example, do you have regular co-conversationalists for informal talk, or can you engage in casual conversation with anyone?

◎ The origin of the word 'conversation' is the Latin *conversari*, 'keep company with'. To what extent is this idea still at the centre of what we call 'conversation', particularly of the casual type?

'REAL' TALK – WHAT IS IT LIKE?

Later in this unit we will be exploring in some detail the idea of how talk has been represented in fictional writing. For now, though, it's important to realise that because ordinary, real talk has been so little researched, we may have notions in our heads about talk that derive more from our experience of made-up dialogues than our real encounters.

Activity

Below are two face-to-face dialogues from a familiar situation – at the hair-dresser's.

The first dialogue would be called a 'service encounter' or 'service trans-action' because it is very goal-oriented (concerned with getting something achieved); the second text is slightly different from this, although in the same setting, because the conversation takes place between two customers, rather than, as in Text 1, customer and stylist.

One of the dialogues is made up, and comes from teaching material aimed at people learning English as a foreign language; the other dialogue is from a real encounter. Can you tell which is which? How do you know?

(For answer and commentary on this activity, see pp. 306–7.)

Text: Hairdressing 1

(A = stylist's assistant; B = customer; C = stylist)
* * = overlapping speech

A: do you want to come over here?
B: right, thanks [3 secs] thank you
A: tea or coffee?
B: can I have a tea, please?
A: do you want any sugar?
B: er, no milk or sugar, just black thanks
C: right
B: I hate it when your hair gets just so, you know a bit *long*
C: *yeah*
B: and it's just straggly
C: right
B: it just gets to that in-between *stage*
C: *yeah*
B: doesn't it where you think oh I just can't stand it any more
    [2 secs] I think when it's shorter it tends to, you notice it
    growing more *anyway*
C: *mm*
B: you know it tends to grow all of a sudden

Text: Hairdressing 2

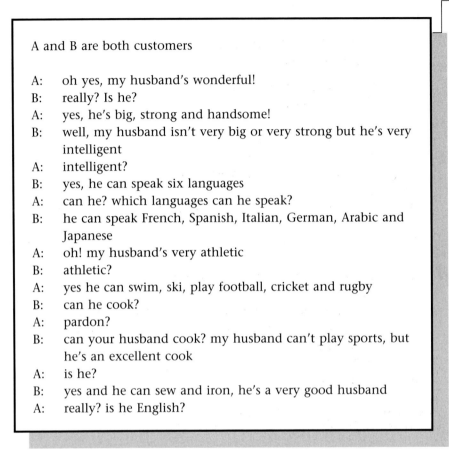

A and B are both customers

A: oh yes, my husband's wonderful!
B: really? Is he?
A: yes, he's big, strong and handsome!
B: well, my husband isn't very big or very strong but he's very intelligent
A: intelligent?
B: yes, he can speak six languages
A: can he? which languages can he speak?
B: he can speak French, Spanish, Italian, German, Arabic and Japanese
A: oh! my husband's very athletic
B: athletic?
A: yes he can swim, ski, play football, cricket and rugby
B: can he cook?
A: pardon?
B: can your husband cook? my husband can't play sports, but he's an excellent cook
A: is he?
B: yes and he can sew and iron, he's a very good husband
A: really? is he English?

CONVERSATIONAL MAXIMS

One area of study that has contributed to our understanding of the assumptions underlying conversation came originally from the discipline of logic and philosophy. This is speech act theory, referred to earlier. An academic figure associated with this school was H. P. Grice, who in 1975 formulated a number of maxims by which he claimed speakers operate in a general sense. Grice posited that conversation was essentially a co-operative enterprise where speakers follow certain unspoken rules that are never spelt out but come to be understood and used as part of the process of language acquisition and early socialisation. He called this the **co-operative principle**, and the associated maxims are as follows:

1   maxim of **quality**: speakers try to tell the truth
2   maxim of **quantity**: speakers give the right amount of information
3   maxim of **relevance**: speakers try to stick to the point
4   maxim of **manner**: speakers try to present their material in an orderly fashion.

Robin Lakoff (1975) added three further maxims which she termed the **politeness principle**:

1   Don't impose
2   Give options
3   Make your receiver feel good.

These scholars were not suggesting that we follow the rules above in any simple way; in fact, just as important in their concept of interaction is the idea that we break the rules as well as keep them. Breaking rules, however, proves that rules exist.

Activity

Below are some expressions that are often heard in conversations. How does each of the expressions show participants' awareness of some of the rules above? Can you add any further expressions like this to the list? (Note: there is no commentary on this activity.)

To cut a long story short
I know you're not going to believe this, but . . .
I'll spare you all the grisly details
Correct me if I'm wrong, but . . .
I know I'm going round the houses here, but . . .
What I forgot to say before was that . . .
I'm not saying we have to discuss this right now, but . . .

Breaking the rules, according to Grice, is a marked activity: it tells us that we need to look for reasons why someone has deviated from what is expected.

Grice calls the process of inference that results from rule-breaking behaviour **conversational implicature**. Rather than being an isolated phenomenon, implicature is at the heart of many of our utterances, including all the language we might call 'non-literal', and much of our humour. For example, metaphor regularly expresses something that cannot be literally true; **hyperbole** rests on wild exaggeration of the truth; and **irony** is all about saying the direct opposite of what you mean.

Activity

Below is the opening of a telephone conversation between participants who know each other well.

How does this conversation illustrate Grice's maxims? Think about:

◎ the operation of implicature, and its role in humour
◎ the way the speakers use ellipsis. How might Grice's maxim of quantity vary according to how well the speakers know each other?

(Note: there is no commentary on this activity.)

Text: Telephone opening

S1 = male speaker
S2 = female speaker

S1:   hello
S2:   hello
S1:   I've died
S2:   what?
S1:   I've died
S2:   what do you mean?
S1:   I've got my Somerset County Cricket club membership through / its annual report / and under obituaries it says / Mr A Nettles
S2:   oh dear
S1:   yeah / unless there's another one / but seems unlikely
S2:   when did you die?
S1:   well it doesn't say / I died in the last year
S2:   I'm going out / with a ghost
S1:   you are / spooky
S2:   full spectral / er yes / so have you got all your fixtures / for the year?
S1:   yep
S2:   gosh
S1:   yep
S2:   do them early / don't they?
S1:   yeah / got my summer holiday sorted out

SEQUENCING IN CONVERSATION

Another area of study that has revealed something of the skill we all employ in understanding conversational practices has come from sociology. An influential figure here was the analyst Harvey Sacks, who is often referred to as the founder of the approach called Conversation Analysis (CA) (see, for example, Jefferson, 1992).

Researchers working in the tradition of CA are interested in how conversation is sequenced: that is, how one element leads to the next and how certain elements can only occur in a particular order. This is termed **adjacency**. For example, a question expects an answer, a greeting calls forth another greeting, a summons may be responded to by an expression of compliance, as follows:

> how are you?
> fine thanks
>
> hello
> hi!
>
> come on Jane, hurry up!
> ok, ok, i'm coming!

This makes conversation appear very simple, but, again, what Sacks and other CA analysts were engaged in was mapping out some of the 'norms' or underlying patterns of conversational routine which are then clearly departed from all the time. For example, the following is a straightforward request–agreement sequence:

> A: will you post this letter for me, please?
> B: ok

but more often than not, we put other utterances between sequences such as the above, for example:

> A: will you post this letter for me, please?
> B: has it got a stamp on?
> A: no
> B: but there's nowhere to buy stamps
> A: there's a machine on the side of the box
> B: have you got some change?
> A: it takes a pound coin, here's one
> B: ok

Such intervening utterances are called **insertion sequences** in CA.

Activity

Schegloff, another researcher working within the CA tradition, has proposed the following routine as that which characterises telephone openings in English-speaking cultures:

summons–answer
identification–recognition
greeting–greeting
initial enquiries

before first topic introduction, usually the responsibility of the caller (Schegloff, 1986).

- **summons–answer:** the ring of the telephone is the summons, and when the called person picks up the receiver, this counts as the answer.
- **identification–recognition:** in English-speaking cultures, the called person is the first to speak. The fact that they do so allows their voice to be recognised by the caller.
- **greeting–greeting:** both speakers exchange greetings, such as 'hello', 'hi', good morning', etc. Speakers don't have to exchange exactly the same words, of course.
- **initial enquiries:** these are about participants' health, general state of things, etc.

Read through the telephone opening below, which is between a student and his/her tutor. The student has phoned the tutor to get some help with an assignment. The tutor has just returned from America.

Which parts of Schegloff's model can you identify, and how do they work? (For commentary on this activity, see p. 307.)

271

Text: Telephone conversation 1

Tutor = Steve
Student = Sam

(Phone rings; tutor picks up the handset)

Tutor: hello
Student: hi Steve / it's Sam
Tutor: hello Sam / hi
Student: how are you
Tutor: I'm alright thanks
Student: have you got over your jetlag yet
Tutor: um / I'm getting there / I still feel a bit strange / but
           I'll probably be alright in a couple of days
Student: yeah
Tutor: it's coming back this way / it seems not to affect me
           going the other way
Student: it's / that's the thing / I can't think of the reason why
           because my brain's so cabbage I can't think / but you
           lose time and it does affect you more coming this way
Tutor: mm / anyway what can I do for you Sam

Activity

Now try the same activity with the data below.

Both speakers are female and know each other well. Heather has phoned Annie for a chat, and to catch up on news because the speakers have not met up for a while.

The phone call opens with Heather laying down a message on Annie's answerphone machine. Then Annie picks up the handset, overlapping with Heather's final 'where are you?'. Heather's repeated 'where are you's are sung.

Make some observations on how the speakers are playing with language routines and features. How typical are these data of phone conversations between close friends, in your experience? (Note: there is no commentary on this activity.)

272

Text: Telephone conversation 2

Heather:	hi Annie / it's Heather / erm / it's quarter past eight / I'm ringing to ring you with / "where are you? / where are you? / where are you? where
Annie:	*hello*
Heather:	*are you?* / hi
Annie:	hi
Heather:	hi hi hi
Annie:	hi hi
Heather:	how are you?
Annie:	I'm very well / I just bought myself a little pair / of Doc Marten sandals
Heather:	aaaaah! / they're good / aren't they?
Annie:	aren't they great? / I'm just admiring my feet
Heather:	oh well what a funny / ni = funny day / to buy them / it's pissing down with rain
Annie:	well / I've been doing some serious shopping / the last few days
Heather:	wow / what have you got?
Annie:	I've bought some luggage / for my holidays
Heather:	oh / right
Annie:	er / what else have I bought? / erm
Heather:	what kind of luggage?
Annie:	things that like / sensible luggage
Heather:	like
Annie:	all the things I've got / are very kind of / squidgy / so I bought / erm / some luggage with hard sides / so you can put clothes in / and they don't get squashed / I'm going to America
Heather:	yeah / I know
Annie:	mm
Heather:	so a suitcase you can have / sit on / that kind of thing
Annie:	yeah
Heather:	right

Other aspects of sequencing in conversation that have been researched are **pre-closings** and **closings**, particularly in telephone discourse.

Pre-closings are those routines where your interlocutor is warned that you are about to leave. This was referred to briefly right at the beginning of this unit (see p. 244–5), where protocols for leaving someone's house were discussed. Pre-closings need to preserve the **positive face** needs of your interlocutor (their need to feel valued), yet satisfy your own **negative face** needs (your right not to be imposed on by someone else). All in all, it's a complicated business, made more complex by the fact that different cultural groups have different rules. **Closings** are the final 'signing-off' routines, where farewells are exchanged.

Activity

Below are some examples of children aged between 3 and 4 years, talking on a simplified telephone system in their nursery classroom (Gillen and Goddard, 2000). They are talking to an adult researcher who is out of sight, in another part of the classroom.

We often think of children as not very able language users compared with us 'perfect' adults, and yet, as you will see, these very young children are going through some of the pre-closing and closing routines that have been described above.

Read each of the data samples and try to describe the various routines that the children are operating, and compare them with your own experience as an adult.

As well as thinking about the two-party talk we engage in on the phone, you might also consider adult behaviour in contexts where we pass the phone on to others who are in our shared physical environment, so that the caller has more than one conversation, sequentially.

It might be useful for you to know that the adult researcher consciously tried not to dominate the conversation in all the phone calls with the children; also, that the children were being videoed while they were using the phone. (For commentary on this activity, see p. 308.)

Text: Telephone conversation 3

K = child (Kirstie); R = researcher

K: yeah
K: right see I go to go now / see ya
R: ok / bye bye
K: bye bye
[K hangs up]

C = child (Callum); R = researcher

C: yeah
R: right
C: bye bye
R: bye bye
C: see you tomorrow
R: ok see you soon
C: um / where do you live?
R: in Burnley
C: bye bye
R: bye bye
C: see you tomorrow
R: see you soon
[C gives phone to another child]

E = child (Edward); R = researcher

E: I / I'm going now
R: ok then
E: I'm coming back on the phone later
R: ok
E: then / come back
[E turns to look at approaching friend who is talking]
E: all right / see you later / see you later
R: ok
[E almost hangs up]
R: bye bye
[E's friend says 'bye bye']
[E brings phone away from its rest and says to friend: 'say hello /
it's a lady']

CMC

CMC stands for 'computer-mediated communication' and refers to all the interactions human beings have via computer terminals.

Although, in the main, computer conversation involves writing, some types of CMC have been likened to spoken language by researchers. For example, 'chatroom' dialogue (often called **Internet relay chat** or IRC) is considered speech-like because it is produced synchronously by participants: that is, people are writing onto the screens of their computer terminals at the same time, with the result that the text is produced quickly, with little time for composition. This fast give-and-take, although nothing like the speed of spoken language, is much quicker and more interactive than traditional forms of writing. (See Werry, 1996, for a more detailed discussion.)

If you have no knowledge of IRC, get some experience of this before you try the next activity. Do this by going to a computer, logging on to the Internet and clicking on any chatroom facility offered by the computer's server. Alternatively, do a search on the word 'chat' and follow one of the links offered.

Activity

Below is a chatroom 'log' of an interaction between two people who know each other outside of the CMC context.

How is this text different from the more traditional forms of paper-based writing?

Would you call any aspects of the text 'speech-like', as the researchers have suggested?

(For commentary on this activity, see p. 308.)

Some useful information

◎ 'cato' and 'regent' are the log-in names of the participants. These names are sometimes referred to as 'nicks'.

◎ In the particular chat facility being used, participants can store a list of their friends. This list is called a 'buddy' list.

◎ When participants are referring to the 'warn button', they are talking about a button by which participants can send each other 'warnings', if they use offensive language. For each warning, the offender in question carries a warning level, expressed in the form of a percentage on their screen. When the person reaches 100%, he or she is 'bounced' automatically from the room.

- Every time a participant sends a message to the screen, the software produces a 'clanging' noise.
- The chat-log has been edited (at the point where . . . occurs) for reasons of space.

Text: Chat-log

cato:	hi buddy!!! :-)
regent:	hiya, wassup?
cato:	I been working SOOOO HARD!
regent:	did you know that your warning level is 0%?
cato:	well when i was on with julia she gave me a 20% warning
regent:	what does it mean?
cato:	if someone misbehaves you can send them a warning
cato:	try it – pretend I said a rude word
regent:	For tea i'm having toad int hole with cabbage
cato:	yum yum you really know how to live well
regent:	you just said a rude word you naughty thing
cato:	what – yum yum?
regent:	no you said to pretend you had said a naughty word so i did
cato:	durrr!
regent:	ok how do you do it
cato:	click on the warn button
cato:	have you died or something?
regent:	all right hold your horses stop rushing me
cato:	sorry ;-)
regent:	SLOW DOWN
cato:	ok, *slow*
regent:	sloooooooow dn
cato:	*sssslllloooowwww*
. . .	
regent:	bye bye everyone, bye bye
cato:	tarra luv!
regent:	good init?
cato:	yeh hehehe
cato:	try a smiley before you go
regent:	i'm off – how do you do smiley
cato:	do a colon dash and right bracket then return
regent:	:-)
cato:	hoorah!
regent:	amazing
regent:	silly tune aint it
cato:	you can go now you passed the smiley test
regent:	bye
cato:	byyyeeee

Extension

1 Research some made-up dialogues in books for foreign learners. If possible, collect some real speech data from the situations proposed in the textbooks, and compare the two sets of data.

2 Research the concept of sequencing and adjacency in some speech from a particular context. For example, it has been suggested (Coulthard, 1992) that the teaching situation often produces three-part exchanges of teacher question, pupil response and teacher feedback. Tape some material from the teaching situation to see whether this pattern is prevalent.

3 Focus on a particular aspect of conversational routine and research its norms and variations, for example, openings or closings in face-to-face, telephone or computer communication. If you are familiar with the routines of another language and culture, you could do a very interesting cross-cultural comparison.

SOME GUIDELINES ON COLLECTING SPEECH

◎ You need to get permission before taping potential informants.

◎ Having got this, and having established the best site for the tape recorder, don't be disheartened if your subjects seem unduly conscious of being recorded, making the early exchanges seem unnatural as spontaneous conversation.

◎ Treat the first few minutes as a 'warm up'; most people will soon forget that a tape recorder or dictaphone is present and relax into 'normal' conversation.

◎ We can never be entirely sure, however, what is 'normal' conversation because once we start to observe or record it we encounter what's known as the 'observer's paradox', that is, how far does the act of observing conversation influence its outcome? Does conversation perform for the observer? Only by recording surreptitiously can we get close to what may be natural conversation.

◎ Having said that, should you inadvertently record someone without him/her knowing beforehand – if, for example, s/he happens to join a group after recording has started – then ask that person's permission to use the material gathered when the recording is over.

◎ Finally, always preserve the anonymity of your informants and change the names.

278

SOME GUIDELINES ON COLLECTING CMC

Participants' contributions to chatrooms and discussion forum spaces belong to them and should be treated in the same way as speech, above. You need to ask permission to use material, and if this is given, you should preserve the anonymity of the contributors. This is particularly important for material from this context because users' locations can be traced if you are sloppy about erasing their details.

SOME GUIDELINES ON TRANSCRIPTION

As you will have noticed in this unit, and perhaps also in your reading of other texts, conventions for the transcription of speech vary considerably. In this unit, the conventions have varied, not because we couldn't make up our minds about which system to use, but because the different sources from which we have drawn our data have themselves used different approaches. The fact is that speech has been researched by people from different academic traditions, and each tradition has its own approach. Also, researchers will mark those features that are important to the research question they are engaged with and not those features that are irrelevant.

So you need to decide yourself which features to mark and how to do it. For example, if you are analysing regional speech, you will need to transcribe at least some of your data using phonemic symbols. However, there are some features that transcribers regularly mark, and they are as follows:

- **Simultaneous speech** (i.e., interruptions and overlaps). The most common way to do this is via either asterisks or square brackets, for example:

  A: *really?*
  B: *are you sure?*

  A: [really?
  B: [are you sure?

- **Pauses.** These are usually marked using round brackets, with a dot for a regular pause (.) and a time in seconds for longer ones (2).

- **Inaudible speech.** This is usually simply described (inaudible).

279

◎ **Intonation.** You will note that in some transcripts in this unit, an intonation boundary marker '/' has also been used. This shows that the words inside the boundary marker were spoken with a distinctive tune. A detailed study of intonation will involve marking intonation units and tunes, but many analysts use a simpler method of marking heavily stressed syllables. Choices here include underlining, capitals or emboldened type, for example:

A: are you <u>sure?</u>
A: are you SURE?
A: are you **sure?**

The representation of talk

So far this unit has focused mainly on what talk is really like when we engage in it on an everyday basis. However, there was some suggestion earlier, when you looked at the made-up dialogue from the English as a foreign language textbook, that we are often presented with constructed versions of talk. Such constructions occur surprisingly frequently: in films and TV programmes, in radio plays, in written texts of all kinds including adverts, newspapers, comics, even in the Bible, talk is presented to us as the result of somebody's creative reconstruction.

The aim of this part of the unit is to consider briefly some of the important issues about the relationship between real and represented talk.

Re-presentation

The first issue to consider is the fact that whenever talk is represented, it is *re-presented* – that is, someone has reworked it. As soon as this happens, effects which are the result of the author's viewpoint and intentions come into play. These intentions may be conscious – the result of deliberate individual decisions – or unconscious – the result of an individual being a member of a certain social group within the larger culture, and learning a particular set of beliefs as part of their socialisation process.

Social groups

The issue of our social-group membership is particularly important when it comes to looking at the representation of talk, because use of language is one of the ways in which we mark out our social groups, and because we all have strong attitudes to the language of the social groups we define as 'other'. At the same time, the people who have had the opportunity to get their ideas into print and onto the screen have traditionally belonged to the more powerful groups, so their versions of what 'other people's talk' is like may come to be accepted wisdom within the wider culture. As was discussed earlier, the exploration of real talk is relatively recent and, while there is still ignorance about what real talk is like, any artificial representations constructed by more powerful social groups can stand unchallenged, as the truth.

In this section, you will be looking at how the spoken language of certain social groups is often represented. These groups are based on the following dimensions: gender; region (and social class); ethnicity. In each case, you will be considering questions about whose viewpoint may be behind representations of spoken language.

GENDERISED TALK: REAL AND REPRESENTED

Studies on language and gender have sought to cast light on people's real experiences of how men and women converse, both in single-sex and mixed-sex groups, in order to investigate the stereotypes we have in our culture – stereotypes such as the trivial, chattering, nagging woman and the strong, silent, long-suffering man. These stereotypes are constantly shored up by a whole range of representations, exemplified by Text: Pub sign and by jokes such as Text: Matchbox jokes.

281

Text: Pub sign

Text: Matchbox jokes

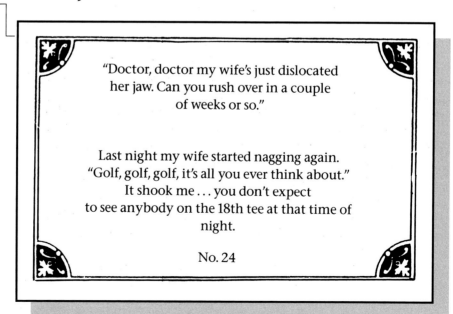

"Doctor, doctor my wife's just dislocated
her jaw. Can you rush over in a couple
of weeks or so."

Last night my wife started nagging again.
"Golf, golf, golf, it's all you ever think about."
It shook me . . . you don't expect
to see anybody on the 18th tee at that time of
night.

No. 24

Such representations are part of a larger picture we have in our culture about how men and women behave: language is one form of behaviour, and we have all sorts of ideas about other forms of behaviour, too. But whose viewpoint is encoded by such stories about the sexes?

Note: see satellite text: *Language and Gender*

Activity

Look back at the pub sign and the jokes, and turn the viewpoint around in them by substituting a male figure for the female in the first, and switching the roles of the male and female figures around in the second: what would be the difference in effect?

Commentary

Turning the texts around reveals the ideology lying behind them.

If the pub sign had been a male figure, surrounded by the words 'soft words turneth away wrath' and QUIET MAN, the effect would have been very different. In its original version, the pub sign acts as a picture of how women should be: it is an exhortation to women to be meek and mild, with the unstated assumption that women are usually garrulous and strident – so the 'quiet woman' is an impossible ideal, achievable only by cutting a woman's head off; as a male figure, the sign would not act in the same way at all. Because men are not normally seen as talkative (male speech is often seen as the 'norm' from which female talk deviates), the idea of a quiet man suggests something rather unremarkable – although, accompanied by a particular image such as a mysterious cloaked figure, this could call up the idea of a spy or other dubious character.

Turning the jokes around produces some interesting effects, where the idea of female talkativeness is also at the centre of the texts in their original form. Female talk is constructed as verbal harassment, so the idea of the husband capitalising on his wife's enforced silence in the 'doctor, doctor' joke (with the implication that she brought the dislocation on herself, by endless talking) is seen as a form of just revenge by a henpecked man. Because men are not supposed to be talkative, the reversed form of this joke loses its point, and leaving the husband with a dislocated jaw appears simply as an act of cruelty.

The 'golf' joke appears comical when reversed, for different reasons than in the original. In reversed form, the comedy is to do with the unlike-

283

liness of the picture created: a woman on the golf course, at dead of night, her husband leaving the kids at home to go looking for her, fretting and getting frustrated by her obsession with a hobby that takes her attention away from him.

Ideologies lying behind common cultural stories are hard to spot because we learn them as part of early socialisation, and they then just seem 'normal' and 'natural'. But when you stand back from them, you can expose the hidden messages that tell us, as men and women, how to behave.

Activity

So far, we have suggested that in our culture we have ideas about the sexes that are constructed around stereotypes, and that these stereotypes often encode the point of view of those who are in a position to get their meanings publicised. The focus now needs to turn to what our own experiences have been about male and female talk, and how this accords with research on real speech.

Discuss your experiences of the following:

◎   Do females talk more than males, and, if so, when?
◎   Do you think men and women follow different rules when they have conversations?

If so, can you give some examples?

Commentary

Contrary to the stereotype of the female as the 'overtalkative' sex who 'gossips' and 'talks a lot' (as reported by Kramer (1977) who surveyed attitudes in the USA), many studies have now been carried out in Britain and the USA which show that, in a variety of contexts, it is men who talk more. Obviously, age, status and context will affect the amount of talk a participant delivers and how much dominance s/he has. Because of the value of access to talk for achievement in education, and because data is arguably easier to collect, many studies in this area have been carried out in educational contexts, and here boys have been shown to speak more than girls. A typical study by Sadker and Sadker (1985) of over a hundred classes in both arts and science subjects found boys talking on average three times more than the girls. One reason for this seems to be the role played by the teacher: there is evidence, for example, that teachers pay more attention to boys, giving them both disapproval and more encouragement and praise.

284

Another reason for the stereotype of the talkative woman is advanced by Deborah Tannen in *You Just Don't Understand: Men and women in conversation* (1992), where it is claimed that men are trained to become familiar with talking in *public* situations, learning how to hold centre stage through verbal performance such as storytelling, joking and imparting information. Women, on the other hand, are more comfortable with *private* speaking: for them, the language of conversation is more about establishing connections and negotiating relationships. Males might therefore *think* females talk a lot because they hear them talking in situations where men would not, for example on the telephone or in social situations with friends.

This means that the idea of the talkative woman may be a view which encodes male perceptions of how women behave in private, personal contexts. If, in contrast, women were able to express their perceptions of men in the workplace and other public situations, this view might well be of men as 'the overtalkative sex'.

Activity

Contemporary research on language and gender does not suggest that male talk is 'normal' while female talk is 'deviant', nor does it indicate that there is anything intrinsically powerful or powerless about male and female talk, respectively.

What it does suggest is that men and women adopt different conversational *styles* because they are trained to understand and operate spoken discourse differently as a part of being socialised for different roles in society. This approach sees male and female groups as different cultures which, when they are brought together in mixed-sex situations, can clash and cause misunderstandings because the participants are operating different rules.

Below are some examples of the misunderstandings that, according to Deborah Tannen's work (1992), often arise in mixed-sex conversations as a result of men and women following different rules. Read through the examples given, and discuss whether similar examples have occurred in your own experience.

Information and consultation

Tannen suggests that many male–female conversations result in difficulty because men think they are simply exchanging information, while women think they are negotiating. As an example, she quotes a couple who are driving home, when the following conversation takes place:

285

Sue: Would you like to stop for a drink?
John: No.

They don't stop, but when they get home they have an argument: Sue says John never consults her feelings, while John says he never knows what Sue really wants because she doesn't tell him – instead, she expects him to guess.

Tannen suggests that, while John thought he was just being asked for information about his needs, Sue thought her question would be the opening move in a conversational sequence where they each would go through the various pros and cons of stopping and not stopping. A negotiated decision would then arise at the end.

Topic raising, interrupting and reinforcing

Much research has suggested that women do more work in conversation than men to raise topics and to get others to take them up; also that women maintain others' contributions by using reinforcers (saying 'yeah', 'mm', and so on) more than men do. At the same time, men appear to interrupt women more than the other way round.

Tannen suggests that because women are trained to look for connection in their interactions, they make an effort to get others to talk and to equalise speakers' turns, even downplaying their own subject knowledge in the process; in contrast, because men are trained to look for power in their interactions, they compete to control topics – interrupting if necessary – and they work to hold their turn against others' interruptions, even when their own subject knowledge is poor.

When these different discourse rules are operating together, women's contributions are likely to be heard less than men's because men will be trying to take the floor and women will be encouraging them to do it. Neither side is deliberately dominating or giving way – each is simply doing what it has been trained to do within its own gender group.

Reporting and rapporting

According to Tannen, one of the biggest complaints women have about men as talkers is that they don't give enough information when they recount incidents – they leave out all the 'juicy bits' of any story, giving just the bare bones; in contrast, men complain that women give too much information when they tell stories – they go on and on when they could really sum up the content of their discourse in one sentence.

Tannen's explanation of these complaints is that men and women think they are doing different things when they relay information: men concentrate on the information content alone (the 'message') because they see the recounting of incidents as reporting, while women pay more attention to the 'metamessage' – recounting experiences is a way to relate to the listener. Such an approach is termed rapporting.

Problem-solving or problem-sharing?

It seems that men and women also respond differently in conversations when a problem is presented. Because men are trained to be active and find solutions to problems, it is argued, they adopt a problem–solution approach when someone articulates personal difficulties; in contrast, women are encouraged to think of themselves as listeners. While listening is certainly not a passive activity, it doesn't necessarily involve making suggestions about how to change situations or take action. In female 'troubles-talk' women often take turns in comparing difficulties and in finding likenesses between their respective situations; when men share difficulties, they appear to be reassured by their male friend's making light of or dismissing their worries as insignificant.

An example of a male 'problem–solution' approach is given at the start of this unit (see 'Speech events', p. 244), where a man responds with a suggested course of action when his female partner says she feels disfigured after breast surgery.

Now here is an example which presents a male perspective: a man expresses a problem to his female partner. The man expects problem-solution, but receives – to his intense annoyance – problem-sharing:

Peter: I'm really tired. I didn't sleep well last night.
Alison: I didn't sleep well either.
Peter: Why are you always trying to belittle me?
Alison: I'm not! I'm just trying to tell you that I understand how you feel!

Commentary

If you found that you recognised some of the ways that men and women were talking in these examples, it means that you have learnt the rules of talk that society has deemed appropriate for your sex. These different approaches to talk are sometimes called 'scripts'. No-one sits a child down and tells them what their 'script' should be; instead, ways of talking are modelled for children by adults and by countless messages in the culture that surrounds them.

Activity

One type of message is carried in the fictional world of media representation. We are all familiar with the old type of sexist joke considered earlier – so what do some of our more modern advertising texts say about male and female talk? Have things changed very much?

Look at Text: Nibz cartoon, then read through Text: BT advert.

◉ What messages are given in the BT text about male and female talk?
◉ How are these messages conveyed by the way the whole text works? (Consider some of the aspects of language you have studied earlier in this book.)

Text: Nibz cartoon

'It would be cheaper if we bought our own communications satellite ..'

Cartoon by 'Nibz', *Daily Mirror*

Why can't men be more like women?

Men and women communicate differently. Have you noticed?

Women like to sit down to make phone calls.

They know that getting in touch is more important than what you actually say.

Men adopt another position.

They stand up.

Their body language says this message will be short, sharp and to the point.

"Meet you down the pub, all right? See you there." That's a man's call.

Women can't understand why men are so abrupt. Why can't they share the simple joys of talking as other men have:

W. Somerset Maugham, for example: "Conversation is one of the greatest pleasures of life. But it wants leisure."

Or, as another writer said, "The talk of women is like the straw around china. It isn't much, but without it everything would be broken."

Even Winston Churchill believed "Jaw, jaw is better than war, war."

This difference between the sexes becomes somewhat more than academic when the phone bill hits the mat.

Some men have a way of making women feel guilty about it.

Would it help, gentlemen, if you knew the true costs?

That a half hour chat at local cheap rates costs less than half a pint, for example?

Or that a five minute call at daytime rates costs about the price of a small bar of chocolate?

Not so much when you think about it.

Particularly compared with the cost of not talking at all.

BT

It's good to talk.

Commentary

Graphology

The image used in the BT advert takes up two-thirds of the advertising space, and is a very arresting one, for a number of reasons:

1   It resembles pruriently 'censored' soft-porn pictures, where the most offensive parts are blocked out, but leaving enough of the image to titillate the reader/viewer.

2   The 'blocked' question, placed where it is, looks as if it is suggesting that the male body could be adapted to become more 'female'. This is a possible reading because of the use of the word 'be' in the question, rather than 'talk'.

3   There are strong contrasts between the way the man and woman are pictured. The man is standing in a comically regimental posture, with a serious and rather pompous facial expression; he is in the act of listening, rather than speaking. The woman, in contrast, is seated in the style of a model from classical art. This idea is reinforced by the drapery that she is sitting on, by her long, flowing hair, by the voluptuousness of her body, and by the serenity of her expression. Her mouth is a generous one. She could either be speaking or, if listening, she is responding to her interlocutor positively and warmly. It is unclear whether these two figures are speaking to each other, but the oppositions outlined so far are further stressed by the line down the middle of the page – familiar to modern viewers from TV advertising's split-screen contrasts of, for example, the effect of two types of washing powder on clothes, or one housewife racing another to clean the kitchen floor with different products. The centre line here could suggest a broken relationship. These two figures are Adam and Eve-like; but the question running across the page offers the startling proposition that there is something wrong with men rather than women.

4   The intriguing question posed by the blocked text carries echoes of the song sung by Rex Harrison in *My Fair Lady*, where one of the lyrical lines was 'Why can't a woman be more like a man?' Traditionally, 'maleness' has been the norm, from which 'femaleness' has been seen as a deviation. The blocked text therefore challenges received wisdom; the italic type and the use of a question suggests a spoken voice here. Italics are used again for the BT slogan: *It's good to talk*. Since the subject of the slogan is talk itself, it seems appropriate that the spoken medium should be suggested.

The layout of the written text underneath the image is unconventional: neither side of each column is justified, leaving a shape that looks rather loosely organised. Within this, some very short sentences stand alone, for dramatic effect: for example, 'They stand up.'

Vocabulary

The main semantic field in the text concerns communication itself, and terms related to this subject are frequent: communicate, getting in touch, body language, talking, jaw, chat, call, conversation.

The text itself is an 'argument' in the discursive sense, putting forward the idea that women are good at talk, and men are bad.

Vocabulary items reflect this line of argument, with male talk being characterised as oppositional and aggressive: men adopt a *position*, are *abrupt*, their talk is *short*, *sharp* and *to the point*; female talk is associated with relationship and emotional bonding: women get in *touch*, *share* the joys of talking, without female talk *everything would be broken*.

This 'argument' offers a crude and partial rendition of what recent academic research in male and female talk has suggested. The use of the word 'academic' in the third column shows the text trying to substantiate its assertions while also suggesting that sex differences in talk behaviour have real outcomes in terms of cost. The word 'cost' itself refers to two different areas: money (associated with men); and emotional wellbeing (associated with women).

The text contains a number of informal terms which help to create the idea that this text, although an academic 'argument', is speech-like: for example, 'getting in touch', 'when the phone bill hits the mat','have a way of', 'a half hour chat', 'half a pint', 'about the price of'. The persona created by these vocabulary choices, plus certain grammatical structures (see below) is someone who is offering friendly exposition. The voice has a degree of irony: for example, the self-conscious double meaning of 'men adopt another position', with an effect of anticlimax as the text descends from this phrase to the bald and literal 'they stand up'; the use of the word 'gentlemen' is also an ironic selection, being over-formal for the rest of the discourse, and occurring straight after the accusation that some men are mean, being an over-polite description of such tight-fisted men.

Grammar and discourse

Much of this text is written in the form of statements, or assertions, giving the effect of authority and knowledge. Since these statements are written in the present tense, they suggest ongoing timeless truths that pertain to all speakers.

291

The questions in the text all ask the reader about the extent of his/her knowledge, making it appear that the reader has a particular need of the so-called 'facts' being offered.

Some of the grammatical structures suggest spoken language rather than written: for example, the sentences that begin with 'or' and 'that'; the last two sentences, both of which show an ellipsis of thought that often characterises speech. This, coupled with the semantic choices helps to establish closeness with the implied reader, who is being cajoled into a point of view by a 'knowledgeable friend'.

There is a shift in terms of address, moving from an implied general reader of either sex (with 'you') to an implied male reader ('would it help, gentlemen . . .?). The text then finally addresses the part of the audience who are thought to pay the phone bill.

Cohesive ties within the text appear to establish the 'argument' by a system of reference: for example, the 'men' who are ungenerous talkers in the first section are contrasted with 'other men' in the second part of the argument. These 'other men' are not the men who are typically the partners of the women mentioned, but are exemplified initially by two writers who appreciated talk. In the face of such artistic figures, whom male readers might find it difficult to identify with, Winston Churchill provides a reassuringly macho figure. Finally, we are asked to focus, not on 'other men' but on 'some men' – those unpleasant individuals who complain at the size of the phone bill run up by their female partners.

'It', 'that' and 'this' are also used as cohesive ties, and are usefully unspecific for texts which do not want the logic of their arguments scrutinised: the reader is encouraged to make links and therefore help construct the argument. For example: 'that's a man's call'; 'this difference between the sexes'; 'some men have a way of making women feel guilty about it'.

The piece as a whole imitates an academic, discursive text where a point of view is put forward and supported. Quotation is used within discursive writing of this type; here, we are offered two literary figures (one unnamed) and a famous statesman who are used to endorse the idea that, as the BT slogan asserts, 'It's good to talk'. While imitating a piece of discursive writing, this text departs from this genre in a number of important ways: the image used interacts with the verbal text, to give veracity to apparently self-evident assertions about male and female talk; the layout allows for a looser organisation than the usual thematically arranged paragraphs, making the text appear more relaxed, and making it possible for some statements to stand alone, accruing a dramatic timing more usually associated with spoken delivery in speeches; style choices of vocabulary and grammar work together to create a spoken voice for the implied writer/speaker to deliver the 'argument' to the implied reader/listener, who turns out to be male. The assumption is that men pay the bill; so it is in the interest of BT to encourage men to do more talking, as well as to 'allow' their female companions to carry on talking themselves. In the end, arguing that women are good at talking turns out to be neither the subject of an academic enquiry, nor any compliment to women; instead, female talk is seen as exploitable, like any other form of consumer behaviour.

Extension

1   *Represented talk:* Collect as many representations as you can find of male and female talk – for example, in literary texts, adverts, TV programmes – and analyse whether the sexes are seen as talking in different ways.

2   *Real talk:* Compare the way men and women (or boys and girls) conduct single-sex conversations in a particular context – e.g. on the phone, at the hairdresser's, playing a game, solving a problem, running a business meeting. If you want to take this further, you could then go on to compare your findings with what happens in an equivalent mixed-sex context – e.g. girls working together on a computer, compared with boys and girls engaged in the same activity.

Note: see satellite text *Language and Gender.*

THE REPRESENTATION OF REGION, SOCIAL CLASS AND ETHNICITY

It should be clear from Unit 1, 'Signs and Sounds', that speech and writing are very different systems, and that it is very difficult to represent spoken language on the page by using a conventional written alphabet. However, writers of literature often try to do just that, in order to construct the idea of a character from a certain region, social class or ethnic group.

Activity

Read through Text: *Silas Marner* (1861), which is from the novel by George Eliot.

It features a confrontation between an upper-class landowner, Godfrey Cass, and a weaver, Silas Marner, who lives on his estate. Many years previously, Silas Marner had found an abandoned baby, and had brought up the child, Eppie, as his own daughter. The baby was illegitimate – fathered by Godfrey Cass as a result of an affair with a local servant girl, who died from illness and poverty as a result of Godfrey's abandonment. Now that Godfrey and his wife are unable to have any children of their own, Godfrey has decided to come and claim his child, now a teenager.

How does the writer convey the spoken language of Silas Marner and Godfrey Cass? Think particularly about the following:

◎ How are their social class differences marked in the language they use?
◎ What region do you think the book is set in?
◎ How do the spoken language features help create the tension in the dialogue, and establish a point of view for the reader?

Text: *Silas Marner*

'But I've a claim on you, Eppie – the strongest of all claims. It's my duty, Marner, to own Eppie as my child, and provide for her. She's my own child: her mother was my wife. I've a natural claim on her that must stand before every other.'

Eppie had given a violent start, and turned quite pale. Silas, on the contrary, who had been relieved, by Eppie's answer, from the dread lest his mind should be in opposition to hers, felt the spirit of resistance in him set free, not without a touch of parental fierceness. 'Then, sir,' he answered, with an accent of bitterness that had been silent in him since the memorable day when his youthful hope had perished – 'then, sir, why didn't you say so sixteen year ago, and claim her before I'd come to love her, i'stead o' coming to take her from me now, when you might as well take the heart out o' my body? God gave her to me because you turned your back upon her, and He looks upon her as mine: you've no right to her! When a man turns a blessing from his door, it falls to them as take it in.'

'I know that, Marner. I was wrong. I've repented of my conduct in that matter,' said Godfrey, who could not help feeling the edge of Silas's words.

'I'm glad to hear it, sir,' said Marner, with gathering excitement; 'but repentance doesn't alter what's been going on for sixteen years. Your coming now and saying . . . "I'm her father . . ." doesn't alter the feelings inside us. It's me she's been calling her father ever since she could say the word.'

'But I think you might look at the thing more reasonably, Marner,' said Godfrey, unexpectedly awed by the weaver's direct truth-speaking. 'It isn't as if she was to be taken quite away from you, so that you'd never see her again. She'll be very near you, and come to see you very often. She'll feel just the same towards you.'

'Just the same?' said Marner, more bitterly than ever. 'How'll she feel just the same for me as she does now, when we eat o' the same bit, and drink o' the same cup, and think o' the same things from one day's end to another? Just the same? that's idle talk. You'd cut us i' two.'

Commentary

Godfrey Cass speaks in Standard English, while Silas Marner uses regional forms of language. While it is never explicitly stated where the book is set, the physical descriptions suggest the newly industrialised cities of the north Midlands. There is nothing in the actual language of the characters that tells us this – the alterations of the spellings and the various pieces of vocabulary and grammar could represent a number of different regional accents and dialects:

> i'stead o', out o', o' the, i' two
> sixteen *year,* the same *bit,* it falls to *them as* take it in.

What the reader does when reading this type of material is to create an appropriate voice in their own head, to fit the region where the book is set and the social class of the respective characters. For Godfrey Cass, this would probably involve the reader creating an RP-sounding voice, since this is associated with middle- and upper-class speakers. Beyond specifically regional features of language, George Eliot has also chosen a particular style of speaking for the two characters: where Silas's language involves many expressions which describe or connote emotion – for example, 'turned your back on her', 'take the heart out o' my body', 'cut us i' two', 'blessing', 'love' – Godfrey Cass's language relates more to ownership and responsibility – 'claim', 'own', 'duty' – and is more formal and politely euphemistic: 'I've repented of my conduct in that matter'. As a result, where Silas Marner is constructed as a warm, straightforward man, Godfrey Cass appears very cold and shifty. These ideas very much support our stereotypes of regional speakers as warm-hearted, while RP-speaking, Standard English users are often constructed as cold and untrustworthy, despite the status accorded them as speakers of a prestige language variety.

The reader is clearly expected to be on Silas Marner's side – there's nothing quite like the honest, working-class hero standing up to the forces of capitalist hypocrisy to raise a cheer from modern readers. The plot there-fore positions the reader to a large extent; but the dramatic tension in this particular scene owes much to the language spoken by the characters, given even more force by George Eliot's 'stage directions'.

George Eliot was doing something rather revolutionary in presenting a working-class figure who uses regional language as the hero of her book. Traditionally, such figures were only allowed to feature as comic characters, faithful servants or villains, and their dialect acted as a signal to the reader to call up expectations of comedy, martyrdom or dirty deeds. They weren't supposed to be 'real people'.

Collect some examples of regionally accented characters from a specific type of text – for example, novels, TV drama, advertisements, comics (e.g. *Viz*). How far are the characters being presented as stereotypes, and how far as complex people with individual characteristics? If they are stereotyped, are certain accents and dialects associated with particular traits? What aspects of regional language are used to convey the idea of regional speech?

If the representation of working-class, regionally accented speakers has been traditionally as figures of comedy, servitude or crime, then that is doubly true of black characters who use a language variety such as Afro-Caribbean Creole (also called Patwa). This type of language has often been presented as a form of 'broken English', with the inference that the speaker is ill-educated and unintelligent, in need of instruction from, and the protection of, figures from white culture: generations of young readers until the 1960s, for example, grew up on comics which conveyed this message, while 'classics' such as *Robinson Crusoe* encode the same ideas.

Read through Text: *Robinson Crusoe* (1719), from the novel by Daniel Defoe.

Before the start of the passage, the narrator has shown Man Friday a boat he built some years previously, in an attempt to escape from the island. The passage then portrays a conversation between Robinson Crusoe and Man Friday, about the possibility of building another boat and going to Man Friday's own country.

What picture is given of Man Friday, and how does his language contribute to that picture?

297

Text: *Robinson Crusoe*

Upon the whole, I was by this time so fixed upon my design of going over with him to the continent, that I told him we would go and make one as big as that, and he should go home in it. He answered not one word, but looked very grave and sad. I asked him what was the matter with him? He asked me again, Why you angry mad with Friday? What me done? I asked him what he meant? I told him I was not angry with him at all. No angry? says he, repeating the words several times; Why send Friday home away to my nation? – Why, says I, Friday, did you not say you wished you were there? – Yes, yes, says he, wish be both there; no wish Friday there, no master there. In a word, he would not think of going there without me. I go there, Friday! says I; what shall I do there? he returned very quick upon me at this: You do great deal much good, says he; you teach wild mans be good, sober, tame mans; you tell them know God, pray God, and live new life. – Alas! Friday, says I, thou knowest not what thou sayest; I am but an ignorant man myself. – Yes, yes, says he, you teachee me good, you teachee them good. – No, no, Friday, says I, you shall go without me, leave me here to live by myself, as I did before. He looked confused again at that word; and running to one of the hatchets which he used to wear, he takes it up hastily, and gives it to me. What must I do with this? says I to him. You take kill Friday, says he. What must I kill you for? said I again. He returns very quick, What you send Friday away for? Take kill Friday, no send Friday away. This he spoke so earnestly, that I saw tears stand in his eyes; in a word, I so plainly discovered the utmost affection in him to me, and a firm resolution in him, that I told him then, and often after, that I would never send him away from me, if he was willing to stay with me.

Commentary

The book is set in the South Seas, so in reality, Man Friday would have spoken a Polynesian language. However, there is no sense of this, as the focus of the narrative is all on Robinson Crusoe's experiences and perceptions rather than on Man Friday's life – the latter even has no name of his own, only the name given to him by his white 'master' (who first encountered him on a Friday). The book assumes the rightness of the white character imposing all the values of white society, including language, on the black character: Man Friday is expected to learn English but there is no suggestion of Robinson Crusoe learning any Polynesian; Man Friday is 'converted' to Christianity, rather than Crusoe learning any interesting new religious beliefs. In the end, the novel reflects the eighteenth-century culture which gave rise to it.

The point of this passage is to demonstrate two main ideas: the good character of Robinson Crusoe, and the devotion of Man Friday to his white companion. Crusoe's character is depicted as modest and humble via his quizzing of Man Friday, protesting as he does so that he is an unworthy moral leader; in turn, this provokes Man Friday to declare his admiration. Crusoe is therefore seen as morally superior.

Man Friday's language is not based on any real code, but is rather a constructed form which suggests a childlike speaker; at certain points, the fact that the narrator feels compelled to 'translate' Man Friday's expressions leads the reader to conclude that the speaker is unclear. This brings the narrator closer to the reader and moves Man Friday further away, encoding him as 'foreign' and 'alien'. Impressions of language therefore support the power relations within the story.

Activity

So far, the focus has been on the representation of the language of non-white speakers from a white point of view. The material that follows will shift its focus to the perspective of black speakers and writers.

Read through Text: 'Home Again', which is an extract from a story written by a Patwa speaker; the story is about being in the Caribbean and contrasting it with life in England. Patwa as a form of language is actually a very complex code, often involving the combination of European vocabulary with African grammatical structures.

Because Patwa is essentially a spoken variety, there is no standardised spelling system, so people who want to construct a written text have to devise a system that will be accessible. The spelling here was devised by the Afro-Caribbean Language Centre in Manchester, where this writer was part of a working group. (Note: the spelling of 'Patwa' is a deliberate change from the former 'Patois', which was thought to suggest a Eurocentric view.)

Compare the Patwa and Standard English versions, and try to trace some of the rules of Patwa.

Text: 'Home Again'

Jamaican Patwa or Creole	Standard English
Winter deh an Inglan	It is winter in England
but mi deh-ya	but I am here
inna de sun all day.	in the sun all day.
And when mi memba how	And when I remember how
Oonu a shiver inna de col	you are all shivering in the cold
mi jus sip mi coconut waata	I just sip my coconut water
an laugh.	and laugh.
Mi av one school frien	I have one school friend
a live inna de country still.	who is still living in the country.
So mi seh to miself,	So I said to myself,
'Mi a go look fi she.'	'I am going to visit her.'
Mi tek de bus fram toun.	I took the bus from town.
De bus pack wid people.	The bus was packed with people.
It so hat me staat fi sweat.	It was so hot I started to sweat.
At laas mi reach fi-mi stap.	At last I reached my stop.
Mi frien a wait deh.	My friend was waiting there.
She come meet mi.	She had come to meet me.
In no time wi reach de house.	In no time we reached the house.
It big an cool an nice.	It was big and cool and nice.
Mi ol frien-dem	My old friends were
glad fi see mi.	glad to see me.

Commentary

Verbs

The past tense is not marked in the verb itself, but is signalled via adverbs or simply the context of use; progressive forms ('was waiting', 'am going') are marked with 'a' in front of the verb; the verb 'to be' is often omitted altogether.

Personal pronouns

mi	wi
yu	oonu
she	dem
im	

(Possessive pronouns: add 'fi': fi-mi, fi-yu, etc.)

Prepositions

'Fi' is also used to mean both 'to' and 'for'.

Nouns

Plurals can be made by adding 'dem' – e.g. frien-dem.

While vocabulary is often similar to English, the pronunciation of words can make them sound unfamiliar when spoken. Important aspects of accent include the use of /t/ for /θ/ and /d/ for /ð/, and /ɑː/ for /ɔː/ and /ɒ/ ('water', 'because', 'stop').

Activity

Now translate the Standard English sentences below into Patwa.
You will need some additional vocabulary, as follows:

picni-dem	children
gi	give
likkle	little
caaz	because
cyar	car
fambli	family

301

mus	must
dat time	in those days
spen time	stay (with)
maaga	thin
nyam	eat
wile	while

1 You (plural) came with her to see the children in those days.
2 His family gave us their car while we stayed with them.
3 He must eat, because he is so thin and little!

(Answers on p. 304)

Activity

Rather than offering a white perspective on black experience, Text: 'The Fat Black Woman Goes Shopping' offers a black perspective on white society. Read the poem through, and discuss how the writer uses aspects of Patwa to construct the voice of the central character.

Text: 'The Fat Black Woman Goes Shopping'

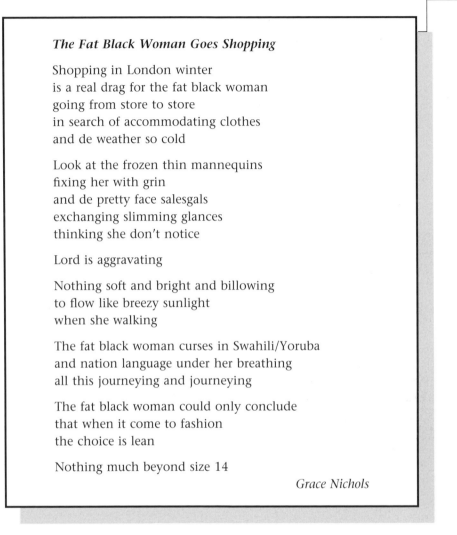

The Fat Black Woman Goes Shopping

Shopping in London winter
is a real drag for the fat black woman
going from store to store
in search of accommodating clothes
and de weather so cold

Look at the frozen thin mannequins
fixing her with grin
and de pretty face salesgals
exchanging slimming glances
thinking she don't notice

Lord is aggravating

Nothing soft and bright and billowing
to flow like breezy sunlight
when she walking

The fat black woman curses in Swahili/Yoruba
and nation language under her breathing
all this journeying and journeying

The fat black woman could only conclude
that when it come to fashion
the choice is lean

Nothing much beyond size 14

Grace Nichols

Commentary

Features of Patwa include the following:

◎ omission of articles – e.g. 'fixing her with grin'
◎ use of base form of the verb instead of the inflected form – e.g. 'when it *come* to fashion'
◎ omission of the verb to be – e.g. 'when she walking'.

The syntax is also contracted, so we find 'pretty face salesgals' and 'Lord is aggravating'.

Pronunciation is suggested in the use of 'de' for 'the', and in the spelling of 'sales*gals*'.

What the Patwa helps to do is to present us with the point of view of the fat black woman and, in the process, to construct a positive picture of her. Her natural environment of the warm Caribbean is suggested in 'breezy sunlight', and this is contrasted favourably with the cold London winter. Another favourable contrast is made between the 'frozen thin mannequins' and the fat, soft and warm black woman. The writer paints a seductive, sensuous picture of the kind of clothes the woman seeks but can't find: 'soft and bright and billowing'. There is a gentle humour in this poem, expressed in the way the woman tolerates the salesgirls and curses with a weary resignation that 'the choice is lean' in their meagre fashion world.

Nichols has created a sense of authentic talk, and this is crucial to the way the fat black woman seems real compared with her lifeless and colourless surroundings. The poem turns the idea of 'fat is bad, thin is beautiful' on its head, to present a positive view of size and gender as well as ethnicity.

Answer to activity

Translation of Standard English into Patwa (p. 302)

1 Oonu come wid she fi-see de picni-dem.
2 Im fambli gi wi fi-dem cyar wile we spen time wid dem.
3 Im mus nyam, caaz im so maaga an likkle!

Commentaries on activities

Speech acts (p. 247)

- 'Waiter, I *insist* on seeing the manager' is an example of a directive.
- 'I'd like to *congratulate* everyone involved in making the show such a success' is an expressive.
- 'I now *pronounce* you husband and wife' is a declarative.
- 'I *vow* to obey the rules of this association' is a commissive.
- 'I *deny* all knowledge of the facts' is a representative.

In reality, in everyday discourse, many speech acts do not directly address the listener. For many reasons – because we might be obeying the politeness principle, for example, and don't wish to impose – we may ask for something to be done *indirectly*. 'Can you pass the salt?' for instance, is not really a question but a directive; an answer of 'Yes' without any attempt to actually *pass* it would seem totally inappropriate. Forms, then, such as 'Can you pass the salt?' in preference to the more direct 'Pass the salt' are known as **indirect speech acts**.

It's possible, of course, to phrase speech acts in various ways – you can, for instance apologise *without* actually using the term 'apologise', as in 'OK I was wrong'; have a bet with someone by saying 'You're on'. Directives can be especially interesting in the gradient they take from direct order to humble question. Imagine that you've got a fly in your soup in a restaurant; a gradient might go something like this:

- Waiter, get the manager immediately
- Waiter, I insist on seeing the manager.
- Waiter, I want to see the manager.
- Waiter, I'd like to see the manager, please.
- Waiter, if it's not too much trouble I'd like to see the manager.
- Waiter, I don't suppose I could see the manager, could I?

Tony Blair's speech (p. 260)

A theme (or semantic field) running through this text is that of a new beginning: 'new era', 'new century', 'Britain renewed', 'the future', 'different and new economic world', 'start once again', 'sense of its own future', 'new millennium'.

Contrasting elements and three-part lists are evident: 'the battles of this past century/the battles of the new century', 'our children'/'our elderly', 'sense of its future'/'sense of its own history'; 'education, technology and

305

enterprise', 'from all walks of life, from all classes of people, from every single corner of our country'.

Use of the first person plural pronoun 'we' is extensive, as is the possessive adjective 'our', suggesting inclusiveness, common beliefs and shared ownership: 'we build a nation united', 'we watch our children', 'the country we have wanted'. However, there is a departure from this in the final line of the extract, which clearly refers to the political party rather than the country. The effect of this shift is to suggest that the ideals of New Labour and of the country as a whole are one and the same, an effect endorsed by the phrase 'the people's party'.

The country is described metaphorically, as though it were a person: it 'stands tall', it is 'certain' and 'confident' in its 'sense of its future', it has 'a sense of its own history'.

This type of metaphor (sometimes called 'personification') can endow abstract entities – here, a country – with the kinds of qualities we associate with living, feeling human beings, offering listeners an emotional connection. Although it has become quite commonplace to describe countries in a gendered way (for example, 'France has let *her* opponents off the hook'), interestingly, Blair does not do this, choosing to use the more neutral 'its' instead. Perhaps this is because using a gendered reference has often been criticised as sexist. It could also be because the use of the female pronoun might not have fitted the description of Britain as 'tall'!

Hairdressing (p. 265)

Text 1 is real; Text 2 is constructed.

Text 1 demonstrates many common features of real conversation, including:

◎ overlaps, many of which involve listener's reinforcements such as 'mm' and 'yeah' which support speakers and encourage them to continue
◎ monitoring features, such as 'you know', where speakers check how their speech is being received
◎ false starts, incompleteness and mid-utterance changes of direction
◎ some long pauses
◎ deictics ('pointing words'), for example, 'here', referring to the physical context
◎ ellipsis, for example 'tea or coffee?'
◎ vagueness, such as 'a bit'

Text 2, on the other hand, presents a neat and tidy picture of question–answer sequences that are often as fully formed as written sentences. There are none of the features listed above. Because Text 2 is teaching material which aims to teach a particular feature (the modal verb 'can'), utterances sound oddly over-specific, repetitive and list-like – in short, rather robotic.

Just as important as the linguistic features in these exchanges, though, is the content, which presents very different pictures of the speakers' concerns. In fact, you may well have decided which text was which simply on this basis. Text 1 presents the familiar routine (at least to female readers who visit hairdressing salons) of the customer being offered a drink by the junior, then customer and stylist engaging in a conversation about the state of the customer's hair, with the customer bemoaning its condition. This is the precursor to the stylist offering to remedy the problem. In contrast, the two customers in Text 2 are playing out what must be a male writer's fond fantasy – the itemising by the speakers of the qualities of their respective husbands. Women who go to the hairdressers know that this venue is in reality a site for the opposite: it is a rare chance to have a good moan about one's relationship, and a good read of the problem pages in magazines in order to be reassured that other people's problems are worse than yours.

If you are a male reader, answer this: what are the routines and familiar topics that occur in a men's hairdressing salon? And a question for both sexes: what happens in unisex salons?

Telephone conversation 1 (p. 272)

Summons and answer, identification and recognition are all present, as are mutual greetings.

Note that the tutor offers three greetings, an opening 'hello' for 'voice display' purposes when picking the phone up, another 'hello' when Sam's voice is recognised, then a 'hi', which acts possibly as a move towards increased informality and friendliness.

The speakers move quickly to the initial enquiries stage, but then this stage is extensive, with the student apparently anxious to show concern for the tutor's health; note that this is not reciprocated. Perhaps the student feels obliged to show this concern because the purpose of the phone call is to ask for help: the student therefore needs the tutor to be positively oriented to the upcoming request. The student's self-disparagement ('my brain's so cabbage . . .') could be seen as further evidence that preparations are being made to ask for help.

Despite the suggestions above that the initial enquiries stage is oriented towards the request for help, the student doesn't seem able to initiate this first topic. (It is normally the caller's responsibility to make the shift from initial enquiries to first topic, remember.) Or perhaps if the tutor had allowed more time, this would actually have happened. In the event, the tutor takes

307

over with a rather more business-like 'what can I do for you', and uses the student's name, which could mark a shift towards increased formality. The rest of the conversation goes on to deal with the real purpose of the phone call – the fact that the student has been struggling with an essay.

Telephone conversations 3 (p. 275)

It is interesting to reflect on how early children now become familiar with the telephone, a piece of technology that was once as strange to people as the equipment we would more regularly call 'modern technology', such as video conferencing and text messaging. Children are often given play phones very early in life, and they observe adults making and receiving phone calls from the word go.

The children in the data are managing some very complex routines. All are paying attention to the adult's need not to be left abruptly, but to be given some warning of impending departure and an explanation of why the child needs to leave. In Callum's case, he introduces a final topic (where the researcher lives) as a pre-closing move; Edward explains that he is going but he will be back later. In two cases (Callum and Edward), children are showing an awareness that the caller can be passed on to others while keeping the line open. In Edward's case, he manages the closure of his own interaction and the opening of his friend's conversation with the researcher at the same time. Such skills are at the basis of the way we manage multi-party talk, both on the phone and face-to-face, in adult life.

Chat-log (p. 277)

There are many examples of participants trying to call up the spoken form of language, for example:

- smileys
- alteration of spelling to suggest sound: SOOOO, byyyeeee
- use of interjections: hoorah, durrr, yum yum
- use of laughter: hehehe
- use of non-standard (regional and ethnic) forms: aint it, init, tarra luv, wassup
- use of punctuation (exclamation marks) and capitalisation to express heightened emotion.

However, it must be remembered that this is still writing, and writing needs typing skills and composition time: note how regent tells cato to slow down. Also, it is writing at a distance: cato says 'have you died?' because until participants send their texts to the screen, there is no evidence that they are still engaged with any activity. In other words, regent has been 'silent' for a long time.

This text is very playful, but that doesn't mean all chatroom interactions have to be so. This type of facility could equally be used for business meetings or health forums on bereavement. In other words, the purpose of the interaction is a powerful factor, as always. In this case, the participants are people who are very relaxed with each other, and are meeting in the chatroom to find out what the IRC medium is like.

309

Unit six

Applications

Aim of this unit

This brief final unit aims to give you some guidance on where to go next in your development of analytical skills.

The core book you have been reading is intended as a foundation course in language analysis. Although in the book's 'Extension' sections we have been signposting some possible directions for research, scope has prevented any detailed consideration of specific topics.

However, now that you have come to the end of this book, you are in a position to think about specialising in particular areas or aspects of language use. Indeed, if you are on a language course involving coursework, it may be part of the course assessment requirements that you undertake a piece of research of your own. So where do you start? Here are some questions to think about.

Which aspects of this book have I found most interesting?

If you are going to do a substantial piece of independent work, it has to be interesting enough for you to stay with it for some time. This means that you need to start by asking yourself which aspects of language you find most ... intriguing, creative, bizarre, humorous, annoying ... in short, those aspects that engage you most strongly. So start by looking back through this book and noting down those texts and discussions that affected you the most: what questions were raised in your mind by them?

311

What types of material would it be possible for me to collect?

It's good to be ambitious in research, but you also need to be realistic, particularly if you have a busy schedule and you are trying to juggle a language assignment with many other demands. So think about the language that you have the means to access, and where there are no ethical problems in the process of collection. Sometimes people assume that they need to go far afield for material, because they interpret the idea of 'objectivity' as a notion that researchers need to be removed from their object of study. This is a false premise. The best studies often tackle data from areas well known to the researcher, but where the analyst is open-minded rather than simply distanced. The important issue is to explain your relationship with the data clearly.

So think about what data you have close to hand. You may well have material that you have overlooked, or that you are discounting because you are assuming you are too involved with it.

What kinds of questions can be asked about different sorts of data?

The 'wh' question words we use in ordinary language are also at the basis of research: for example, *What* tends to happen in interactions such as these?; *How* does this text work?; *Where* do texts like these come from?; *Who* uses this kind of language?; *When* do we use language like this? However, the particular type of data you are going to research will tend to lend itself to certain questions.

What other resources can help me?

You need to focus on texts not as objects that have dropped out of the sky, but as pieces of communication that exist within a system of discourses. The smaller topic-based books that are part of the INTERTEXT series each focus on a type of discourse, present some of its important aspects, and suggest ways to research it.

In discussing the three sample texts that follow, we raise questions that have been touched on in this book but which are taken much further in the satellite titles indicated. For reasons of space, it isn't possible to discuss all of the satellite titles in the series; for a current list, see the front of this book or refer to the Routledge catalogue.

Sample text 1: BT, GO HOME

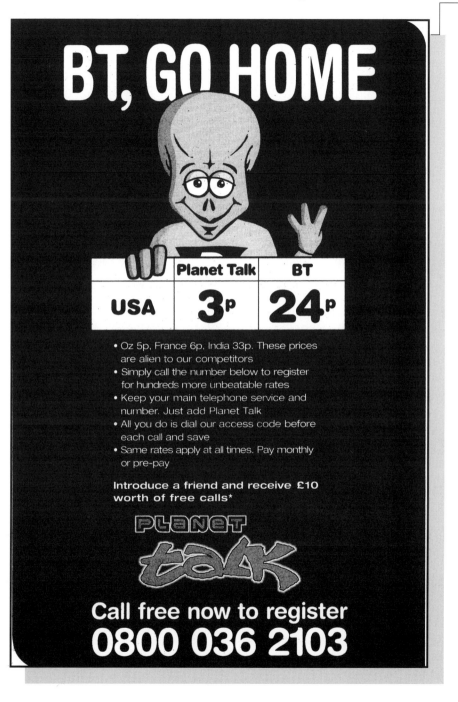

313

Commentary

Advertisements often refer to other texts as part of the way they construct their messages. This was referred to earlier as intertextuality. As well as referring outside the system of advertisements (for example, where an advert might imitate a newspaper article or an advice column in a magazine), adverts also refer to each other. This makes their comprehension particularly difficult for people outside of the culture in question, since understanding intertextual references of the latter sort requires the reader to be familiar with many different advertising texts, which in turn might be based on texts outside of advertising discourse. This is the case with Text: BT, GO HOME.

The text assumes that readers are familiar with BT's advertising campaign featuring the alien ET. The character ET derives from Spielberg's film of the same name, short for 'Extra Terrestrial'. So BT's advertising campaign is based on an American film text, and Planet Talk's advertisement refers intertextually to BT's campaign.

But there are further interesting complexities. The Planet Talk text is not simply referring, it is also undercutting BT's message, and not just by claiming to undercut the BT call rates. For example, the hook-line 'BT, GO HOME' is a direct reference to the film *ET*, where the loveable alien expressed his homesickness via the phrase 'ET phone home' (tellingly prompted by the humans' use of the telephone to communicate with each other).

However, the phrase 'go home' is also another way of saying 'get lost', a message reinforced by the alien's ambiguous three-fingered salute. So the Planet Talk text, by directly referring to BT's source but subverting it, is being disruptive of its competitor's position and profile. This same idea of serious disruption encoded playfully is also suggested by the graffiti-like lettering of 'talk' at the bottom of the ad, and by the expression of goofy mischief on the alien's face.

The idea of intertextuality and the ways in which advertising messages are constructed can be explored further by reading *The Language of Advertising*; a very particular form of advertising – the magazine front cover – is discussed in some detail in *The Language of Magazines*; if you are interested in the way new communication technology is used and marketed, see *The Language of ICT: Information and Communication Technology*. All titles are in the INTERTEXT series.

Krajicek has confidence to walk tall

BY RICHARD EDMONDSON
at Wimbledon

AS HE was about to serve at match point yesterday Richard Krajicek, the 1996 Wimbledon champion, heard an aeroplane overhead and backed off. He was probably afraid he might hit it with the rim of his racket.

When it comes to physical advantages for his sport there are few as generously blessed as the Dutchman. The 14st of his body is wrapped in a 6ft 5in frame, dimensions built to damage. Todd Woodbridge was in the shy yesterday and he failed to lay a racket on 18 Krajicek services, which took the latter's total to 38 for the tournament. Some of these projectiles reached 133mph and it made you realise that the tennis balls used must have been very wicked indeed in a past life to deserve this.

Woodbridge himself is not a man you would want to nudge while he had a pint in his hand but, as he crouched to receive serve yesterday, he looked like a fieldmouse in the path of a combine harvester. By the end the Australian had the slightly distracted look of a man wandering around the trenches. He left with the sound of service reports ringing in his ears, the victim of a 7-5, 6-4, 6-4 scoreline.

At the outset, there were plentiful spare places in the crowd on Court No 2 because while you can admire Krajicek it is not that easy to be entertained by him. His powerful gifts make the rally obsolete. He is one of the handful of men who have made the game largely redundant as a spectacle on grass. He is almost too efficient.

At the other end of the pitch was Woodbridge, who has always been a couple of gun turrets short of the battleship you need to be successful in singles around these parts. It is another format of the game, though, in which the man has made his name. Todd, of course, is one of the Woodies, the doubles team which has won five consecutive titles here. When Woodbridge is on court, Mark Woodforde is usually within his whispering distance. Yesterday it was a bit like watching Emu out there without Rod Hull.

It was certainly not the easiest of assignments for whenever he managed to return service he would see a huge shadow bearing down on him. Krajicek fills the space at the net like a bouncer in a nightclub doorway. It is territory in which the Dutchman is feeling particularly at ease.

"I feel more comfortable at the net and I miss very few volleys," he said. "I feel sharp and if I have a good preparation then I feel it's very tough to pass me and I get a lot of confidence at the net. I feel taller."

Krajicek looks better because he feels better. His meringue kneecaps no longer bring him pain following surgery, and there has been no recurrence either of the back spasms which almost forced him out of the game several years ago. Winning Wimbledon three years ago was too much for Richard Krajicek and subsequent defeat in the first round of the US Open, followed by other bleak results, darkened an already suspect temperament.

That gloomy character is hard to recognise these days. Krajicek marries his girlfriend, Daphne Deckers, next month and is close to being sickeningly happy. He is tickled most by his 15-month-old daughter Emma's recent smiling recognition of her father on television.

Krajicek has already beaten Pete Sampras both here and this season, in the Lipton, and is one of the few men who can be held up against the American as a creditable alternative. Prior to Wimbledon, Krajicek's form was not outstanding, but the pacing of his improvement is seductive. "The confidence is there and I don't have to play my best tennis at the beginning," he said. "You don't want to peak too early and at least I don't have to worry about that the way I'm playing at the moment."

Krajicek then continued to tell us that he is some way short of championship-winning form and while it is a story he delivers well, it comes from an ambassador sent abroad to be less than candid about his prospects. Privately, Krajicek believes he has quite a chance this year. He also believes he is building towards the best tennis of his life. The peak may be reached a week on Sunday.

Preening Frenchwoman uses physical prowess to sweep past Grande

Pierce's array of grand gestures

RICHARD WILLIAMS
AT WIMBLEDON

THIS HAS not been a great week for photojournalism. First there was the nonsense about Prince William's head. And now there is the business of Mary Pierce's shoulders.

At a minute or two before noon yesterday, Mary Pierce removed her cardigan. For Pierce, this pre-match unveiling has always been an important part of the show. Who could forget that sultry Monday afternoon at the Stade Roland-Garros, three or four years ago, when she slowly disrobed to reveal a black dress with chalk-stripes, strapless and cut startlingly low?

But that was a matter of pure physical display, the sort of thing Pierce seems to relish more than most of her contemporaries. Yesterday's unveiling, prefacing her match against Rita Grande, had an entirely different meaning. For most of those clustered around the court, it was their first chance to examine the effect of creatine on the human body.

A dietary supplement that aids recovery in training, creatine is a sort of legal steroid. Rugby players and racing cyclists are big fans of it, and so is Pierce. "It helps to rebuild the muscle tissues and the fibres you tear a little bit," she told journalists during this year's French Open. "It gives you a little bit of extra energy that you feel like maybe you don't have, so you can push yourself a little more."

The fuss arose when Pierce and her fellow Frenchwoman Amelie Mauresmo appeared at the start of this season with significantly enhanced musculature. In the case of the 19-year-old Mauresmo, who is not at Wimbledon, the interest was stoked by the presence of her girlfriend at the Australian Open. With Anna Kournikova at one end of the spectrum and a teenage lesbian bodybuilder at the other, the tabloids were enjoying a Grand Slam of their own.

Juxtaposed with pictures of the authentically beefy Mauresmo in the many instant articles on the new breed of pumped-up woman tennis player was a new photograph of Pierce. It showed her on the attack, swinging into a two-fisted

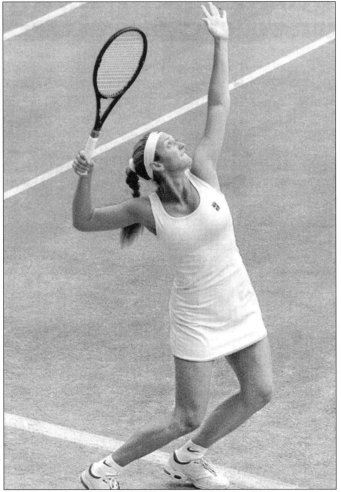

Mary Pierce shows yesterday that use of creatine has had no significant effect on her physique   *David Ashdown*

backhand, her face grimacing and her shoulders and biceps massively bunched. She looked, not to put too fine a point on it, like a runaway truck.

So it was a bit of a relief when she removed her cardy yesterday and revealed the unmistakable upper structure of a woman. A fraction thicker around the upper arms, perhaps, but no more. A formidable embonpoint, for sure, but Pierce-watchers would find nothing new there.

Her opponent did not stoop to the tactic

employed by Billie Jean King when facing the similarly well-endowed Ann Jones. "Ladies," King once wrote, "here is a hint when you're playing and opponent with big boobs: bring her to the net and maker her hit backhand volleys. 'I've got to hit over them or under them, but I can't hit through them,' Ann used to moan to me." Instead Grande, a slender Neapolitan, currently ranked No 56 in the world, chose to counter Pierce's assets by trying to maker her bend, feeding her soft, sliced backhands that died on the grass.

Commentary

The topic of language and gender has surfaced at various points during the core book: for example, in the section of Unit 5 sub-titled 'The Representation of Talk'. But the comments made there were quite generalised. How does gender work in a particular arena?

A real arena where gender is at work is the sporting one. How are men and women described within the discourse of sport? The texts above are from the same day's sporting fixtures – Wimbledon tennis – and from the same newspaper. They are from a well-known sports genre, the 'match write-up'.

The texts make for an interesting comparison because they both focus on the physical aspects of the players. But their emphasis is quite different, and they contain embedded ideas about how male and female players should look and act.

To a certain extent, both articles are critical of the idea of simple physical strength as worthy of approval, but for very different reasons in the two cases. While Krajicek's physical power is criticised because it is seen as leading to a boring game, Pierce's is criticised for its unnaturalness – the apparent result of chemical enhancement. There is no parallel discussion as to whether the male player has taken any supplements: his physique is assumed to be natural – he is 'generously blessed'. While Krajicek has the 'confidence to walk tall', Pierce is 'preening' in her 'physical prowess', the latter connoting a kind of self-regarding egotism.

Although both players are compared with machinery, the descriptions of Krajicek betray a sneaking admiration: he is 'a combine harvester' bearing down on his opponent, who is reduced to the level of a 'fieldmouse'; he plays in a game where you need to be a 'battleship'. Krajicek is seen as a deadly war machine, targeting his opponent with 'projectiles' in a ruthlessly efficient manner. Pierce, on the other hand, is described as looking like a 'runaway truck' – a force, but out of control. The writer's aside – 'not to put too fine a point on it' – reveals his own knowledge of this as an insult.

The writer's mock-relief that Pierce is still femininely proportioned when she takes off her 'cardy' to demonstrate 'the unmistakeable upper structure of a woman' (evidenced by the picture – note that there is no picture of Krajicek) contrasts with his comments on the lesbian Mauresmo, who is 'authentically beefy'. In short, Pierce, as a heterosexual woman, is still 'acceptably' proportioned, while the gay Mauresmo isn't assumed to be womanly at all: she has shifted category, so it's seen as appropriate for her physique to resemble that of a man.

As well as constructions of gender and sexuality, there are potential stereotypes of nationality at work: the coquettish Frenchwoman, the passive

317

Dutchman. Depictions of gender, nationality and race interweave in accounts such as these, and emerge in most other sporting arenas.

Aside from the sports-oriented content of these articles is the relationship between the various newspapers within the newspaper industry. You'll have noticed that the 'tabloids' are disparagingly referred to in the Pierce article as having had a 'Grand Slam' of their own on the subject of femininity. However, this doesn't stop *The Independent* journalist from using their comments as part of his copy.

The INTERTEXT series devotes a whole text to the topic of gender, in *Language and Gender*, but this subject is also covered in many of the other titles, such as *The Language of Magazines*, *The Language of Newspapers*, *The Language of Fiction* and *The Language of Sport*. *The Language of Sport* focuses on the different discourses underlying sport, such as the metaphor of warfare referred to above, and explores the ways in which different media – such as radio, TV and fanzines – approach sports reportage. In *The Language of Newspapers*, you will find more exploration of the ways in which different newspapers construct their narratives and make assumptions about their readers.

Bus stop. Kelly-Marie Tunstall and her pal

Kelly	So he walked over, right, big 'I am' and he had tattoos up his arms right, an anchor here and a microwave here.
Pal	He didn't.
Kelly	He did. He said do you want a drink or do you want a kick up the bum with an open-toed sandal. I said get you Eamonn Andrews.
Pal	You didn't.
Kelly	I did. I said I'll have a pint of babycham, some pork scratchings and a yellow cherry and if I'm not here when you get back I'll be in t' toilet putting hide and heal on my love bites.
Pal	You didn't.
Kelly	I did. So I come out of toilets, right, and he says hey scallop face your skirt's all caught up in your knickers at back, I said I pity you do you know why, he says why, I says 'cos it happens to be the latest fashion, I read it in a book, he says what book, I said *Vogue* that's what book, he said oh likely likely when do you read *Vogue*, I said when I'm in the hospital having exploratory surgery that's when. So he said oh.
Pal	He didn't.
Kelly	He did. And he sits there, right, picking the quiz off his beer-mat, and he says what were they exploring for, I said well it wasn't the Left Bank of the blinking Limpopo.
Pal	You didn't.
Kelly	I did. I said if you must know Magnus Magnusson I was rushed in last Wednesday when I swallowed the upholstery attachment of an Electrolux 567. He said how did you do that, I said I were hoovering a pelmet with my mouth open. Like that.
Pal	You weren't.
Kelly	I was. He said was it a long operation, I said it was a bit longer than normal because while they were stitching me I said could they put a new zip in my drainpipes.
Pal	You didn't.
Kelly	I did. Anyway, he stands up and he says do you want to come for a Chinese or do you want a clip round the ear with a wrestler's braces? I said I'll come for a Chinese because I've had a clip round the ear with a wrestler's braces and there's nowt to it.
Pal	You didn't.
Kelly	I did. He fell about laughing. Like this. I could see all cheese and onion crisps in his fillings.
Pal	You couldn't.
Kelly	I could. So we sit down and he says right I'm bloke I'm ordering, I says haven't you ever heard of Women's Lib he says no, I said oh. Anyway, we get t'end of meal, right, he's having a crack at burping and I'm chasing a lychee round a saucer, he says can I walk you home?
Pal	He didn't.
Kelly	He did. I said what's brought this on, bird bath? I said you needn't get any funny ideas because my mum and dad'll be up, I don't fancy you, and surgeon says I can't joggle about for a fortnight.
Pal	He didn't.
Kelly	Who?
Pal	Surgeon
Kelly	He did. So I said you can walk me home, but you're not pressing me up against the doorbell. So he puts down his banana fritter, he says Kelly-Marie Tunstall, just because I have tattoos and a hairy navel button does not mean I do not have the instincts of an English gentleman. Please believe me when I say I will be happy to escort you to your abode of residence, asking nothing in return but the chance of seeing you again.
Pal	He didn't.
Kelly	No, he didn't. He caught his bus and I had to pay for my own lychees.

Commentary

This sketch bases itself on some well-known aspects of real interactions, and exaggerates them to comic effect. For example:

◎ The 'didn't–did' exchanges mimic the routines we use in casual chat where speakers reveal something scandalous or shocking. These exchanges build throughout the sketch, so that we expect them to occur at regular intervals. Having set up expectations, there are departures towards the end, first where there is an 'insertion sequence' (he didn't/who?/surgeon/he did), then in the final line, where Kelly-Marie reverses polarity (he didn't/no, he didn't). These departures contribute to the comic 'finale'.

◎ A similarly familiar structure is the 'he said/I said' routine, staple of the gossipy 'report' genre. Comically, this is taken to an extreme level of detailed reportage (I said 'cos it happens to be the latest fashion, I read it in a book/he says what book/I says Vogue that's what book/).

◎ Parody of the detail that close friends (stereotypically, female friends) sometimes go into in their accounts is not simply restricted to the 'he said/ I said' sequences. This detail extends to some wonderfully comic minutiae, such as 'an Electrolux 567', and 'the Left Bank of the blinking Limpopo'. It is also at the centre of the play on expressions that echo 'better than a poke in the eye with a sharp stick': 'a kick up the bum *with an open-toed sandal*', 'a clip round the ear *with a wrestler's braces*'.

◎ Speakers regularly report the speech of others for dramatic effect. This is at the basis of the 'he said/she said' routines that we all know and use. However, there is a clever shift in the formality of Kelly-Marie's report at the end ('I will be happy to escort you to your abode of residence'), signalling either a change in the behaviour of her 'date', or her own fantasy of such. In the end, of course, it turns out to be the latter.

◎ The filler, 'right', along with certain features of regional dialect, such as 'nowt', 'I were', 't'end', establish Kelly-Marie as a regional speaker. Of course, in the performed sketch, the characters' accents would also be heard. Such aspects of language signal the 'ordinariness' of the characters, helping to construct Kelly–Marie as a working-class northern girl 'telling all' about her date to her mate. Performances of this type are in a long tradition of regional comedy, and the playful depiction of female gossip sits squarely with this tradition, too. But the characters are not simply regional and gender stereotypes. The energetic ways in which the features of so-called 'ordinary' language are played with, as outlined above, ensure that we see Kelly-Marie as more than a match for the young man with the tattoo of a microwave on his biceps.

If you are interested in the way people fashion language for comic purposes, read *The Language of Humour* in the INTERTEXT series.

further reading

Unit 1

Knowles, G. (1987) *Patterns of Spoken English* (Longman, Harlow).

Unit 2

Aitchison, J. (1994) *Words in the Mind,* 2nd edn (Basil Blackwell, Oxford).

Carter, R. (1998) *Vocabulary: Applied linguistic perspectives*, 2nd edn (Routledge, London).

Carter, R. and McCarthy, M. (1997) *Exploring Spoken English* (Cambridge University Press, Cambridge).

McCarthy, M. (1990) *Vocabulary* (Oxford University Press, Oxford).

Unit 3

Carter, R. and Nash, W. (1990) *Seeing Through Language: A guide to styles of English writing* (Basil Blackwell, Oxford).

Woods, E. (1994) *Introducing Grammar* (Penguin, Harmondsworth).

Unit 4

Bex, T. (1996) *Variety in Written English* (Routledge, London).

Hughes, R. (1996) *English in Speech and Writing* (Routledge, London).

Nunan, D. (1994) *Introducing Discourse Analysis* (Penguin, Harmondsworth).

Unit 5

Carter, R. and McCarthy, M. (1997) *Exploring Spoken English* (Cambridge University Press, Cambridge).

Cook, G. (1990) *Discourse* (Oxford University Press, Oxford).

Unit 6

Goddard, A. (2000) *Researching Language*, 2nd edn (Heinemann, Oxford).

Goodman, S. and Graddol, D. (eds) (1997) *Redesigning English: new texts, new identities* (Routledge, London).

Maybin, J. and Mercer, N. (eds) (1996) *Using English: from conversation to canon* (Routledge, London).

Montgomery, M. *et al.* (eds) (2000) *Ways of Reading*, 2nd edn (Routledge, London).

Widdowson, H. G. (1992) *Practical Stylistics* (Oxford University Press, Oxford).

Books for teachers

Bain, R., Taylor, M. and Fitzgerald, M. (1992) *Looking into Language* (Hodder & Stoughton, Sevenoaks).

Carter, R. (1997) *Investigating English Discourse: Language, Literacy, Literature* (Routledge, London).

Carter, R. and McRae, J. (eds) (1996) *Literature, Language and the Learner: Creative classroom practice* (Longman, Harlow).

Fairclough, N. (1988) *Language and Power* (Longman, Harlow).

McCarthy, M. (1991) *Discourse Analysis for Language Teachers* (Cambridge University Press, Cambridge).

McCarthy, M. and Carter, R. (1994) *Language as Discourse: Perspectives for Language Teaching* (Longman, Harlow).

McRae, J. (1991) *Literature with a Small 'l'* (Macmillan, Basingstoke).

Simpson, P. (1993) *Language, Ideology and Point of View* (Routledge, London).

Van Lier, L. (1995) *Introducing Language Awareness* (Penguin, Harmondsworth).

references

Carter, R. and McCarthy, M. (1997) *Exploring Spoken English* (Cambridge University Press, Cambridge).

Coulthard, M. (ed.) (1992) *Advances in Spoken Discourse Analysis* (Routledge, London).

Crystal, D. (1995) *The Cambridge Encyclopedia of the English Language* (Cambridge University Press, Cambridge).

Giddens, A. (1993) *Sociology* (Polity Press, Oxford).

Gillen, J. and Goddard, A. (2000) 'Medium management for beginners', paper presented at the 8th IADA Conference, Bologna, Italy, 15–17 June.

Grice, P. (1975) 'Logic and conversation', in Cole, P and Morgan, J. (eds) *Syntax and Semantics, vol. 3: Speech acts* (Academic Press, New York), pp. 41–58.

Halliday, M.A.K. and Hasan, R. (1976) *Cohesion in English* (Longman, Harlow).

Jefferson, G. (ed.) (1992) *Harvey Sacks: Lectures on conversation*, vol. II (Blackwell, Oxford).

Kramer, C. (1977) 'Perceptions of male and female speech', *Language and Speech*, 20: 151–61.

Labov, W. (1972) 'The transformation of experience in narrative syntax', in Labov, W. (ed.) *Language in the Inner City* (University of Philadelphia Press, Philadelphia, PA), pp. 354–96.

Lakoff, R. (1975) *Language and Woman's Place* (Harper & Row, New York).

Montgomery, M. (1999) 'Speaking Sincerely: public reactions to the death of Diana', *Language and Literature* 8, 1: 5–33.

Sadker, M. and Sadker, D. (1985) 'Sexism in the schoolroom of the 80's', *Psychology Today*, March: 54–7.

Schegloff, E. (1986) 'The routine as achievement', *Human Studies*, 9 (2–3): 111–51.

Schmitt, N. (2000) *Vocabulary and Language Teaching* (Cambridge University Press, Cambridge).

325

Searle, J. (1969) *Speech Acts: An essay in the philosophy of language* (Cambridge University Press, Cambridge).

Tannen, D. (1992) *You Just Don't Understand: Men and women in conversation* (Virago, London).

Werry, C. (1996) 'Linguistic and interactional features of Internet Relay Chat', in Herring, S. (ed.) *Computer Mediated Communication* (John Benjamins, Amsterdam).

Wolfson, N. (1982) *CHP: The conversational historic present in American English narrative* (Foris Publications, Cinnaminson, NJ).

list of URLS

You should be aware that URLs can change quickly. At the time of writing, these URLs were accurate. However, you may well find that some of the addresses are no longer in existence, or that you are redirected to a new address. This is part of the world of the Internet. Get used to keeping your own list of useful addresses, and regard these as a starting point rather than as the final word.

Sound symbolism

Dictionary of English phonesthemes:
http://www.geocities.com/SoHo/Studios/9783/phond.html

Animal sounds:
http://www.georgetown.ed/cball/animals/animals.html

Emoticons

http://www.randomhouse.com/features/davebarry/emoticon.html

Images

Almost any website could be explored for its use of images. A good starting point might be a newspaper site:

Press Association (news agency):
http://www.pa.press.net

an advertising site (with a difference):
http://www.adbusters.com

or a magazine site. For magazines, try typing the name of the magazine, followed by .com or .co.uk

Dictionary sites

Web of online dictionaries:
   http://www.yourdictionary.com

Language of computer-based communication:
   http://www.netlingo.com

Corpus search sites

British National Corpus:
   http://info.ox.ac.uk/bnc

Collins Cobuild:
   http://titania.cobuild.collins.co.uk/form.html

Collections of resources for language, literature, media and communication

   http://www.june29.com/HLP
   http://eserver.org
   http://www.bartleby.com
   http://lion.chadwyck.co.uk
   http://www.aber.ac.uk/media/index
   http://web.syr.edu/~mdtaffet/student_sites.html

index of terms

This is a form of combined glossary and index. Listed below are some of the main key terms used in the book, together with brief definitions for purposes of reference. The page references will normally take you to the first use of the term in the book where frequently used terms will be shown in **bold**. In some cases, however, understanding of the term can be helped by exploring its uses in more than one place in the book and accordingly more than one page reference is sometimes given.

Not all terms used in the book are glossed here as a limited number of terms in the book receive extensive discussion and explanation in particular units. This is also by no means a full index of linguistic terms, so it should be used in conjunction with other books, dictionaries and encyclopaedias which are indicated in the Further Reading section.

accent 42–44, 49–51, 294–7
An accent is a speaker's distinctive pronunciation which marks his or her regional or social identity.

acronym 21
A word composed of the initial letters of the name of something, usually an organisation and normally pronounced as a whole word. For example, NATO (North Atlantic Treaty Organization).

active (see **voice**)

adjacency 270
The positioning of elements in a conversational exchange so that one follows on from another. For example, greetings are nearly always followed by greetings in an 'adjacency pair'.

adjective 130
Adjectives frequently modify nouns or noun phrases (the *beautiful* girl) and can themselves be modified by **adverbs** (underlined) (the extremely competitive team). Adjectives can have morphemes added to them to express degrees of comparison (the *oldest* pupil in the school); and they can also stand alone to describe the qualities and features of a noun (the house was very *old* and *spooky*).

affricate 47, 48, 55–6
There are only two of these sounds in English. They begin with a sound which resembles a stop consonant (e.g. *d*, *t*) and end with a sound which resembles a

fricative; for example, ju*dge*, bri*dge*, scra*tch*.

ambiguity (lexical)   79, 80–1, 93
Words and phrases which can be interpreted as having more than one meaning; for example, a politician who says 'Europe isn't working' can convey, by the use of the word 'working', two meanings at the same time.

amelioration   116
A process by which a word acquires increasingly positive meanings; for example, words such as 'lord' and 'master'.

anaphoric reference   (see **reference**)

anthropomorphism   8
A view that an animal or an object has feelings like those of a human being. Anthropomorphic descriptions occur regularly in literary texts where a similar term used is personification.

approximant   47, 54
An approximant is a term used to describe how we produce sounds which are somewhere between **vowels** and **consonants**; for example, the *y* in *young*.

assonance   62, 65
A sequence of repeated vowel sounds: for example, 'bl*o*wing *o*ld c*o*ld shad*o*ws away'.

bound morpheme   (see **morpheme**)

cataphoric reference   (see **reference**)

clause   156–8
A structural unit which is part of a **sentence** either as a main clause which can stand alone and be equivalent to a sentence or as a

subordinate or dependent clause. For example, 'The owner, who lives abroad, has written to all the neighbours' consists of a main clause 'The owner . . . has written to all the neighbours' and a subordinate clause 'who lives abroad'.

closing   274
Words and phrases used to indicate that a conversational sequence is ending. For example, routine expressions like farewells (*bye then*) are closings. (See also **pre-closing**)

cohesion   170, 173–5, 187, 292
The patterns of language created within a text, mainly within and across sentence boundaries and which collectively make up the organisation of larger units of the text such as paragraphs. Cohesion can be both lexical and grammatical. Lexical cohesion is established by means of chains of words of related meaning linking across sentences; grammatical cohesion is established mainly by grammatical words such as 'the', 'this', 'it' and so on.

comparative   (see **reference**)

conjunction   212–14
A general term which describes words which link sentences and clauses together, indicating temporal, spatial, logical and causal relationships. Words such as 'and', 'but', 'therefore', 'because' are conjunctions. Conjunctions are also termed 'connectives'.

connotation   4, 102
The connotations of a word are the associations it creates. For example, the connotations of December, mainly within British

and North American culture, would be of 'cold', 'dark nights' and 'Christmas parties'. Connotations are often either individual or cultural.

consonant 44 ff.
A consonant is produced when we close our airstream or it is blocked in such a way as to cause friction. *B, p, t, d* are consonants.

co-operative principle 267
Refers to the way in which most conversations are conducted in a coherent manner with participants acting towards one another as efficiently and collaboratively as possible.

deictic 149, 199
Deictics are words which point backwards, forwards and extratextually and which serve to situate a speaker or writer in relation to what is said. For example, in the sentence 'I'm going to get some wine from that shop over there' the main deictic words are 'that' and 'there'.

demonstrative (see **reference**)

denotation 102
The literal, dictionary definition of a word.

derivational morpheme (see **morpheme**)

dialect 294 ff.
A variety of a language, marked by a particular grammar and vocabulary and used by speakers with a common regional and social background.

diphthong 58
A vowel sound in which there is a kind of glide during its

pronunciation between one sound and another. For example, h*ouse* and *ear* are diphthongs.

discourse 238, 291–2
A term used in linguistics to describe the rules and conventions underlying the use of language in extended stretches of text, spoken and written. (Such an academic study is referred to as 'discourse analysis'.) The term is also used as a convenient general term to refer to language in action and the patterns which characterise particular types of language in action; for example, the 'discourse' of advertising.

ellipsis 158, 209
Ellipsis refers to the omission of part of a structure. It is normally used for reasons of economy and, in spoken discourse, can create a sense of informality. For example, in the sentence 'She went to the party and danced all night' the pronoun 'she' is elliptted from the second clause; in the dialogue

'You going to the party?'
'Might be'

the verb 'Are' and the pronoun 'I', respectively, are omitted with the ellipsis here creating a casual and informal tone.

endophoric/exophoric (see **reference**)

face (see **positive face** and **negative face**)

filler 96
Fillers are items which do not carry conventional meaning but which are inserted, usually in spoken discourse, to allow time to

331

think, to create a pause and so on. Examples are items such as: 'erm', 'er', 'ah'.

finite verb 141–2

A finite verb or verb phrase can occur on its own in a clause or sentence and is normally marked for tense and mood. A non-finite verb only occurs in a subordinate clause and normally lacks explicit reference to time or person. For example, 'Walking through the town, we came across an old pub' contains a non-finite verb 'walking' and a finite verb 'came'.

foregrounding 174

Language is foregrounded when a particular form or structure is highlighted or draws attention to itself in some way, for example by being placed in an unusual order or by being repeated several times.

formality 111, 177ff.

A level of language use which refers to a particular social context or situation. Formal language is used in social situations which are distant and more impersonal; informal language is used in social situations which are intimate and casual.

free morpheme (see **morpheme**)

fricative 46, 48, 54, 56

A sound in which air passes through a narrow space and produces a hissing noise. *V* and *f* are fricatives in the sentence 'It was very fair'.

generic 195

A term which is used to refer to a particular example of a general class or category. For example, the sentence 'bats can see in the dark' contains a generic noun 'bats'. Some generic nouns such as 'man' to refer to both men and women are sexist.

genre 33, 40

Another word for text-type. Examples of a genre are: narrative; report; argument.

grammatical ambiguity
(see **ambiguity, grammatical**)

grammatical cohesion
(see **cohesion**)

hedge(s) 95

Hedges are words and phrases which soften or weaken the force with which something is said. Examples of hedges are: 'kind of', 'sort of', 'by any chance', 'as it were', 'admittedly'.

homophone 62–3, 121–2

Words which have the same pronunciation but which differ in meaning; for example, 'threw/through'.

hyperbole 267

Exaggeration for purposes of emphasis, expressing emotion, etc. 'I waited hours for that bus', 'It'll take you years to photocopy all that' would be examples of hyperbole in everyday conversation.

hypernym (see **hyponym**)

hyponym 104

Hyponymy is the relationship which exists between specific and general words. For example, 'rose' is a hyponym of the more general word 'flower'. General words such as 'flower', 'animal' and 'vehicle' are also sometimes called hypernyms.

modal verb 143

Modality is normally conveyed by means of modal verbs (also known as modal auxiliary verbs – see **verb**). Examples of modal verbs are: 'must', 'can', 'may', 'will', 'should', 'could'.

modality 143

A general term which describes unrealized states and possible conditions and the forms of language which encode them, such as 'possibly', 'perhaps', 'could be', 'ought to be'. (See also **modal verb**)

modifier (pre-modifier/post-modifier) (see **noun phrase**)

monosyllabic 56

Words such as *cat, bite, disk, film* have only one syllable and are monosyllabic. (By contrast, words such as *biscuit, committee* have two and three syllables respectively and are polysyllabic.)

morpheme 75–6

A morpheme is a basic unit of grammar in that it can function to mark a grammatical feature or structure. For example, 'walks' contains two morphemes: 'walk' and 's', the latter morpheme marking the tense and person of the basic or root morpheme 'walk'. Morphemes are normally divided into 'free' and 'bound' morphemes, the former occurring also as single words and the latter only occurring meaningfully when joined to the 'free' morpheme. Thus, 'unselfish' is a word made up from three morphemes, a 'free' morpheme 'self' and two bound morphemes 'un' and 'ish'.

Morphemes are often studied as inflectional or derivational forms: inflectional morphemes are morphemes such as 's' and 'ed' (bound morphemes) which indicate grammatical meanings; derivational morphemes are morphemes such as 'ship', 'dom' which can form specific grammatical categories – in these cases nouns such as 'friend*ship*' and 'king*dom*'.

morphology (see **morpheme**)

narratee 35

The imagined recipient of a text, including a story. In texts the narratee can be distinct from the reader.

narrative structure 250 ff.

Narratives are normally structured with a beginning, middle and end and should normally contain a clear action or plot, an evaluation of the point of the narrative and, sometimes, an indication of the moral we should draw from the events narrated.

narrator 198

The implied teller of a story or presenter of a text. In texts the narrator can be distinct from the author of the text.

nasal 48, 54

Nasal sounds are consonant sounds such as *m* and *n* in which we produce air through the nose as well as through the mouth.

negative face 274

Speakers try to avoid negative face by not allowing themselves to be imposed upon. 'I'd rather not but just for you' or 'Well, I'm a bit busy this weekend but . . .' are typical phrases which avoid too much negative face.

non-finite verb (see **finite verb**)

noun 127

Nouns are a major class of words which are regularly inflected or otherwise marked to show plurals (ship/ships; mouse/mice; child/children) and to indicate possession (the dog's lead).

noun phrase 129–31

A group of words which describe a *noun*. 'Old pop-singers with long hair are still making records' contains a noun phrase with the core noun 'pop-singers' pre-modified with the word 'old' and post-modified with the words 'with long hair'.

onomatopoeia 51

The connection of a sequence of sounds with the action(s) to which they refer.

pararhyme 64

The rhyming of words with the same consonants but with different vowel sounds. For example, *France* and *once* are half-rhymes.

participle (see **verb**)

passive (see **voice**)

pejoration 116

A process by which words increasingly acquire negative meanings. For example, the word 'spinster' has a basic meaning of unmarried woman but has acquired pejorative **connotations**.

phoneme 44

A minimal speech unit in a language which is often described in terms of the way it contrasts with another closely related speech sound. For example, *d*in and *b*in are closely related in articulation but are distinguished by the contrasting phonemes *b* and *d*.

plosive 44, 48, 54–7

A plosive is a sound produced when our passage of air is obstructed and then suddenly released. Examples of plosive sounds would be *b* and *p*. Plosives are sometimes called 'stops'.

politeness principle 268

A principle of conversation in which speakers indicate respect for each other by adopting appropriate strategies to maintain polite and smooth-running interaction.

polysemy 121

A semantic process by which certain words have several meanings. For example, the word 'lap' is polysemous.

positive face 274

Speakers try to preserve the positive face of the people they are talking with by not, for example, seeming to impose on them. Phrases, 'Do you mind if . . .' or 'I know this is inconvenient but . . .' help to preserve positive face. (See also **negative face**)

pre-closing 274

Words and phrases which are used to indicate that a conversation is about to be brought to a closing. For example, 'I must be going, I'm late already' is a pre-closing move. (See also **closing**)

preposition 301

A preposition is normally a short particle such as *with, in, across, for* which introduces nouns and noun phrases and pronouns as well as other words and which expresses a relationship between it and the

335

rest of the phrase. For example, *in* debt; *with* him; *across* the road; *for* the sake *of* Jennifer.

progressive (see **verb**)

pronoun 104, 134, 194–7
Words which normally substitute for nouns and noun phrases. For example, 'I', 'you', 'it', 'they', 'their', 'some', 'any', 'this', 'myself', 'which'. Personal pronouns such as 'I', 'you', 'we', 'they', 'us' are especially significant in texts.

RP (received pronunciation) 42, 60, 294–7
An accent of English which is not associated with any region of the country and which carries a high social status.

reference 4, 187 ff., 197 ff., 207
The act of referring to something (often called a referent). Many words also allow reference to each other and establish links and patterns across a text. Different types of reference include: 'anaphoric' and 'cataphoric' reference. Anaphoric reference points backwards; for example, the grammatical word 'he' in the following sentence 'I saw the man. *He* was wearing . . .'; 'cataphoric reference' points forwards; for example, the word 'here' in the following sentence '*Here* is the nine o' clock news'. Reference within a text is generally referred to as 'endophoric' reference; reference to the world outside the text is generally referred to as 'exophoric' reference. 'Demonstrative reference' involves **deictics** such as *these, those, here, there* which refer back and forth within a text or **speech event**. 'Comparative reference' involves

reference within a text when one thing is compared to another; for example, 'Ann is *fitter than* Jill'.

reverse rhyme 62, 65
The repetition of initial rather then final syllables; for example, *st*ar, *st*one.

semantic change 115
A change in a word's meaning over time. For example, in the English of Jane Austen's time the word 'injury' means emotional upset.

semantic field 89, 172, 291
A group of words which are related in meaning, normally as a result of being connected with a particular context of use. For example, 'chop', 'sprinkle', 'salt', 'dice', 'wash', 'simmer', 'boil', 'herbs' are all connected with the semantic field of cookery.

semiotic 3
Human communication by means of signs and symbols.

sentence 141, 215
A difficult term to define because the structure of sentences differs according to whether spoken or written language is used. Traditionally, a sentence has a subject and a main **verb**, though in literary texts a sentence can be a single word; in spoken English, however, structures such as 'over here', 'if you like','perhaps'can constitute a sentence. (See **clause**)

signifier 11 ff., 35
The use of words to represent rather than simply to convey meanings. For example, the use of lower-case letters signals that a communication is high-tech or computer-related.

sound symbolism 9 ff.

The linking of sounds with particular ideas; for example, the 's' sound is associated with the sound of the sea.

speech act 245–7, 305

A speech act refers to what is done when something is said (for example, warning, threatening, promising, requesting). 'I declare the meeting open' in this sense does what it says. An 'indirect speech act' has a meaning which is different from its apparent meaning. For example, the question: 'Is that your coat on the floor?' could *indirectly* suggest that the coat should be picked up.

speech event 243

A use of language in a social context in which the speakers normally follow a set of agreed rules and conventions. For example, telling a joke, recounting a story, purchasing stamps in a post office are all speech events.

Standard English 296–303

The prestige variety of English which is used in written forms and in institutional contexts such as government, the law and education. There are many varieties of Standard English in the world and, although there are not major differences between their written forms, Standard American or Standard Australian English are different in certain aspects of grammar and vocabulary from Standard British English.

subject 132

The subject of a sentence is normally the noun, noun phrase or pronoun which appears before the verb in statements and after the first verb in questions; for

example, '*I* shouted to him' and 'Are *the children in the bus* coming to the cinema?' (See also **theme**)

subordinate clause 156–8

A subordinate clause is a clause which cannot normally stand on its own. For example, the subordinate clause 'who is very young' is dependent on a main clause (That is the captain of the team) for its full understanding. (That is the captain of the team, *who is very young*.) Subordinate clauses are also called dependent clauses. (See also **clause**)

substitution 208

Substitution allows a speaker or writer to substitute one word or phrase for another in a text. 'Do' is normally used to substitute for verbs or verb phrases, whereas words like 'so' can be used to substitute for whole clauses. For example:

'Are you going to the party? I would do but I'm a bit tired.'

symbolic 3

Something is symbolic when it suggests associations rather than refers to something directly.

synonymy 79

Synonyms are words which have equivalent meanings. For example, 'cheap' and 'inexpensive'.

tense 133, 219

Tense is a very important grammatical category and is mainly associated with the **verb** in a sentence. English has two primary tenses, the present tense and the past tense. (The future is normally referred to by means of **modal verbs** such as 'will' and by adverbs or adverbial phrases such as 'tomorrow' or 'on Monday'.)

theme 223

The theme of a clause is normally the first complete word unit in a sentence, for example:

Mr Kipling makes exceedingly good cakes.

has the unit 'Mr Kipling' as its theme. If the structure of the sentence is altered to form:

Exceedingly good cakes Mr Kipling makes.

then the phrase 'Exceedingly good cakes' becomes the theme; indeed, in some definitions of theme the word 'exceedingly' alone is the theme and is marked because it does not normally appear in this position and is put to the front of the sentence for purposes of emphasis. The theme of the clause signals what the clause is going to be about, marking out a topic for our attention. The grammatical subject of the sentence is normally also the theme, as in '*Mr Kipling* makes exceedingly good cakes'. (See also **subject**)

verb 132–3, 219

A verb is a major category of grammar. Verbs can be either main verbs or auxiliary verbs. For example in the sentence:

I do intend to go to the match.

'intend' is a main verb and 'do' is an auxiliary verb. Auxiliary verbs cannot normally stand on their own, whereas main verbs can (e.g., I intend to go to the match). Verbs also have other forms.

Here, for example, 'to go' is an infinitive form of the verb 'go'.

Verbs can be inflected to show tense. For example:

She works hard (present tense).
She worked hard (past tense).

– and can also form present and past participles: working (present participle); worked (past participle). Participles can be used as modifiers:

The working day.
A worked example.

A progressive form of the verb indicates an action which is continuous. For example, 'I was walking home' is a past progressive form of the verb 'walk'.

voice 160–3, 221–3, 242

Voice is a grammatical feature which indicates whether a subject in a sentence is the agent of an action or is affected by the action. Voice can normally be either active or passive. For example:

The dog bit the man (active).
The man was bitten by the dog (passive).

In the passive sentence it is of course still the dog which bites and in this sense the dog remains the underlying subject of the sentence; but the man is given greater emphasis in the passive sentence. The passive voice also allows the 'by-phrase' to be omitted, thus deleting any reference to an agent. For example:

The man was bitten.

Such structures allow the responsibility for an action or event to be concealed. In a text the choice of active or passive forms is often connected to questions of **theme** and **cohesion**.

voiced 52–4

Voiced and voiceless consonants contrast with each other. Voiced consonants are produced when your vocal cords vibrate. Thus, *t*

and *d* are contrasting consonants, the former being voiceless (or unvoiced) and the latter voiced.

voiceless (see **voiced**)

vowel 43, 58–61

A vowel is a sound which is normally produced by a free flow of air through the mouth. In written form there are five vowels: *a, e, i, o, u.*

index of main texts

Menus

Newspapers and journalism

Oral narratives and dialogues

Signs, slogans and logos

Speeches and political rhetorics